FODOR'S BED & BREAKFASTS
AND COUNTRY INNS

The Upper Great Lakes' Best Bed & Breakfasts

2nd Edition

*Delightful Places to Stay and Great
Things to Do When You Get There*

Fodor's Travel Publications, Inc.
New York • Toronto • London • Sydney • Auckland

Copyright © 1995
by Fodor's Travel Publications, Inc.

ISBN 0–679–02697–5

Second Edition

The Upper Great Lakes'
Best Bed & Breakfasts

Editor: Chelsea Mauldin
Editorial Contributors: Robert Blake, Linda Schmidt
Creative Director: Fabrizio La Rocca
Cartographer: David Lindroth
Illustrators: Alida Beck, Karl Tanner
Cover Design: Guido Caroti
Cover Photograph: Zane B. Williams

Special Sales

MANUFACTURED IN THE UNITED STATES OF AMERICA

10 9 8 7 6 5 4 3 2 1   3 9082 05696763 4

NOV 8 1995

Contributors

Richard Bak, who lives in suburban Detroit, wrote the Southeast, Southwest, and Upper Peninsula sections of the Michigan chapter. He has written three books and contributed to *The Wall Street Journal Guides to Business Travel: USA & Canada.*

Tom Davis updated the section on Door County, Wisconsin, where he makes his home. The author of two books, he also serves as Senior Editor for *Wisconsin Trails* and for *Sporting Classics.* His freelance writing and photography has appeared in *Cross-Country Skier, Country Inns/Bed & Breakfasts, Milwaukee Magazine, Gray's Sporting Journal,* and *New England Review/Bread Loaf Quarterly.*

Deborah Hawkins is a freelance writer whose articles appear regularly in various regional newspapers and magazines; she is also the co-founder of *Traverse, The Magazine.* She lives in Traverse City and wrote the Little Traverse Bay Region, Grand Traverse Region, and Mackinac Island sections of the Michigan chapter.

Oliver McCurnin, who updated the Mississippi River Valley and Bluff Country and the Duluth and North Shore sections of the Minnesota chapter, is a North Dakota native who has lived in Minnesota for four years. He recently moved to Poland to travel, to observe, and to pursue a teaching career.

Brenda Steinbring, a third-generation Minnesotan, lives in uptown Minneapolis. She updated the Twin Cities Area, the Northwest and the Cuyana Iron Range, and the Southwestern Prairie sections of the Minnesota chapter.

Kristin Visser is a travel writer based in Madison, Wisconsin. Her articles have appeared in regional and national publications. She is the author of four travel books: *Wisconsin with Kids, Frank Lloyd Wright and the Prairie School in Wisconsin,* the *Acorn Guide to Door County,* and *Wisconsin Trivia.* She updated every section of the Wisconsin chapter but Door County.

Contents

Foreword

While every care has been taken to ensure the accuracy of the information in this guide, the passage of time will always bring change, and, consequently, the publisher cannot accept responsibility for errors that may occur.

All prices and listings are based on information supplied to us at press time. Details may change, however, and the prudent traveler will avoid inconvenience by calling ahead.

Fodor's wants to hear about your travel experiences, both pleasant and unpleasant. When an inn or B&B fails to live up to its billing, let us know and we will investigate the complaint and revise our entries where the facts warrant it.

Send your letters to: Editor, The Upper Great Lakes' Best Bed & Breakfasts, Fodor's Travel Publications, 201 East 50th Street, New York, NY 10022.

Introduction

*You'll find bed-and-breakfasts in big houses with turrets and
little houses with decks, in mansions by the water and cabins
in the forest, not to mention structures of many sizes and
shapes in between. B&Bs are run by people who were once
lawyers and writers, homemakers and artists, nurses and
architects, singers and businesspeople. Some B&Bs are just a
room or two in a hospitable local's home; others are more like
small inns. So there's an element of serendipity to every B&B
stay.*

*But while that's part of the pleasure of the experience, it's also
an excellent reason to plan your travels with a good B&B
guide. The one you hold in your hands serves the purpose
neatly.*

*To create it, we've hand-picked a team of professional writers
who are also confirmed B&B lovers: people who adore the
many manifestations of the Victorian era; who go wild over
wicker and brass beds, four-posters and fireplaces; and who
know a well-run operation when they see it and are only too
eager to communicate their knowledge to you. We've instructed
them to inspect the premises and check out every corner of the
premier inns and B&Bs in the areas they cover, and to report
critically on only the best in every price range.*

*They've returned from their travels with comprehensive
reports on the pleasure of B&B travel, which may well become
your pleasure as you read their reports in the pages that
follow. These are establishments that promise a unique
experience, a distinctive sense of time and place. All are
destinations in themselves, not just spots to rest your head at
night, but an integral part of a weekend escape. You'll learn
what's good, what's bad, and what could be better; what our
writers liked and what you might not like.*

At the same time, Fodor's reviewers tell you what's up in the area and what you should and shouldn't miss—everything from historic sites and parks to antiques shops, boutiques, and the area's niftiest restaurants and nightspots. We also include names and addresses of B&B reservation services, just in case you're inspired to seek out additional properties on your own. Reviews are organized by state, and, within each state, by region.

In the italicized service information that ends every review, a second address in parentheses is a mailing address. A double room is for two people, regardless of the size or type of its beds. Unless otherwise noted, rooms don't have phones or TVs. Note that even the most stunning homes, farmhouses and mansions alike, may not provide a private bathroom for each individual. Rates are for two, excluding tax, in the high season and include breakfast unless otherwise noted; ask about special packages and midweek or off-season discounts.

What we call a restaurant serves meals other than breakfast and is usually open to the general public.

Where applicable, we note seasonal and other restrictions. Although we abhor discrimination, we have conveyed information about innkeepers' restrictive practices so that you will be aware of the prevailing attitudes. Such discriminatory practices are most often applied to parents who are traveling with small children and who may not, in any case, feel comfortable having their offspring toddle amid breakable bric-a-brac and near precipitous stairways.

When traveling the B&B way, always call ahead; and if you have mobility problems or are traveling with children, if you prefer a private bath or a certain type of bed, or if you have specific dietary needs or any other concerns, discuss them with the innkeeper. At the same time, if you're traveling to an inn because of a specific feature, make sure that it will be available when you get there and not closed for renovation. The same goes if you're making a detour to take advantage of specific sights or attractions.

It's a sad commentary on other B&B guides today that we feel obliged to tell you that our writers did, in fact, visit every property in person, and that it is they, not the innkeepers, who wrote the reviews. No one paid a fee or promised to sell or promote the book in order to be included in it. (In fact, one of the most challenging parts of the work of a Fodor's writer is to persuade innkeepers and B&B owners that he or she wants nothing more than a tour of the premises and the answers to a few questions!) Fodor's has no stake in anything but the truth. If a room is dark, with peeling wallpaper, we don't call it quaint or atmospheric—we call it run-down, and then steer you to a more appealing section of the property.

So trust us, the way you'd trust a knowledgeable, well-traveled friend. Let us hear from you about your travels, whether you found that the B&Bs you visited surpassed their descriptions or the other way around. And have a wonderful trip!

Karen Cure
Editorial Director

Michigan

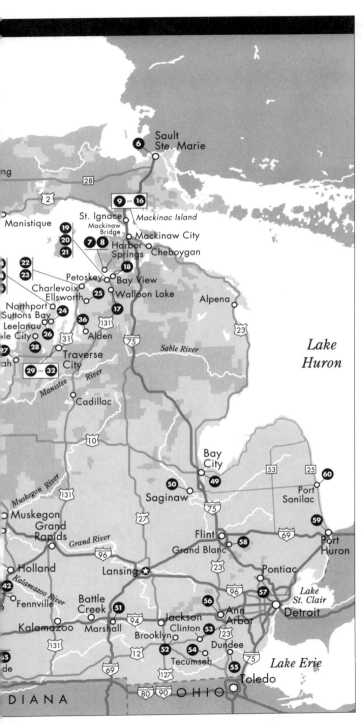

Special Features at a Glance

Name of Property	Accessible for Disabled	Antiques	On the Water	Best Value	Car Not Necessary	Historic Building	Romantic Hideaway	Luxurious	
MICHIGAN									
Bay View at Mackinac		✓	✓		✓		✓	✓	
Bear River Valley									
Belvedere Inn					✓	✓			
The Benson House	✓						✓		
Big Bay Point Lighthouse			✓			✓	✓		
Birch Brook	✓								
Blanche House Inn		✓	✓			✓	✓		
Bogan Lane Inn				✓	✓				
Botsford Inn	✓	✓				✓	✓		
Bowers Harbor Bed & Breakfast			✓						
The Bridge Street Inn		✓				✓			
Brookside Inn							✓	✓	
Centennial Inn				✓		✓			
Chateau Chantal	✓						✓	✓	
Cherry Knoll Farm									
Chicago Pike Inn	✓	✓				✓	✓	✓	
Chicago Street Inn		✓		✓			✓		
Clinton Inn	✓	✓		✓					
Cloghaun Bed & Breakfast		✓			✓	✓			
Crane House	✓	✓				✓	✓		
Dundee Guest House		✓		✓					
Eagle's Nest Bed & Breakfast		✓		✓		✓	✓		
Fairchild House		✓					✓	✓	
The Gingerbread House	✓			✓		✓			
Haan's 1830 Inn		✓		✓	✓	✓			

	Pets Allowed	No Smoking Indoors	Good Place for Families	Boating Nearby	Beach Nearby	Cross-Country Ski Trails	Golf Within 5 Miles	Fitness Facilities	Good Biking Terrain	Skiing	Horseback Riding	Tennis	Swimming on Premises	Fishing Nearby	Hiking Nearby
		✓		✓	✓				✓		✓				✓
		✓			✓	✓	✓		✓	✓					✓
		✓	✓		✓		✓		✓	✓					
		✓		✓	✓		✓		✓	✓					✓
		✓		✓	✓	✓			✓			✓		✓	✓
		✓			✓	✓			✓	✓			✓	✓	✓
		✓	✓	✓			✓					✓		✓	✓
		✓	✓	✓	✓	✓			✓		✓				✓
							✓					✓			
		✓		✓	✓				✓	✓				✓	✓
		✓		✓	✓		✓		✓	✓					✓
		✓			✓				✓	✓				✓	✓
		✓			✓	✓			✓	✓				✓	✓
		✓			✓	✓			✓	✓					
		✓			✓				✓	✓				✓	✓
			✓		✓		✓								
				✓	✓		✓		✓					✓	
			✓						✓					✓	✓
		✓	✓	✓	✓				✓			✓			✓
				✓	✓	✓			✓					✓	✓
		✓							✓						✓
				✓	✓	✓			✓					✓	✓
				✓	✓	✓	✓		✓				✓	✓	✓
		✓	✓	✓	✓		✓		✓	✓					✓
		✓	✓	✓	✓				✓		✓				✓

Special Features at a Glance

Name of Property	Accessible for Disabled	Antiques	On the Water	Best Value	Car Not Necessary	Historic Building	Romantic Hideaway	Luxurious	
The House on the Hill		✓					✓	✓	
The Inn at Union Pier	✓	✓	✓	✓			✓		
The Inn on Mackinac	✓			✓	✓				
Kimberly Country Estate		✓					✓	✓	
Kingsley House		✓	✓				✓		
Laurium Manor Inn		✓		✓		✓	✓	✓	
Leelanau Country Inn									
Lee Point Inn			✓						
Linden Lea			✓	✓			✓		
Main Street Bed & Breakfast				✓					
Maplewood Hotel	✓		✓		✓	✓	✓		
Metivier Inn	✓					✓	✓	✓	
Michigamme Lake Lodge	✓	✓	✓			✓	✓		
Montague Inn	✓	✓				✓			
Murray Hotel	✓				✓				
National House Inn	✓	✓				✓	✓		
Neahtawanta Inn			✓			✓			
1900 Market Street Inn					✓				
North Shore Inn	✓		✓				✓		
Old Mill Pond Inn				✓			✓		
Parsonage 1908		✓				✓	✓		
Pebble House	✓	✓	✓				✓		
Pine Garth Inn			✓				✓		
Pinewood Lodge	✓	✓	✓	✓			✓		
Raymond House Inn						✓			
South Cliff Inn		✓	✓				✓	✓	

Pets Allowed	No Smoking Indoors	Good Place for Families	Boating Nearby	Beach Nearby	Cross-Country Ski Trails	Golf Within 5 Miles	Fitness Facilities	Good Biking Terrain	Skiing	Horseback Riding	Tennis	Swimming on Premises	Fishing Nearby	Hiking Nearby
	✓			✓	✓	✓		✓	✓					✓
			✓	✓	✓			✓					✓	✓
	✓	✓	✓	✓				✓		✓				✓
	✓			✓	✓	✓		✓	✓			✓		✓
	✓		✓	✓		✓		✓	✓	✓			✓	✓
	✓	✓		✓	✓	✓		✓			✓		✓	✓
	✓			✓	✓			✓	✓				✓	✓
	✓		✓	✓	✓	✓		✓	✓				✓	✓
	✓	✓	✓	✓		✓		✓	✓			✓	✓	✓
	✓	✓	✓	✓		✓		✓	✓					
	✓	✓	✓	✓	✓	✓		✓		✓		✓	✓	✓
	✓		✓	✓				✓		✓				✓
	✓	✓	✓	✓	✓			✓				✓	✓	✓
			✓				✓						✓	✓	✓
	✓		✓	✓				✓		✓				✓
		✓			✓	✓		✓			✓		✓	✓
	✓	✓	✓	✓				✓	✓				✓	✓
	✓		✓	✓				✓		✓				✓
	✓		✓	✓	✓			✓	✓			✓	✓	✓
	✓		✓	✓				✓					✓	✓
	✓		✓	✓	✓	✓		✓			✓		✓	✓
	✓		✓	✓	✓	✓		✓			✓		✓	✓
			✓	✓	✓			✓					✓	✓
	✓	✓	✓		✓			✓				✓	✓	✓
	✓		✓	✓		✓		✓					✓	✓
			✓	✓	✓	✓		✓				✓	✓	✓

Special Features at a Glance

Name of Property	Accessible for Disabled	Antiques	On the Water	Best Value	Car Not Necessary	Historic Building	Romantic Hideaway	Luxurious	
The Stacy Mansion	✓	✓				✓	✓	✓	
Stafford's Bay View Inn						✓			
Torch Lake Bed & Breakfast									
The Victoriana 1898		✓			✓	✓	✓		
Victorian Inn		✓				✓	✓	✓	
Victorian Villa Inn		✓				✓	✓	✓	
Walloon Lake Inn			✓						
Water Street Inn	✓	✓	✓				✓		
Wickwood Country Inn	✓	✓					✓	✓	
William Clements Inn	✓	✓		✓		✓		✓	
Yelton Manor		✓	✓			✓	✓	✓	
MINNESOTA									
The Afton House Inn	✓		✓			✓			
The Anderson House				✓		✓			
The Ann Bean House		✓			✓	✓	✓	✓	
The Archer House	✓		✓		✓	✓			
Asa Parker House		✓				✓	✓	✓	
Barnum House Bed & Breakfast		✓				✓	✓	✓	
Battle Hollow Bed and Breakfast		✓			✓	✓	✓	✓	
Bearskin Lodge			✓				✓		
Bridgewaters Bed and Breakfast		✓	✓						
The Brunswick Inn		✓			✓	✓			
The Candle Light Inn		✓			✓	✓	✓	✓	
Caribou Lake B&B	✓		✓	✓			✓		
Carriage House Bed & Breakfast		✓		✓	✓	✓			

	Pets Allowed	No Smoking Indoors	Good Place for Families	Boating Nearby	Beach Nearby	Cross-Country Ski Trails	Golf Within 5 Miles	Fitness Facilities	Good Biking Terrain	Skiing	Horseback Riding	Tennis	Swimming on Premises	Fishing Nearby	Hiking Nearby
	✓						✓		✓					✓	
		✓		✓	✓		✓		✓	✓					✓
		✓		✓	✓		✓		✓	✓					✓
		✓		✓			✓		✓	✓		✓			
				✓	✓	✓	✓	✓				✓		✓	✓
		✓	✓	✓	✓		✓		✓	✓					✓
		✓		✓	✓	✓	✓		✓	✓				✓	✓
				✓	✓	✓	✓		✓		✓	✓		✓	✓
				✓	✓		✓		✓					✓	
				✓	✓	✓	✓		✓					✓	✓
			✓	✓	✓	✓	✓		✓	✓				✓	✓
	✓			✓	✓		✓		✓					✓	✓
		✓		✓	✓	✓	✓		✓			✓		✓	✓
			✓	✓	✓		✓		✓			✓		✓	✓
		✓		✓	✓	✓	✓		✓			✓		✓	✓
		✓		✓	✓	✓	✓		✓	✓		✓		✓	✓
		✓		✓	✓	✓	✓		✓		✓	✓		✓	✓
			✓	✓	✓	✓			✓				✓	✓	✓
		✓			✓	✓	✓		✓	✓		✓			
		✓		✓	✓		✓		✓			✓		✓	✓
		✓		✓		✓	✓		✓	✓		✓		✓	✓
		✓		✓	✓	✓			✓	✓	✓	✓	✓	✓	✓
		✓		✓	✓	✓	✓		✓		✓	✓		✓	✓

Special Features at a Glance

Name of Property	Accessible for Disabled	Antiques	On the Water	Best Value	Car Not Necessary	Historic Building	Romantic Hideaway	Luxurious
Carrington House		✓	✓					
Carrolton Country Inn				✓		✓		
Chatsworth B&B					✓	✓		
Cottonwood Inn				✓		✓		
Dr. Joseph Moses House					✓			
The Ellery House		✓		✓	✓	✓	✓	
Evelo's Bed & Breakfast		✓		✓	✓			
Fering's Guest House								
Fitger's Inn	✓		✓	✓	✓	✓		
The Garden Gate Bed and Breakfast				✓	✓			
Hallett House		✓					✓	
Heartland Trail Inn								
The Heirloom Inn		✓		✓	✓	✓	✓	
Historic Scanlan House		✓		✓		✓		
Hungry Point Inn		✓		✓		✓	✓	
The Inn at Palisade Bed & Breakfast			✓	✓			✓	
JailHouse Inn		✓		✓		✓	✓	✓
James A. Mulvey Residence Inn		✓		✓	✓	✓	✓	
Le Blanc House		✓		✓	✓	✓	✓	
Lindgren's Bed & Breakfast			✓					
Log House on Spirit Lake and Homestead		✓	✓				✓	
The Mansion Bed & Breakfast Inn			✓	✓		✓	✓	
Martin Oaks		✓		✓		✓		
Mathew S. Burrows 1890 Inn		✓			✓	✓	✓	✓
Mrs. B's Historic Lanesboro Inn			✓	✓		✓		
Naniboujou Lodge	✓		✓	✓		✓	✓	

	Pets Allowed	No Smoking Indoors	Good Place for Families	Boating Nearby	Beach Nearby	Cross-Country Ski Trails	Golf Within 5 Miles	Fitness Facilities	Good Biking Terrain	Skiing	Horseback Riding	Tennis	Swimming on Premises	Fishing Nearby	Hiking Nearby
	✓	✓		✓	✓	✓	✓		✓		✓	✓	✓	✓	✓
		✓	✓	✓			✓		✓					✓	✓
		✓							✓						
		✓		✓			✓		✓	✓				✓	✓
		✓		✓		✓	✓		✓		✓				✓
		✓	✓	✓	✓	✓	✓			✓		✓		✓	✓
		✓		✓	✓				✓			✓		✓	✓
		✓		✓			✓							✓	✓
			✓	✓	✓	✓	✓		✓	✓		✓		✓	✓
	✓	✓	✓			✓	✓		✓			✓			
		✓		✓	✓	✓	✓		✓					✓	✓
		✓		✓	✓	✓	✓		✓		✓			✓	✓
		✓		✓		✓	✓		✓		✓	✓		✓	✓
		✓		✓		✓	✓		✓		✓	✓		✓	✓
		✓	✓			✓	✓		✓	✓	✓			✓	✓
		✓	✓	✓	✓	✓			✓					✓	✓
		✓		✓		✓			✓					✓	✓
		✓		✓	✓	✓	✓		✓			✓		✓	✓
		✓		✓					✓			✓		✓	✓
				✓	✓	✓	✓		✓	✓	✓	✓		✓	✓
		✓		✓	✓	✓	✓		✓		✓	✓	✓	✓	✓
				✓	✓	✓	✓		✓	✓		✓		✓	✓
		✓		✓		✓	✓		✓					✓	✓
		✓		✓	✓	✓	✓			✓		✓		✓	✓
				✓		✓	✓		✓		✓	✓		✓	✓
			✓	✓	✓	✓			✓					✓	✓

Special Features at a Glance

Name of Property	Accessible for Disabled	Antiques	On the Water	Best Value	Car Not Necessary	Historic Building	Romantic Hideaway	Luxurious	
Nicollet Island Inn	✓		✓	✓	✓	✓	✓		
Nims' Bakketop Hus			✓						
1900 Dupont		✓		✓	✓	✓	✓		
Oakhurst Inn									
Park Row Bed and Breakfast		✓		✓			✓		
Park Street Inn		✓				✓	✓		
Peace Cliff		✓	✓				✓		
Peters' Sunset Beach		✓	✓			✓			
Pincushion Mountain Bed & Breakfast				✓			✓		
Prairie House on Round Lake		✓	✓						
Prairie View Estate		✓		✓					
Pratt-Taber Inn		✓		✓	✓	✓	✓		
Quill & Quilt	✓	✓		✓		✓	✓		
Red Gables Inn		✓		✓	✓	✓			
The Rivertown Inn		✓				✓	✓		
The Robards House		✓				✓			
The Rose Bed and Breakfast				✓			✓	✓	
St. James Hotel	✓		✓		✓	✓			
Schumacher's New Prague Hotel						✓	✓	✓	
Sod House on the Prairie		✓							
Spicer Castle		✓	✓			✓	✓	✓	
The Stone Hearth Inn Bed & Breakfast		✓	✓	✓		✓	✓		
Stonehouse Bed and Breakfast									
The Superior Overlook B&B			✓	✓		✓	✓		
Thorwood Historic Inns		✓				✓	✓	✓	
Tianna Farms			✓			✓			

Pets Allowed	No Smoking Indoors	Good Place for Families	Boating Nearby	Beach Nearby	Cross-Country Ski Trails	Golf Within 5 Miles	Fitness Facilities	Good Biking Terrain	Skiing	Horseback Riding	Tennis	Swimming on Premises	Fishing Nearby	Hiking Nearby
✓		✓	✓					✓			✓		✓	✓
✓	✓		✓	✓	✓			✓		✓		✓	✓	✓
	✓		✓	✓				✓			✓		✓	✓
		✓	✓	✓	✓	✓		✓			✓		✓	
	✓		✓	✓	✓	✓		✓			✓		✓	✓
	✓		✓	✓	✓					✓			✓	✓
	✓		✓		✓	✓		✓				✓	✓	✓
			✓	✓		✓		✓			✓	✓	✓	✓
	✓		✓		✓	✓		✓					✓	✓
	✓		✓							✓	✓	✓	✓	✓
✓	✓		✓		✓	✓						✓	✓	✓
✓		✓	✓		✓	✓		✓	✓		✓		✓	✓
			✓		✓	✓		✓	✓		✓		✓	✓
	✓		✓	✓	✓	✓		✓	✓		✓		✓	✓
	✓		✓	✓	✓	✓		✓			✓		✓	
	✓		✓	✓	✓	✓		✓		✓	✓		✓	✓
	✓				✓	✓		✓			✓			
		✓	✓		✓	✓	✓	✓	✓		✓		✓	✓
					✓	✓		✓			✓			✓
	✓	✓								✓				✓
			✓	✓	✓	✓	✓	✓		✓		✓	✓	✓
	✓		✓	✓	✓			✓					✓	✓
		✓	✓	✓	✓	✓		✓		✓			✓	✓
	✓	✓	✓	✓	✓	✓		✓			✓		✓	✓
	✓		✓		✓	✓		✓	✓		✓		✓	✓
			✓	✓	✓	✓		✓		✓	✓	✓	✓	✓

Special Features at a Glance

Name of Property	Accessible for Disabled	Antiques	On the Water	Best Value	Car Not Necessary	Historic Building	Romantic Hideaway	Luxurious	
The Victorian Bed & Breakfast		✓	✓	✓	✓	✓	✓		
Walden Woods		✓	✓	✓			✓		
Whistle Stop Inn		✓		✓			✓		
The William Sauntry Mansion		✓			✓	✓	✓	✓	
WISCONSIN									
Allyn Mansion Inn		✓				✓	✓	✓	
American Country Farm	✓	✓				✓	✓		
Arbor House		✓				✓	✓		
The Barbican Guest House		✓				✓	✓	✓	
Bettinger House		✓		✓		✓			
The Boyden House		✓				✓	✓	✓	
Breese Waye		✓		✓		✓			
Candlewick Inn		✓				✓	✓		
Canterbury Inn	✓				✓		✓	✓	
Cedar Trails Guesthouse		✓		✓					
The Church Hill Inn	✓	✓					✓	✓	
Collins House		✓	✓		✓	✓			
The Country Manor		✓				✓			
The Creamery			✓			✓			
Dreams of Yesteryear		✓			✓	✓	✓		
The Duke House		✓		✓		✓			
The Eagle Harbor Inn	✓	✓							
Eleven Gables Inn on the Lake		✓	✓		✓	✓			
Elizabethian Inn	✓	✓	✓		✓	✓			
Enchanted Valley Garden									

Pets Allowed	No Smoking Indoors	Good Place for Families	Boating Nearby	Beach Nearby	Cross-Country Ski Trails	Golf Within 5 Miles	Fitness Facilities	Good Biking Terrain	Skiing	Horseback Riding	Tennis	Swimming on Premises	Fishing Nearby	Hiking Nearby
	✓		✓	✓	✓	✓		✓	✓		✓		✓	✓
	✓	✓	✓	✓	✓	✓		✓	✓	✓	✓		✓	✓
	✓		✓	✓							✓		✓	
	✓		✓	✓	✓	✓		✓			✓		✓	✓
	✓		✓	✓	✓	✓		✓	✓	✓	✓		✓	✓
			✓	✓	✓	✓		✓	✓	✓	✓		✓	✓
	✓		✓	✓	✓	✓		✓			✓			
			✓	✓	✓	✓		✓		✓	✓		✓	✓
			✓	✓	✓	✓		✓	✓				✓	✓
	✓		✓	✓	✓	✓		✓	✓				✓	✓
	✓		✓	✓	✓	✓		✓	✓				✓	✓
	✓				✓	✓		✓						
	✓	✓	✓		✓	✓		✓	✓		✓		✓	✓
	✓		✓	✓	✓	✓	✓	✓			✓	✓	✓	✓
		✓	✓	✓	✓	✓		✓	✓		✓		✓	✓
	✓		✓	✓	✓	✓		✓	✓		✓		✓	✓
		✓	✓		✓	✓		✓	✓				✓	✓
	✓		✓	✓	✓	✓		✓	✓		✓		✓	✓
	✓		✓		✓	✓		✓	✓				✓	✓
	✓	✓	✓	✓	✓	✓		✓		✓	✓		✓	✓
			✓	✓	✓	✓		✓	✓	✓	✓	✓	✓	✓
	✓		✓	✓	✓	✓		✓	✓	✓	✓	✓	✓	✓
✓		✓	✓	✓	✓	✓		✓	✓				✓	✓

Special Features at a Glance

Name of Property	Accessible for Disabled	Antiques	On the Water	Best Value	Car Not Necessary	Historic Building	Romantic Hideaway	Luxurious	
The Ephraim Inn	✓	✓	✓			✓	✓		
Fargo Mansion Inn		✓				✓	✓	✓	
48 West Oak		✓				✓	✓	✓	
The Franklin Victorian		✓							
The French Country Inn of Ephraim		✓		✓		✓			
The Gallery House			✓	✓		✓			
The Geiger House		✓		✓					
The Gray Goose Bed and Breakfast		✓		✓		✓			
Great River Bed & Breakfast		✓				✓	✓		
The Griffin Inn	✓	✓		✓		✓	✓		
The Harbor House Inn	✓	✓	✓	✓		✓			
The Harrisburg Inn		✓							
Hill Street		✓							
Historic Bennett House		✓			✓	✓	✓	✓	
The Hitching Post		✓				✓			
The Inn at Cedar Crossing		✓				✓	✓		
The Inn at Wildcat Mountain		✓							
Jackson Street Inn		✓		✓		✓			
The Jefferson-Day House		✓				✓	✓		
The Jones House		✓				✓	✓	✓	
Just-N-Trails	✓						✓		
The Knollwood House		✓		✓		✓			
Lakeside Manor	✓		✓	✓			✓		
The Manor House	✓	✓	✓			✓	✓	✓	
The Mansards on-the-Lake		✓	✓	✓		✓			
Mansion Hill Inn		✓			✓	✓	✓	✓	

Pets Allowed	No Smoking Indoors	Good Place for Families	Boating Nearby	Beach Nearby	Cross-Country Ski Trails	Golf Within 5 Miles	Fitness Facilities	Good Biking Terrain	Skiing	Horseback Riding	Tennis	Swimming on Premises	Fishing Nearby	Hiking Nearby
	✓		✓	✓	✓	✓		✓		✓	✓		✓	✓
	✓	✓	✓	✓	✓	✓		✓	✓				✓	✓
	✓		✓	✓	✓	✓		✓	✓	✓	✓		✓	✓
✓		✓	✓	✓	✓	✓		✓	✓				✓	✓
	✓		✓	✓	✓	✓		✓		✓	✓		✓	✓
	✓		✓	✓	✓	✓		✓	✓		✓		✓	✓
	✓		✓	✓	✓	✓		✓	✓				✓	✓
			✓	✓	✓	✓		✓		✓	✓		✓	✓
	✓	✓	✓		✓			✓						
			✓	✓	✓	✓		✓		✓	✓		✓	✓
	✓		✓	✓	✓	✓		✓		✓	✓		✓	✓
✓		✓	✓	✓	✓	✓		✓	✓				✓	✓
	✓		✓	✓	✓	✓		✓	✓		✓		✓	✓
	✓		✓	✓	✓	✓		✓	✓		✓		✓	✓
	✓	✓	✓		✓			✓	✓		✓			
			✓	✓	✓	✓		✓		✓	✓		✓	✓
✓		✓	✓	✓	✓	✓		✓	✓	✓			✓	✓
	✓	✓	✓	✓	✓	✓		✓	✓		✓		✓	✓
	✓		✓	✓	✓	✓		✓	✓		✓		✓	✓
	✓		✓	✓	✓	✓		✓	✓		✓		✓	✓
	✓	✓	✓	✓	✓	✓		✓	✓				✓	✓
	✓		✓	✓	✓	✓	✓	✓	✓			✓	✓	✓
	✓		✓	✓	✓	✓		✓	✓	✓	✓	✓	✓	✓
			✓	✓	✓	✓		✓	✓		✓		✓	✓
	✓		✓	✓	✓	✓		✓	✓		✓		✓	✓
			✓	✓	✓	✓	✓	✓	✓		✓		✓	✓

Special Features at a Glance

Name of Property	Accessible for Disabled	Antiques	On the Water	Best Value	Car Not Necessary	Historic Building	Romantic Hideaway	Luxurious	
Martindale House		✓				✓	✓	✓	
Mascione's Hidden Valley Villas	✓						✓		
Middleton Beach Inn	✓	✓	✓				✓		
Nash House				✓		✓			
Oak Hill Manor		✓		✓		✓			
The Oak Street Inn		✓				✓			
Parkview		✓		✓		✓			
The Parson's Inn		✓		✓		✓			
Past and Present Inn	✓	✓					✓		
The Peterson Victorian Bed & Breakfast		✓		✓		✓			
The Phipps Inn		✓				✓	✓	✓	
Pine Creek Lodge	✓						✓	✓	
Pinehaven				✓					
Riley House Bed and Breakfast		✓				✓			
Rosenberry Inn	✓	✓			✓	✓	✓		
The Ryan House		✓		✓		✓			
The Scofield House		✓				✓	✓	✓	
Sherman House						✓			
Stagecoach Inn	✓	✓				✓	✓		
Stewart Inn		✓				✓			
Sugar River Inn		✓	✓	✓					
The Swallow's Nest				✓					
T. C. Smith Inn		✓			✓	✓	✓	✓	
Thorp House Inn		✓				✓	✓		
Trillium	✓	✓		✓			✓		
Trillium Woods				✓			✓	✓	

Pets Allowed	No Smoking Indoors	Good Place for Families	Boating Nearby	Beach Nearby	Cross-Country Ski Trails	Golf Within 5 Miles	Fitness Facilities	Good Biking Terrain	Skiing	Horseback Riding	Tennis	Swimming on Premises	Fishing Nearby	Hiking Nearby
	✓		✓	✓	✓	✓		✓	✓		✓		✓	✓
			✓	✓	✓	✓		✓	✓	✓		✓	✓	✓
	✓		✓	✓	✓	✓	✓	✓	✓		✓	✓	✓	✓
	✓	✓	✓		✓	✓		✓	✓				✓	✓
	✓	✓	✓		✓	✓		✓	✓				✓	✓
	✓		✓	✓	✓	✓		✓	✓				✓	✓
		✓	✓	✓	✓	✓		✓	✓				✓	✓
	✓	✓	✓	✓	✓	✓		✓	✓				✓	✓
	✓	✓	✓	✓	✓	✓		✓	✓				✓	✓
	✓					✓		✓	✓	✓				
	✓		✓	✓	✓	✓		✓	✓		✓		✓	✓
	✓				✓	✓		✓						
	✓	✓	✓	✓	✓	✓		✓	✓				✓	✓
	✓	✓	✓	✓	✓	✓		✓	✓		✓		✓	✓
		✓	✓	✓	✓	✓		✓	✓				✓	✓
	✓	✓	✓	✓	✓	✓		✓	✓				✓	✓
	✓		✓	✓	✓	✓		✓					✓	✓
		✓	✓	✓	✓	✓		✓	✓	✓			✓	✓
	✓		✓	✓	✓	✓		✓	✓	✓	✓		✓	✓
	✓		✓	✓	✓	✓		✓	✓				✓	✓
	✓		✓	✓	✓	✓		✓	✓			✓	✓	✓
	✓		✓	✓	✓	✓		✓	✓				✓	✓
					✓	✓		✓	✓		✓			
	✓	✓	✓	✓	✓	✓		✓			✓	✓		✓	✓
		✓	✓	✓	✓	✓		✓	✓				✓	✓
	✓	✓				✓		✓						

Special Features at a Glance

Name of Property	Accessible for Disabled	Antiques	On the Water	Best Value	Car Not Necessary	Historic Building	Romantic Hideaway	Luxurious	
University Heights Bed and Breakfast		✓				✓			
The Victorian Belle		✓				✓			
Victorian Garden		✓				✓	✓		
Victorian Swan on Water		✓		✓	✓	✓			
Victoria-on-Main		✓		✓		✓			
Viroqua Heritage Inn		✓		✓		✓			
Washington House Inn	✓	✓				✓	✓	✓	
Westby House		✓				✓			
The Whistling Swan		✓				✓	✓		
The White Apron		✓		✓		✓	✓		
The White Gull Inn	✓	✓				✓	✓		
White Lace Inn	✓	✓				✓	✓	✓	
William's		✓							

Pets Allowed	No Smoking Indoors	Good Place for Families	Boating Nearby	Beach Nearby	Cross-Country Ski Trails	Golf Within 5 Miles	Fitness Facilities	Good Biking Terrain	Skiing	Horseback Riding	Tennis	Swimming on Premises	Fishing Nearby	Hiking Nearby
	✓	✓		✓	✓	✓		✓						
	✓		✓	✓	✓	✓		✓	✓				✓	✓
	✓	✓	✓	✓	✓	✓		✓	✓				✓	✓
	✓		✓	✓	✓	✓		✓	✓		✓		✓	✓
	✓		✓	✓	✓	✓		✓	✓	✓			✓	✓
	✓	✓	✓	✓	✓	✓		✓	✓		✓		✓	✓
			✓	✓	✓	✓		✓	✓	✓	✓		✓	✓
		✓	✓	✓	✓	✓		✓	✓				✓	✓
	✓		✓	✓	✓	✓		✓		✓	✓		✓	✓
	✓		✓	✓	✓	✓		✓	✓				✓	✓
	✓	✓	✓	✓	✓	✓		✓		✓	✓		✓	✓
			✓	✓	✓	✓		✓		✓	✓		✓	✓
	✓		✓	✓	✓	✓		✓	✓	✓	✓		✓	✓

Michigan

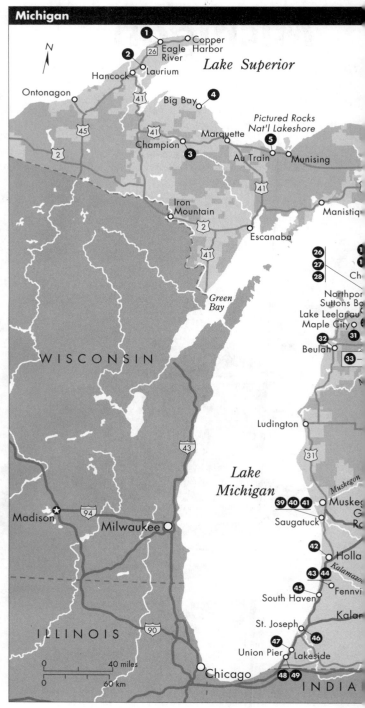

Michigan

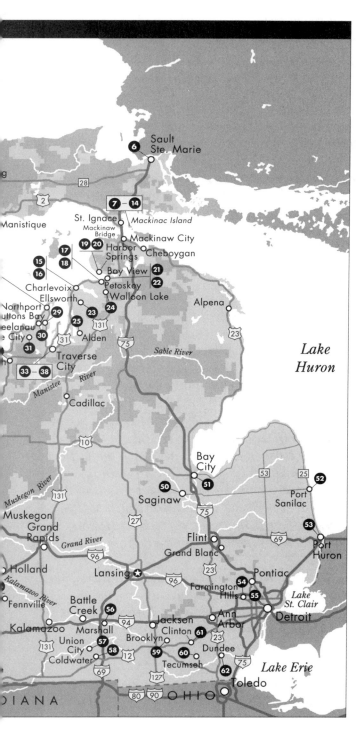

Southeastern Michigan
Including Ann Arbor and Detroit

First-time visitors to this part of Michigan are surprised to find more than post-industrial forests of cold smokestacks. Although the region's two major urban centers, Detroit and Flint, struggle with the same socioeconomic problems that afflict most Rust Belt cities, no other part of the state offers a greater mix of natural, cultural, and recreational resources. Row a boat on a quiet lake in the morning, browse in rural antiques shops in the afternoon, take in a professional sporting event, dine at a world-class restaurant in the evening, even visit another country for a nightcap—all usually within an hour's reach of your lodging.

Although one-third of the state's population lives here, an excellent network of freeways and secondary roads allows travelers to zip easily out of city centers and into the surrounding countryside. If you find shopping in the cavernous Renaissance Center in downtown Detroit frustrating, drive northbound on I–75 for 45 minutes until you reach Holly, a pastoral pocket of old stores. Port Huron is an hour away from Flint or Detroit, and once there, you can watch freighters pass so close you can almost touch them. Port Huron is at the base of the largely rural "Thumb" region (lower Michigan is shaped like a mitten), honeycombed with farms, sleepy ports, and superb county and state parks. U.S. 25 traces the thumb's outline from Bay City to Port Huron and affords exquisite views of Lake Huron and Saginaw Bay.

Detroit, of course, anchors the region. The Motor City, ringed by some of the most affluent suburbs in the country, is dissected by three major interstate highways. Interstate 75 will take you to Monroe (home of General George Custer) in the south and to Bay City, a port town on Saginaw Bay, to the north. Interstates 96 and 94 will carry you west to Lansing and Jackson, respectively. Running north from the Ohio border, U.S. 127 strings these two cities together and forms a logical western boundary to the region. Urban sprawl is minimal here, and the little there is blends easily into miles of open country.

Despite its lunch-bucket reputation, Detroit actually has a very cosmopolitan feel that befits the oldest city west of the Appalachians. The flags of three nations—France, Britain, and the United States—have flown over this onetime trading post. As a chief port of entry for settlers heading for the interior in the mid-1800s, then later as a magnet drawing a multitude of immigrants and South Americans to its booming auto plants, Detroit has always been a polyglot community. At one time an exasperated Henry Ford was obliged to post work signs in eight languages in his factories.

Today, this diversity is evident in the scores of ethnic restaurants sprinkled throughout the region. Many are in such ethnic enclaves as Hamtramck, a large community of Polish-Americans within Detroit city limits, and Dearborn, a western suburb that has the largest Arab population outside the Middle East. A growing colony of transplanted Japanese—a sign of the increasing interdependence between U.S. and Asian car makers—has materialized, resulting in a rash of Oriental restaurants and karaoke bars. The village of Frankenmuth, an hour's drive north of Detroit, remains more German than American.

To add to the mix, Canada is just a short bridge or tunnel ride away. Americans and Canadians move freely back and forth; passports are not necessary for citizens of either country. Spectacular annual events such as the Detroit Grand Prix auto race, the Montreaux Detroit Jazz Festival (the largest free jazz fest in the world), the Port Huron–Mackinac Island sailing regatta, the North American International Auto Show, the Gold Cup powerboat races, and the International Freedom Festival draw hundreds of thousands of people apiece and help to maintain the region's international flavor.

Countless chain motels and luxury hotels have been built to handle the business and convention trade. As a result, historic inns and bed-and-breakfasts are not nearly as numerous in southeastern Michigan as in other parts of the state. Those that do exist, however, typically have been around for a long time and are very good, their owners having learned how to weather the boom-and-bust cycles that are so much a part of this area's history.

Places to Go, Sights to See

Ann Arbor. Home to the University of Michigan, this leafy, liberal community is a 45-minute drive from downtown Detroit via westbound I–94. Ann Arbor is the quintessential university town: drowsy neighborhood bookshops and funky street performers peacefully co-exist with respected arts centers and world-class research facilities. Sidewalk cafés operate past midnight, and the 101,000-seat Michigan Stadium, the nation's largest college-owned stadium, makes Ann Arbor a great place for tailgate parties on football weekends in the fall.

Auto Racing. The Detroit Grand Prix (tel. 313/259–5400), held every June since 1981, has evolved into a three-day weekend party interrupted periodically by the main event and support races. The Michigan International Speedway (tel. 313/961–1922), 60 miles west of Detroit on U.S. 12 in Brooklyn, features NASCAR and Indy-style races.

Detroit. Once the nation's fourth-largest city, Detroit has lost half of its population since the 1950s. The shrinking tax base has caused one of the country's truly great museums, the **Detroit Institute of Arts** (5200 Woodward Ave., tel. 313/833–7900), to juggle hours of operation, so call ahead. But while the core city has struggled as jobs and people have moved elsewhere, downtown and surrounding suburbs continue to offer first-class shopping, dining, cultural, and entertainment experiences. **Belle Isle** (tel. 313/267–7115), a 1,000-acre island park, sits in the Detroit River, 3 miles from the heart of the city, connected by a bridge to the mainland. The multipurpose park has facilities for baseball, golf, swimming, cycling, hiking, basketball, tennis, and many other recreational activities. Other attractions are an aquarium, a zoo, a nature center, a conservatory, and the Dossin Great Lakes Museum. The Detroit Grand Prix is held here in June. **The Fox Theatre** (2211 Woodward Ave., tel. 313/965–7100), which opened in 1928 as America's largest movie palace, today showcases big-name musical acts and large-screen movies. The **Henry Ford Museum & Greenfield Village** (Village Rd. and Oakwood Blvd., Dearborn, tel. 313/271–1620) are two world-famous collections of Americana in the western suburb of Dearborn. Especially noteworthy is "The Automobile in American Life," a lavish, upbeat collection of chrome and neon devoted to the evolution of the automobile and roadside culture. Detroit's chapter of the American Dream comes alive in a tour of **Historic Homes of the Auto Barons** (tel. 313/644–2060), which includes several mansions that once belonged to auto pioneers such as Henry and Edsel Ford and the Dodge brothers. To round out the experience, you can schedule a guided tour of old factories and other historic sites relating to Detroit's auto and labor past through the Detroit Labor History Tour Project (tel. 313/822–6426). The **Motown Museum** (2648 W. Grand Blvd., tel. 313/875–2264) is an unassuming two-story house on West Grand Boulevard where Berry Gordy, Jr., started the "Motown Sound" in the late 1950s. It's stuffed with memorabilia, including album covers, costumes, gold records, and, yes, one of Michael Jackson's gloves. You can squeeze into the small recording studio where such acts as the Temptations, Smokey Robinson and the Miracles, and Diana Ross and the Supremes cranked out hit after hit. The Detroit Tigers and their predecessors have been playing baseball at the corner of Michigan and Trumbull streets in **Tiger Stadium** (tel. 313/962–4000) since 1896, making this professional sports' oldest address. Prices are reasonable and acquiring tickets is almost never a problem, making it easy to enjoy a summer game.

Frankenmuth. "Little Bavaria," founded by German immigrants in 1845, sits just off the I–75 corridor between Flint and Saginaw. The town markets its heritage through scores of gift shops, lodgings, and restaurants that groan under the weight of flower boxes and gingerbread trim. The village's most popular attraction is Bronner's Christmas Wonderland (25 Christmas La., Frankenmuth, tel. 517/652–9931), where more than 50,000 lights and ornaments are for sale year-round.

Port Huron. Situated at the confluence of the St. Clair River and Lake Huron, the hometown of inventor Thomas Edison has changed very little since he was young. The 1858 Grand Trunk Depot from which he sold newspapers on the Detroit-bound train has been restored in a riverside park. Here visitors get incredible close-up views of freighters from all over the world passing through the narrow, ¼-mile-wide passageway. Other maritime treats include the 152-foot-high Blue Water Bridge, from which pedestrians can enjoy panoramic views while waiting for freighters to pass underneath; and the Lighthouse Park complex, which includes an 1874 lightkeeper's dwelling, a white clapboard Coast Guard station, and the oldest surviving lighthouse in Michigan.

Tecumseh. This town, about 30 miles east of Jackson on Route 50, is the antiques center of the region. Founded in 1824, it has three antiques malls among its many historic buildings and restored train depot. One of the state's largest antiques fairs is held on the third Sunday of every month from April to November at the fairgrounds (tel. 313/429–1131) in nearby Saline.

Boating

Michigan has more registered boat owners than any other state, so the Great Lakes and inland waters become crowded playgrounds in warm weather. Most county and state parks offer boat and canoe rentals and have beaches with supervised swimming. Bay City, a freighter port on Saginaw Bay, has speedboat and offshore powerboat racing and other water sports. River cruising is gaining popularity. You can cruise, dine, and view the skylines of Detroit and Windsor on the *Detroiter* (tel. 313/567–1400) or eat while enjoying the breezes of Lake St. Clair on the 100-foot yacht the *Infinity* (tel. 313/778–7030).

Fishing

With almost 100 lakes in the metro Detroit area alone, you'll never be far from a fishing hole. The Detroit River, especially around Belle Isle, is popular with anglers. Generally, the waters throughout the region are rated good to excellent for trout, yellow perch, bluegills, crappies, bass, walleye, panfish, and northern pike. Charter-boat fishing for salmon, walleye, and lake trout is available on Lakes Huron, St. Clair, and Erie.

Golf

Michigan's golf season stretches from April through October. New courses continue to spring up, including Marion Oaks Golf Club (2255 Pinkey Rd., Howell, tel. 517/548–0050), halfway between Lansing and Detroit on I–96 in Howell. Desmond Muirhead designed the course at Bay Valley Inn (2470 Old Bridge Rd., Bay City, tel. 517/686–5400, and Cascades Golf Course (1992 Warren Ave., Jackson, tel. 517/788–4323) in Jackson is considered one of the best golf values in the state. In the Thumb, Verona Hills (3175 Sand Beach Rd., Bad Axe, tel. 517/269–8132), with an excellent layout, is just east of Bad Axe on Route 142. For a complete listing, contact the **Michigan Association of Public Golf Courses** (Box 612, Plymouth, MI 48170, tel. 313/582–8860 or 800/223–5877).

Skiing

Downhill resorts can be found just off I–75 north of Detroit at Pine Knob Ski Resort (tel. 313/625–0800) in Clarkston and Mt. Holly (tel. 313/582–7256) in Holly. Mt. Brighton Ski Area (tel. 313/229–9581) in Brighton and Alpine Valley (tel. 313/887–4183) in Milford also are popular. Many county and state parks, as well as a growing number of golf courses, have groomed trails for cross-country skiing.

Restaurants

The region is chock-full of good restaurants. The cavernous **Bavarian Inn** (713 S. Main St., tel. 517/652–9941) in Frankenmuth specializes in hearty, homemade chicken dinners. Ann Arbor's most popular restaurant, **Chuck Muery's Gandy Dancer** (401 Depot St., tel. 313/769–0592), serves fresh seafood dishes in an old fieldstone train station. Some of the favorites in Detroit include downtown's **Fishbone's Rhythm Kitchen Cafe** (400 Monroe St., tel. 313/965–4600), home of New Orleans–style gumbo and whiskey ribs; the classically Italian **Roma's Cafe** (3401 Riopelle St., tel. 313/831–5940), the city's oldest restaurant; and **The Whitney** (4421 Woodward St., tel. 313/832–5700), where American food and music are served inside a pink-stone mansion that once belonged to lumber baron David Whitney. **The Lark** (6430 Farmington St., tel. 313/661–4466) in suburban West Bloomfield is famous for its crisp service, superb Continental cuisine, and genuinely warm hospitality. World travelers Jim and Mary Lark have transformed their interestingly decorated country inn into the best dining experience on this side of the state.

Tourist Information

The umbrella organization for the entire state is the **Michigan Travel Bureau** (333 S. Capitol Ave., Lansing, MI 48933, tel. 800/543–2937). For information on boating, fishing, and hunting, contact the **Michigan Department of Natural**

Resources (530 N. Allegan St., Lansing, MI 48933, tel. 517/373–1204). Site-specific tourist information can be found through the **Ann Arbor Convention and Visitors Bureau** (211 E. Huron St., Ann Arbor, MI 48104, tel. 313/995–7281); **Flint Area Convention and Visitors Bureau** (400 N. Saginaw St., Flint, MI 48502, tel. 313/232–8900); **Frankenmuth Chamber of Commerce** (635 S. Main St., Frankenmuth, MI 48734, tel. 517/652-6106); **Greater Lansing Convention and Visitors Bureau** (119 Pere Marquette, Box 15066, Lansing, MI 48901, tel. 517/487–6800 or 800/648–6630); **Metropolitan Detroit Convention and Visitors Bureau** (100 Renaissance Center, Suite 1950, Detroit, MI 48243, tel. 313/259–4333); **Port Huron/Marysville Chamber of Commerce** (920 Pine Grove Ave., Port Huron, MI 48060, tel. 313/985–7101); and the **Saginaw County Convention and Visitors Bureau** (901 S. Washington St., Saginaw, MI 48601, tel. 517/752–7164).

Montague Inn

Robert Montague was a respected businessman and civic leader when he built his 12,000-square-foot Georgian house in 1929. He made his fortune developing a way to use sugar beet byproducts to make hand creams and soaps, a process later sold to the Andrew Jergens Company.

Saginaw's historic Grove District was once an enclave of stunning residences. The city bought the house in the early 1960s and demolished several of the surrounding properties. Then a group of five couples bought it in 1985. Eight months later, they reopened the restored mansion and the adjacent carriage house as the Montague Inn. Not only has the three-story brick mansion been named to the State Register of Historic Places, but it is also considered one of Michigan's best inns, a designation that's hard to dispute.

The inn's location on 8 gently rolling acres overlooking Lake Linton is a mixed blessing. There is usually a lot of activity on the grounds, and on days when the city park across the water is staging a concert or a raft race, there can be a large volume of traffic in the area. That said, the inn is still a champion. A winding staircase connects the three floors of guest rooms. The Georgian-style quarters typically contain four-poster beds and wing chairs and are tastefully decorated in subtle hues and patterns. The most compelling is the Montague Suite, which features a fireplace, green Pewabic tile, and great views of the impeccably landscaped grounds.

Guests enjoy a Continental breakfast of oatmeal, cereals, juice, and baked goods in either of two dining rooms, one of which has a welcoming fire on cold mornings. Lunches and candlelight dinners are first-class affairs, too, with an expansive (and expensive) menu and wine list. After meals, a fire is lit in the fireplace of the main-floor library, and guests can look for the hidden cabinets inside the library walls, where Montague stashed his expensive supply of liquor during Prohibition, or sink back into couches to smoke and talk. Others sit at the antique writing desk to pen a postcard: Those who scrawl "Wish you were here" know what they're talking about.

Address: *1581 S. Washington Ave., Saginaw, MI 48601, tel. 517/752–3939, fax 517/752–3951.*
Accommodations: *16 double rooms with baths, 2 doubles share bath, 1 suite.*
Amenities: *Air-conditioning, phone and TV in guest rooms, restaurant.*
Rates: *$65–$120, Montague Suite $150; Continental breakfast. AE, MC, V.*
Restrictions: *Smoking in library only, no pets.*

Raymond House Inn

As Shirley and Ray Denison, owners of the inn, enjoy pointing out, there is no McDonald's in Port Sanilac. The 60-ish couple do what they can to keep the golden arches at bay by heading a movement to have this old port village declared a Historic Maritime District, thereby limiting commercial development.

Port Sanilac sits halfway up the eastern edge of the "Thumb" region on Route 25, about 30 miles north of Port Huron and less than two hours from Detroit. It was one of Lake Huron's first ports of call during the heyday of the steamship. Its colorful history includes lumberjacks, lake storms, rum-running, and forest fires that more than once destroyed the town.

The background of the comfortable, impressive Victorian house, which is listed on the State Register of Historic Places, is a little calmer but nevertheless significant. In 1850, Uri Raymond, the original owner, opened what is reputed to be the first hardware store in the state. (Raymond Hardware, just a block down the road, is still in business.) Raymond built his two-story brick residence in 1871, adorning it with classic Victoriana: elaborate moldings and a winding oak staircase on the inside, a gingerbread facade and white icicle trim dripping on the outside. It stayed in the family for the next 112 years until Ray and Shirley—he's a lobbyist for the AFL–CIO, she's a restorative artist who in 1976 reframed the Constitution for the

Bicentennial—bought it in 1983 and moved here from Washington, D.C.

The house, set on an acre planted with trees and gardens of wildflowers, was in good condition and is now full of family heirlooms, antiques, and numerous examples of Shirley's considerable artistic and restorative skills. She has recaned the chairs, restored the frames that hold a collection of old family photos in an upstairs hallway, and designed the grandfather clock in the dining room. The upstairs quarters are authentically furnished, down to crocheted lacework on the shades, handmade quilts, and hand-crocheted rugs. Lake Huron, a block away, can be spied from the upstairs porch and, in the winter, from three of the guest rooms.

Address: *111 S. Ridge St., Port Sanilac, MI 48469, tel. 313/622–8800 or 800/622–7229.*
Accommodations: *7 double rooms with baths.*
Amenities: *Air-conditioning, radio/cassette player in rooms; fireplace, cable TV, and phone in parlor.*
Rates: *$65–$75; full breakfast. D, MC, V.*
Restrictions: *No smoking, no pets; closed Jan.–Mar.*

The Stacy Mansion

The story of one of the state's grandest homes can be gleaned from a quick look inside its first-floor library. On a desktop, *The 1874 Historical Atlas of Lenawee County* is opened to a sketch of the four-story brick mansion as it looked when Judge C. A. Stacy owned it. Directly above the open book hangs a buffalo head, provided by the current owners, Sonny and Joyce Lauber, who, among their other business interests, run one of the few bison farms in the country.

Stacy, newspaper publisher, businessman, and the first probate judge in the county, built the 9,000-square-foot house in the mid-1850s in anticipation of using it as the governor's residence. He lost the gubernatorial election but held on to the house, which has fine examples of 19th-century craftsmanship such as a foyer with marbled wood and a rare cantilevered oak staircase.

"Sonny drove past the house for 25 years and always talked about buying it," says Joyce. When the badly neglected building on the outskirts of Tecumseh came on the market in 1988, the Laubers didn't think twice. The house had been stripped of nearly everything—from the furnishings to the brass doorknobs and gingerbread trim—so restoration has been a slow, expensive process. To their credit, they have taken time to research and spent the money necessary to recall its 19th-century ambience. They tore out the carpeting and restored the floors

and woodwork and replicated the plasterwork and hand-printed wallpaper. They were even able to buy back some of the furniture. All told, the house "is about 95% antiques," says Joyce. One bedroom has a double-mirrored wardrobe and another an 8½-foot-high, ornately carved walnut headboard. The only incongruous item is the water-filled mattress in the master bedroom. "We couldn't find a mattress that would fit the odd-sized cherry full-tester bed," she explains.

The 3-acre site is expertly landscaped. Judge Stacy, who owned a local brickyard, would certainly approve of the 25,000 bricks the Laubers used to create the paths that wind through the yards and gardens. A 130-year-old pine tree shades a court of geranium-filled stone planters and wrought-iron garden furniture, while old-fashioned streetlamps and red maple trees flank the circular drive and help to make the outdoors an appealing retreat in itself.

Address: *710 W. Chicago Blvd., Tecumseh, MI 49286, tel. 517/423–6979.*
Accommodations: *5 double rooms with baths.*
Amenities: *Air-conditioning, phone in sitting room.*
Rates: *$75–$120; full breakfast. MC, V.*
Restrictions: *No smoking indoors, small pets only.*

Victorian Inn

L ynne Secory and Vicki Peterson were neighbors busily renovating their own homes when they got the impulse to breathe new life into what had once been one of Port Huron's most magnificent houses, the old James A. Davidson residence. Davidson, founder of a large furniture company that bore his name, had built the elaborate Queen Anne house in 1896 and lived in it until his death in 1911. In 1983, Lynne and Vicki persuaded their husbands to buy the property. Enlisting the aid of many preservation-minded friends, relatives, and craftsmen, and working from the architectural plans and spec sheets, they managed to accomplish their mission by the end of the year. Halfway through the project, the house was placed on the State Register of Historic Places. The result of their efforts is a harmonious combination of luxurious lodging and fine dining in a neighborhood of well-maintained Victorian-era buildings that has become a travel destination in itself.

Immediately to the right of the foyer as you walk in is the parlor. Its green velvet valances, antique lace window curtains, green and gold floral wallpaper, pincushion settee, and hurricane lamps are invitingly elegant. The second-floor guest rooms are similar blends of antique furnishings and little flourishes: a needlepoint headboard, a papier-mâché picture frame. Two rooms have modern private baths, while the Victoria and Edward rooms share a pedestal sink, claw-foot tub (no shower), and pull-chain toilet.

Guests can eat breakfast in the main-floor 50-seat restaurant, also open for lunch and dinner Tuesday through Saturday. The service is attentive, the staff is immaculately attired in crisp white uniforms, and the mainly American menu is well executed. The inventive soups and desserts are especially popular.

The inn is just a couple of blocks from the St. Clair River, which carries freighter traffic and cool breezes. The Museum of Arts and History is one block over, on Court Street, and houses one of the finest collections of marine lore in the state. Travel the dozen or so blocks to the Fort Gratiot Lighthouse, the first one on the Great Lakes, and return to the inn and wet your whistle at the stone-walled Pierpont Pub. Originally a cellar, it features an old red oak bar that used to be a dry-goods counter.

Address: *1229 7th St., Port Huron, MI 48060, tel. 313/984–1437.*
Accommodations: *2 double rooms with baths, 2 doubles share bath.*
Amenities: *Air-conditioning, room service, fireplace in parlor, restaurant, pub.*
Rates: *$55–$65; Continental breakfast. AE, D, MC, V.*
Restrictions: *No pets.*

William Clements Inn

his gray Queen Anne–style mansion in Bay City is what eccentric Great-Aunt Emily's house always looked like, at least in the movies: Ornately carved staircases and ceilings, heavy oak furniture, and voluminous velveteen drapes establish the look. The house, built by industrialist/inventor/banker William Clements in 1886 during the peak of the lumber era, was bought in early 1994 by Brian and Karen Hepp, a local couple with a great appreciation of history.

The second-floor guest rooms are spacious and filled with period furnishings, including iron or brass beds, marble-topped tables, and oak armoires. In three rooms, claw-foot tubs have been equipped with showers. The most impressive room is the elegant master bedroom. The king-size brass bed has a Matelasse spread in a classic Elizabethan motif, elegantly complemented by brass fixtures, a cast-iron fireplace, and gold velvet jabots at the windows. The room also includes a queen-size sofa bed. The sunniest guest room is called James's Room after the Clements' youngest son. Light pours through a floral-lace-curtained bow window onto the queen-size Canterbury brass bed. The private bath across the hall features china tiles bordered with hand-painted morning glories.

As the quintessential 19th-century man of industry and culture, Clements exhibited a respect for music, equipping the music room with a magnifi-

cent Steinway grand piano. But Clements's true passion was collecting books. A few volumes of his impressive collection of books and manuscripts, which formed the nucleus of the library at the University of Michigan that bears his name, remain in the richly paneled main-floor library. A Victorian tea with muffins, scones, and live entertainment is held here the first Wednesday of each month. Guests, however, are more likely to be found in the screened-in back porch, shaded by a 200-year-old beech tree. There they play cards and talk of the sea captains and lumber barons who built the other grand mansions that fill this historic district.

Address: *1712 Center Ave., Bay City, MI 48708, tel. 517/894–4600, fax 517/895–8535.*
Accommodations: *6 double rooms with baths.*
Amenities: *Air-conditioning, TV, and phone in rooms; fireplaces in 2 rooms.*
Rates: *$70–$125; Continental breakfast served weekends only, evening refreshments. AE, D, MC, V.*
Restrictions: *No smoking, no pets.*

Blanche House Inn

When Mary Jean Shannon sold her suburban house in 1988 to buy a run-down mansion in Detroit, no one thought that a bed-and-breakfast could make it anywhere in Motor City, much less in the depressed center-city area. Today, there's still only one, but the Blanche House is a beautiful example of Detroit's grand past and an inspiration for its eventual renaissance. Designed by Louis Kemper and built in 1905, the Colonial Revival structure once served as a prep school for Henry Ford II, former governor G. Mennen Williams, and other local notables.

Mary Jean, aided by her son, Sean, has done a commendable job restoring the towering porch pillars, 10-foot etched-glass doors, oak woodwork and floors, and ornate plasterwork. The guest rooms, all named after someone who has figured in the inn's history, are fitted with antiques, including an 1850s brass British army bed in the Bell Parker Room. There is a back porch where guests can relax in hammocks that overlook a marina and the Stanton Canal.

Address: *506 Parkview Dr., Detroit, MI 48214, tel. 313/822–7090.*
Accommodations: *13 double rooms with baths, 1 suite.*
Amenities: *Air-conditioning, cable TV and phone in rooms, hot tubs in 3 rooms.*
Rates: *$60–$115; full breakfast. AE, D, DC, MC, V.*
Restrictions: *No smoking, no pets.*

Botsford Inn

The unofficial motto of Michigan's oldest continuously-operating inn, built as a stagecoach stop in 1836, is "History never goes out of style." So says Creon Smith, a North Carolina native who purchased the National Historic Landmark in late 1993 and has lovingly maintained its high ranking among preservationists and lovers of fine cuisine.

At one time the inn was owned by Henry Ford, whose wife Clara stocked the place with such antiques as a spinet piano that once belonged to General Custer's sister, Abraham Lincoln's writing desk, a Simon Williams grandfather clock, and original Currier & Ives prints. However, the restaurant and banquet facilities are the main attraction today. The hearty meals are based on American heritage recipes, and Smith insists that the full breakfast include extra-thick bacon, Triple-A eggs, and freshly squeezed orange juice. So you can burn off those calories, the inn hosts ballroom or country dances on a cushioned floor designed by Ford himself.

The rooms are decorated traditionally (four-poster beds, quilts) with an eye toward modern practicality (coffeemaker, cable TV).

Address: *28000 Grand River, Farmington Hills, MI 48336; tel. 810/474–4800.*
Accommodations: *10 double rooms with baths.*
Amenities: *Cable TV, coffeemaker, phone in rooms.*
Rates: *$65–$75; full breakfast. AE, D, DC, MC, V.*
Restrictions: *No pets.*

Chicago Street Inn

If you like auto racing, you can hardly do better than to stay at this bed-and-breakfast at the foot of touristy Irish Hills, just 3 miles from the Michigan International Speedway. On summer weekends, the air is alive with the sound of engines, and the tiny downtown is swamped with young racing fans.

In this casual environment, innkeepers Bill and Karen Kerr have obviously decided that authenticity should take a back seat to comfort. Aluminum siding and a contemporary veranda do nothing for the Queen Anne–style house, especially when compared with the beautifully restored brick residence next door. Your stay, however, is made pleasant by the easygoing atmosphere and an interior graced by hand-wrought oak moldings and fretwork, stained-glass windows, and a striking cherry-wood and ceramic-tile fireplace. Guest rooms are extremely feminine but tastefully done. Shades of rose, teal, cinnamon, peach, and cream bring out the best in the antique beds and accessories.

Address: *219 Chicago St., Brooklyn, MI 49230, tel. 517/592–3888, fax 517/592–9025.*
Accommodations: *3 double rooms with baths, 2 doubles share bath.*
Amenities: *Air-conditioning, cable TV in sitting room, phone in entranceway, fireplace in sitting room.*
Rates: *$55–$65; full breakfast. MC, V.*
Restrictions: *No smoking upstairs, no pets.*

Clinton Inn

This is basic lodging in a drowsy town that had its heyday nearly a century ago. Settlers from New York came to the region in the early 1800s and named the village after their state governor, DeWitt Clinton. The three-story brick hotel officially opened Thanksgiving Day, 1901, and was a popular way station for salesmen traveling Michigan Avenue, now U.S. 12. Vestiges of the building's former glory can be found in the golden oak staircase and oak trim, which new owners Mark and Laurie Pederson are restoring.

The Clinton Inn is a work-in-progress, and the Pedersons are striving to replace the uninspired modern furnishings in the second-story guest rooms with period pieces. (The third floor is still given over to apartments.) The village is near the antiques meccas of Saline and Tecumseh. The place remains a bargain, especially if you're in town to visit the historic Southern Michigan Railroad, which offers rides between Clinton and Tecumseh on weekends and holidays.

Address: *104 W. Michigan Ave. (Box 457), Clinton, MI 49236, tel. 517/456–4151.*
Accommodations: *6 double rooms with baths, 4 single rooms share bath.*
Amenities: *Air-conditioning and cable TV in guest rooms.*
Rates: *$30–$45; Sunday brunch only. D, MC, V.*
Restrictions: *No pets.*

Dundee Guest House

The greatest asset of Karen and Jerry Glover's gingerbread-trimmed brick house in Dundee is its location. The sleepy village sits on the River Raisin, near wineries, historic sites, and a meandering stream, and is just 15 miles east of Monroe, home of General George Custer. Dundee is also near the university towns of Ann Arbor and Ypsilanti.

The Glovers—who bought the 120-year-old house in 1989—run a friendly establishment. Jerry, forced into early retirement by Eastern Airlines, has time to linger over what is truly a bottomless cup of coffee. (Karen still works at Michigan Bell.) The decor here strives to be Victorian, but undistinguished wallpaper, modern bathrooms, and the plush pink carpet in one of the guest rooms compete with such authentic touches as crocheted lace curtains, a bentwood cradle, a carved oak staircase, and Karen's collection of handmade porcelain dolls. Still, there's a good feeling here, the kind of unhurried pleasantness thought to characterize this country back when it was a collection of small towns like Dundee.

Address: *522 Tecumseh St., Dundee, MI 48131, tel. 313/529–5706.*
Accommodations: *2 double rooms with baths.*
Amenities: *Croquet and gazebo in backyard.*
Rates: *$45–$85; Continental breakfast. MC, V.*
Restrictions: *No smoking, no pets; closed Dec. 24–25.*

Southwestern Michigan
*Including Battle Creek, Grand Rapids,
Kalamazoo, and Saugatuck*

*The southwest quadrant of Michigan offers travelers a wide
range of diversions, from a leisurely afternoon drive to pick
raspberries in the country to a week of carefully orchestrated
relaxation at a tony lakeside retreat. In fact, thanks to
growing media attention that has resulted in a number of
travel-magazine pieces, the region is fast becoming recognized
as a four-season vacation area. This "discovery" would have
amused such old-time aficionados as Al Capone and L. Frank
Baum, who knew the Lake Michigan shoreline as a salve for
troubled spirits. Baum wrote some of his Wizard of Oz books
here; perhaps Scarface came here to sort out his thoughts
about Bugs Moran or the Purple Gang.*

*The advent of air-conditioning and affordable air travel to
more exotic places made some of the area's features less
compelling. But southwestern Michigan's cool summers and
mild winters are starting to draw visitors again, thanks to a
blossoming of individual entrepreneurs and increasingly
promotion-minded communities. Along the Red Arrow
Highway, which runs north from the Indiana border through
towns like New Buffalo, Union Pier, and Lakeside, cottages
and storefronts are finding new life as bed-and-breakfasts, art
galleries, and antiques shops.*

*Farther up the coast, nearly everything revolves around sand
and water, from beach volleyball and kite-flying tournaments
to breakneck dune-buggy rides. Such upscale ports as South
Haven and Saugatuck do land-rush business from Memorial
Day to Labor Day, with a 50-50 mix of Chicagoans and
Michiganders vying for space in the harbor inns and B&Bs.
Saugatuck is particularly trendy, with a large number of fine
restaurants and shops. The combination of berthed sailboats,
ancient shade trees, and old houses reminds visitors of New
England coastal villages, and its thriving gay community sets*

*it apart from the more conservative towns typical of the area.
A few miles north is the delightful city of Holland, noted for its
tulip farms and its streets that undergo daily scrubbing.*

*Inland, orchards parade across the gently rolling, fertile
terrain. Spring produces an explosion of fragrance and
color—and numerous festivals. July ushers in picking season.
You can drive down just about any back road and come across
a U-Pick farm, cider stand, or winery. In the fall, the orange
globes of pumpkins and squash splash the roadsides with
color. During the winter, cross-country skiers glide silently up
and down the mild, undulating hills, later heading for inns
that are nearly always empty in midweek.*

*The countryside is a jumble of farms, small manufacturing
centers, and a few crossroads communities that have yet to
recover from the decline of the railroad. If you're lost, don't be
afraid to approach someone for directions. Even in the larger
cities—Kalamazoo, Grand Rapids, and Battle Creek—people
are unmistakably, hospitably Midwestern. Not only do they
talk to you; they listen. And those traveling the area's
highways should know that strangers are trusted enough to
keep the rest room doors unlocked.*

Places to Go, Sights to See

Battle Creek. Dubbed the "Cereal Capital of the World" with Post Cereals,
Ralston Purina, and the Kellogg companies located here, Battle Creek is host to a
pair of fun annual events: Every June, thousands participate in what is described
as the world's largest breakfast; in July some 200 hot-air balloonists compete in
the weeklong International Balloon Championship (tel. 616/962–0592). Ten miles
to the east is the well-preserved town of Marshall, whose Historical Society (tel.
616/781–5163) presents a tour of nationally recognized 19th-century homes every
September.

Cherry County Playhouse. A fixture in Traverse City for many years, the theatrical company moved to the Frauenthal Theatre in downtown Muskegon in
1991. Summer stock productions include children's plays, musicals, comedies,
and celebrity concerts. Call 616/727–8000 or 800/686-9666 after April 15 for the
schedule.

Flower Festivals. Every spring 30 communities work together to produce the
Blossomtime Festival (tel. 616/926–7397), which includes a floral parade through

Boston Harbor and St. Joseph. More than 400,000 people attend the Tulip Time Festival (tel. 616/396–4221) in Holland, held for 10 days every May when the blooms are at their peak.

Grand Rapids. The state's second-largest city is a clean, well-ordered manufacturing community 30 minutes east of Lake Michigan. It has an amazing number of churches per capita and is a conservative, friendly place with quite a few things to see. The Gerald R. Ford Museum (303 Pearl St. NW, tel. 616/456–2674) traces the life and times of the 38th president. Self-guided walking tours of Heritage Hill (tel. 616/459–8950), a historic district of some 1,300 buildings east of the rejuvenated downtown, are well-liked, as is the exotic John Ball Zoological Gardens (1300 W. Fulton St., tel. 616/776–2591).

Kalamazoo. This pleasant college town, roughly halfway between Chicago and Detroit on I–94 and just an hour's drive from Lake Michigan, is popular as a way station or as a destination in itself. The immaculate Kalamazoo Aviation History Museum (2101 E. Milhan Rd., tel. 616/382–6555) features rare, operational World War II aircraft, memorabilia, and restoration work of vintage planes. Aircraft buffs and casual visitors flock to the Michigan International Air Show (tel. 616/383–1000 or 616/381–1692), which attracts more than 100,000 people every June.

Michigan's Adventure Amusement Park (Russell Rd. exit off U.S. 31, tel. 616/766–3377), 8 miles north of Muskegon, is the state's largest amusement and water park with more than 20 thrill rides, 10 water slides, a wave pool, a children's activity pool, shows, games, food, and the only two roller coasters in Michigan.

Paw Paw. A dozen miles west of Kalamazoo, the village has several wineries, including Frontenac Vineyards (tel. 616/657–5531), St. Julian Winery (tel. 616/657–2964), and Warner Vineyards (tel. 616/657–3165), Michigan's largest. Each offers free tours and samplings. The Wine Country Scenic Train (tel. 616/657–5963) has 90-minute excursions year-round, including autumn-color tours and Santa Trains.

Saugatuck and Douglas. A thriving arts colony has developed in these two lakefront communities, which sit on opposite sides of the mouth of the Kalamazoo River. The Ox-Bow Art Workshop in Saugatuck is the Midwest's oldest summer school of painting, but artists are in evidence everywhere—from the tasteful downtown shops and galleries to the boardwalk pier, one of the Great Lakes' longest. Picturesque beaches and the area's relaxed lifestyle have helped create one of the state's most fashionable vacation spots.

SS *Keewatin*. One of the last of the Great Lakes' classic passenger steamboats is permanently docked in Douglas as a maritime museum (south of the Saugatuck–Douglas Bridge, tel. 616/857–2151 or 616/857–2107). Guided tours of this luxuriously appointed 1907 vessel are available from Memorial Day through Labor Day.

Veldheer Tulip Gardens/DeKlomp Wooden Shoe & Delft Factory. Two million bulbs exhibit their color every spring at Veldheer's (12755 Quincy at U.S. 31, Holland, tel. 616/399–1900), making it one of the premier attractions for Holland-area visitors. At the DeKlomp factory next door, visitors can watch workers carve wooden shoes and hand-paint the famous blue-and-white Delftware.

Beaches

The best beaches are in state parks such as Grand Haven, Holland, and Van Buren. The state's longest stretch of beach—2½ miles—is at Warren Dunes State Park (Red Arrow Hwy., tel. 616/426–4013), south of Bridgman. However, because of eroding shorelines, some of the area's public beaches may be partially restricted.

Boating

No one in Michigan is ever more than 6 miles from a lake or stream, so you won't have to work hard to find a place to either launch or rent a boat. Marina activity, particularly in major yachting and sportfishing ports like South Haven and Muskegon, is frenzied through the peak summer months, but slows down considerably with the cool weather. For those who prefer to leave the driving to someone else, you can cruise the Kalamazoo River and Lake Michigan aboard *The Queen of Saugatuck* (tel. 616/857–4261), a 67-foot-long stern-wheeler, or the *City of Douglas* (tel. 616/857–2107), a 60-foot yacht.

Fishing

Whether you cast your line from a boat or off a pier, southwest Michigan offers some reel opportunities. The waters hold panfish, trout, walleye, bass, northern pike, bullheads, catfish, and, especially, yellow perch. Visiting anglers will find some of Michigan's finest fishing in the center of Grand Rapids, where the Grand River is kept stocked with chinook, steelhead, and coho salmon. Also worth noting are Reeds Lake in East Grand Rapids, which has bluegills, crappies, and northern pike, and the Muskegon River, popular for its annual perch and salmon runs. Charter fishing on Lake Michigan is available at marinas up and down the shoreline.

Golf

The state is known for its large number of fine courses, many on the "Golf Coast" of Lake Michigan. You can play 18 holes among dunes and pines at the Grand Haven Golf Club (1700 Lincoln Rd., Grand Haven, tel. 616/842–4040), rated one of the country's top public courses. Clearbrook (135th Ave., Saugatuck, tel. 616/857–1766) in Saugatuck is the southwest shoreline's only championship public golf and fine dining complex. Tee off at Winding Creek Golf Course (8600 Ottafan St., Holland, tel. 616/396–4516) in Holland or Grand Island Golf Ranch (6266 W. River Dr., Belmont, tel. 616/363–1262) in Grand Rapids. A complete listing of all golf courses in the state is available through the **Michigan Association of Public Golf Courses** (Box 612, Plymouth, MI 48170, tel. 313/582–8860 or 800/223–5877).

Restaurants

You can have your steak and scampi prepared tableside at **Churchill's** (3927 28th St. SE, tel. 616/942–0590), an elegant favorite in downtown Grand Rapids. The city features another fine dining experience at **Schnitzelbank** (342 Jefferson St., tel. 616/459–9527), where German fare and paneled rooms transport you to the Old World. In Macatawa, just west of Holland, the sophisticated but unpretentious **Sandpiper Restaurant** (2225 S. Shore Dr., tel. 616/335–5866) offers a full range of reasonably priced American cuisine and a bird's-eye view of the harbor. Orchard country farther south offers more than just roadside cider stands. In Bridgman, sautéed chicken breast with chopped pecan crust is a specialty of the **Tabor Hill Winery Restaurant** (185 Mt. Tabor Rd., tel. 616/422–1161), which overlooks the surrounding vineyards. And "monster" Reuben sandwiches and chunky wedges of homemade pie make **Wick's Apple House** (52281 Indian Lake Rd., tel. 616/782–7306) in Dowagiac a delicious detour.

Tourist Information

The Michigan Travel Bureau (333 S. Capitol Ave., Lansing, MI 48933, tel. 800/543–2937) has statewide tourist information. To learn more about boating, fishing, and hunting opportunities and regulations, contact the **Michigan Department of Natural Resources** (530 N. Allegan St., Lansing, MI 48933, tel. 517/373–1204). The following cover more specific areas: **Greater Battle Creek Visitors and Convention Bureau** (34 W. Jackson St., Battle Creek, MI 49017, tel. 616/962–2240); **Greater Grand Rapids Convention Bureau** (245 Monroe NW, Grand Rapids, MI 49503, tel. 616/459–8287); **Holland Area Chamber of Commerce** (272 E. 8th St., Holland, MI 49422, tel. 616/392–2389); **Kalamazoo County Convention and Visitors Bureau** (128 N. Kalamazoo Mall, Kalamazoo, MI 49007, tel. 616/381–4003); **Muskegon County Convention and Visitors Bureau** (349 W. Webster Ave., Muskegon, MI 49440, tel. 616/722–3751); **Saugatuck/Douglas Chamber of Commerce** (303 Butler St., Saugatuck, MI 49453, tel. 616/857–5801); **Lakeshore Convention and Visitors Bureau** (Box 890, South Haven, MI 49090, tel. 616/637–5252); **West Michigan Tourist Association** (136 E. Fulton St., Grand Rapids, MI 49503, tel. 616/456–8557).

Chicago Pike Inn

Parental love is the simple story behind this large yellow inn, which sits on U.S. 12 halfway between Detroit and Chicago. Looking to lure their daughter Becky back to Michigan, Harold and Jane Schultz dangled a carrot: They would buy one of Coldwater's most elegant mansions and convert it into a B&B if she would come home to run it. Becky, who had studied hotel management in college and was working at a plush Florida resort at the time, immediately agreed.

The 7,500-square-foot mansion was built in 1903 by local mercantilist Morris G. Clarke, who hired Asbury Buckley to design it. The Chicago architect was responsible for many of the fine homes built on Mackinac Island in the 1890s. Although the mansion was being used as a boarding house when the Schultzes bought it, it was still in marvelous condition. Today, such elegant touches as the built-in mirrored buffet in the cherry-paneled dining room, the double mantel fireplace in the reception room, and the oak parquet floors can make you feel almost guilty about showing up in jeans and a T-shirt.

Guest rooms in the main house are appointed with period wall coverings and such Victorian antiques as marble-top tables. All but one are on the second floor; the exception is the Clarkes' "Own" Room (as it was labeled on the original architectural drawings). Located off the library—a restful refuge with a marble fireplace and century-old tea table—this room is furnished with a ornately carved, lace-covered canopy bed. At the top of the stairs is Miss Sophia's Suite, the inn's most popular room, which has a yellow-tiled fireplace with an oak mantel and a private balcony. The velvet-covered sofa and large table make private breakfasts here a favorite option. A gambrel-roofed, two-story carriage house contains the two newest rooms. Decorated in the same style as the main house, these lodgings also include air-conditioning, whirlpools, refrigerators, and private balconies.

The antiques centers of Allen and Marshall are nearby, and northern Indiana—home to the famous Shipshewana auctions and a thriving Amish community—is just a half-hour's drive away. Or you can hop on one of the inn's bicycles and explore Coldwater, a drowsy town filled with 19th-century statuary and Victorian-era homes.

Address: *215 East Chicago St., Coldwater, MI 49036, tel. 517/279–8744.*
Accommodations: *6 double rooms with baths, 2 suites.*
Amenities: *Cable TV, fireplace, and phone in common area; fireplace in 1 room; air-conditioning, refrigerator and whirlpool in 2 rooms; bicycles.*
Rates: *$80–$165; full breakfast, afternoon refreshments; AE, MC, V.*
Restrictions: *No pets; smoking in common areas only.*

Crane House

Bob and Lue Crane are fourth-generation Fennville fruit farmers whose sprawling homestead comprises a restaurant, a 120-year-old farmhouse painted white with green shutters, and 310 acres of apple, cherry, raspberry, blueberry, and peach orchards. The farmhouse is a large, two-story wooden structure that Bob and Lue bought from Bob's cousin and renovated five years ago. "The place was empty and ready to fall down," says their daughter, Nancy Crane-McFarland, who today serves as innkeeper. "To help defray some of the costs of fixing it up, we decided to turn it into a bed-and-breakfast."

In many ways, the Cranes seem as if they've stepped right off a *Saturday Evening Post* cover—along with the house. The interior is a pleasant mix of farm antiques, Americana, and primitive art. The upstairs guest rooms have stenciled walls, ceiling fans, and wooden, iron, and brass beds, each with a handmade quilt and a feather mattress. The rooms overlook the orchards—a truly splendid sight in the spring and fall. The parlor boasts Nancy's great-grandmother's curved-glass oak curio cabinet and a 1900 stove, and the breakfast room has a pine hanging dry sink. "The only other time I've seen one was in an old episode of 'Bonanza,'" says Nancy, whose own young family lives in the house.

The Cranes are genuine, neighborly, family-centered, and industrious. They also have a fair amount of business savvy. Across the highway from the house is their Pie Pantry Restaurant, which Bob and Lue started as an alternative way to make money when American agriculture suffered reverses in the early 1970s.

The restaurant, in an old barn, is a cheerful jumble of worn chairs and tables under a folksy burlap-sack ceiling, with a Round Oak stove and a wall of framed Charles Lindbergh clippings. In summer, the gravel drive becomes a turnstile as pleasure drivers take time out to pick fruit, buy cider, or sample some of the outstanding sandwiches, soups, and fruit pies. The orchards, restaurant, and B&B are truly a family operation, with three generations of Cranes pitching in wherever they're needed.

Address: *6051 124th Ave., Fennville, MI 49408, tel. 616/561-6931.*
Accommodations: *3 double rooms with baths, 2 doubles share shower.*
Amenities: *TV and phone in den.*
Rates: *$65–$95; full breakfast. AE, D, MC, V.*
Restrictions: *No smoking indoors, no pets.*

Kingsley House

David and Shirley Witt tout their impressive Queen Anne house in tiny Fennville as being "as American as apple pie," an example of truth in advertising if ever there was one. It was built in 1886 by Harvey Kingsley, who introduced fruit trees to this area around Lake Michigan. Tipping their caps to Kingsley, the Witts have placed his picture in the living room and named each of the guest rooms after a variety of apple. The winding oak stairway leads to six second-story chambers, two of which are dubbed McIntosh and Golden Delicious. The most interesting is the Jonathan Room, a former stableboy's room, with a century-old sleigh bed and an 1850 platform rocker. Nestled in the tower is the Dutchess Room, which, with five windows, is the brightest, and is regally decorated in cranberry and antique lace. Immediately above it is Northern Spy, a honeymoon suite that features a fireplace, a whirlpool bath, and a calming view of miles of rolling countryside.

Shirley, who was born in the Netherlands, runs the household with smooth efficiency and simple elegance. The guest rooms and common areas are spacious and immaculately clean. The furnishings are a tasteful blend of oak and cherry antiques that harmonize with such family ornaments as the shadowboxes the Witts made.

Breakfast is a fancy affair, served on linens and Royal Doulton china in the formal cherry-wood dining room. The Delftware and silver are typical of Dutch touches throughout the house. Five menus are rotated but meals usually include country ham, farm-fresh eggs, hash browns, and homemade muffins and bread. Coffee and the morning paper are set out by 7:30 AM, and tea, cold drinks, cookies, and snacks are available all day.

With busy Route 89 close at hand, traffic noise can be a problem in the front rooms. To escape, hop on one of the four 18-speed Peugots the Witts provide and pedal 8 miles south to the Allegan State Game Area, famous as a rest stop for geese and other migrating waterfowl. Once there, you can hike, canoe, swim, cross-country ski, or pick wild blueberries, strawberries, and other fruit.

Address: *626 W. Main St., Fennville, MI 49408, tel. 616/561–6425.*
Accommodations: *8 double rooms with baths, 3 suites.*
Amenities: *Air-conditioning, whirlpool tub, TV, VCR, fireplace, and phone in suites; 2 phones in common areas.*
Rates: *$75–$125; full breakfast, refreshments all day. AE, D, MC, V.*
Restrictions: *No smoking, no pets.*

National House Inn

The he National House Inn in Marshall is more than a magnificently preserved and smooth-running period hostel; it's a centerpiece of what many consider the finest cross-section of 19th-century architecture in the country. The oldest inn in the state opened as a stagecoach stop in 1835, two years before Michigan was admitted to the Union. For many years it served double duty as one of the final stops on the Underground Railroad that spirited escaped slaves to Canada, 120 miles to the east. In 1878, it was converted into a wagon and windmill factory. The inn was drawing its final breath as an apartment house when a consortium of local business people bought it and restored it for the nation's Bicentennial.

For the past 12 years, innkeeper Barbara Bradley has watched a parade of tourists, business travelers, and honeymooners pass through the rustic entryway, which is warmed by a massive beam-and-brick open-hearth fireplace. The rough-hewn ceiling beams and aged plank floors are the framework for the selection of country antiques found in every room. There are punched-tin chandeliers; Windsor, ladderback, and herringbone wing chairs in the living room; spindle-legged tables and hurricane lamps in the dining room; and gilt-framed oil portraits throughout. Thanks to a unique warming fireplace set into handcrafted, paneled cabinets, the upstairs lounge is comfortable and inviting, although in warmer weather guests prefer sitting in the back porch and gardens.

Guest rooms are attractively wallpapered and carpeted, with the decor ranging from country style to the Victorian style of the Ketchum Suite, which overlooks a handsome garden and the village circle. There's plenty of elbow room in the dining room, where a Continental breakfast of boiled eggs, fruit bowls, wheat bread, coffee, and a wide variety of fruit juices and teas are served.

Marshall is right off I–94, 10 miles east of Battle Creek. In 1991, the village—frequently referred to as "the Williamsburg of the Midwest"—was designated a National Historic Landmark District. The district encompasses some 850 structures (and nearly 50 historical markers), including striking examples of Queen Anne, Italianate, and Gothic Revival architecture. The town hall itself is a century-old stone livery.

Address: *102 Parkview St., Marshall, MI 49068, tel. 616/781–7374, fax 616/781–4510.*
Accommodations: *16 double rooms with baths; no-smoking rooms available.*
Amenities: *Air-conditioning, cable TV and phone in rooms.*
Rates: *$66–$120; Continental breakfast. AE, MC, V.*
Restrictions: *No pets.*

South Cliff Inn

Five years ago, Bill Swisher left behind a 10-year career as director of the Cassopolis, Michigan Probate Court and opened the South Cliff Inn. "I grew up in the area, and I suppose I was always looking for an excuse to come back," Bill says.

In the pre-air-conditioning days of the early 1900s, St. Joseph ("St. Joe," as it's sometimes called) and its sister city, Benton Harbor, were among the Midwest's most popular lakefront summer resorts. The collapse of the area's manufacturing base led to a decline of fortunes in the 1970s, especially in Benton Harbor, always the more blue-collar of the two. South Cliff Inn, a salmon-colored brick English cottage, is a small but important representative of an economic renaissance that once again is capitalizing on the therapeutic breezes of Lake Michigan.

The 80-year-old inn is perched on a bluff, giving all but one of the seven guest rooms superb views of the water. The largest room, the Sunset Suite, is perhaps the most popular. The queen-size bed, sofa, and wing chair are dressed in complementary teal English-chintz fabrics; the private bath features a custom-designed marble tub. In the adjacent Harbour Room, guests can lie back in a bubbling whirlpool bath and watch the sun melt into the lake in the evening. The entire place is decorated in English country style, with plenty of bold prints, chintz fabrics, and a large number of antiques. One of the guest rooms

houses an imposing 150-year-old oak armoire that is so large it had to be hoisted through the windows.

The trouble was worth it: The inn is comfortable, sun-filled, and, with just one part-time staffer to assist Bill, commendably unhurried. A Continental breakfast includes juice, homemade bread and muffins, and—this being orchard country—plenty of fresh fruit. That's enough carbohydrates to fuel a short walk to the downtown of this pleasant harbor town, whose turn-of-the-century storefronts and monuments, landscaped brick streets, and Lake Michigan backdrop combine to make it perhaps the most picturesque in the entire state.

Address: *1900 Lakeshore Dr., St. Joseph, MI 49085, tel. 616/983–4881, fax 616/983–7391.*
Accommodations: *7 double rooms with baths.*
Amenities: *Air-conditioning, whirlpool bath in 1 room, fireplace in 1 room, cable TV in den.*
Rates: *$70–$110; Continental breakfast, refreshments all day. AE, D, MC, V.*
Restrictions: *Smoking in den only, no pets; 2-night minimum on weekends, 3-night minimum on holidays.*

Wickwood Country Inn

Guests at Saugatuck's oldest bed-and-breakfast are in for a treat, both figuratively and literally. The new owner, Julee Rosso-Miller, is the co-author of *The Silver Palate Cookbook*. With 2 million copies sold, it's the second-best-selling cookbook in the history of publishing, behind *The Joy of Cooking.*

Julee came to her new career as innkeeper in much the same way she became a well-known gourmet writer: serendipity. Her mother's heart attack in 1986 forced her to reappraise her own hectic lifestyle as half-owner of one of the first-ever gourmet takeout shops in the country, New York's Silver Palate. She moved to Saugatuck and fell in love with the sunsets over Lake Michigan—and with Ray Miller, a local builder. They married, then persuaded their neighbors to sell what has long been regarded as the best B&B in town. Of course, the location doesn't hurt: It's two blocks from downtown's many fine shops and restaurants, and a short walk from the beach and other lakefront attractions.

With its brick floors, cedar walls, and vaulted ceilings, the circa-1940 inn resembles one of those small toasty hotels that dot the English countryside. The main-floor rooms, filled with overstuffed chairs, French and English antiques, fresh flowers, and original art, surround a courtyard blooming with perennials, roses, and herbs. The guest rooms have individual themes but are uniformly captivating, with plenty of antique lace, Ralph Lauren and Laura Ashley fabrics, and cabbage-rose patterns on the walls and beds.

Guests are pampered from daybreak to dusk. A buffet breakfast is served and a newspaper is supplied weekday mornings on the old English pine buffet table in the dining area, which is filled with antique toy trains, boats, and trucks. On weekends, a hearty brunch is prepared. Hors d'oeuvres, which might include a light salmon mousse, bruschetta, Chinese ribs, and crudites with low-fat dip, are put out at 6 PM. As if this weren't enough, candies and jars of spiced nuts are placed in each room. Calorie counters can relax, though: most items are selections from Julee's recent low-fat cookbook, *Great Good Food.*

Address: *510 Butler St. (Box 1019), Saugatuck, MI 49453, tel. 616/857–1097, fax 616/857–4168.*
Accommodations: *11 double rooms with baths, 2 suites.*
Amenities: *Air-conditioning, fireplace in 1 suite, phone in common room, cable TV in library.*
Rates: *$140–$190; full breakfast, evening refreshments. MC, V.*
Restrictions: *No pets; 2-night minimum on weekends, closed Dec. 24–25.*

Fairchild House

In an area fairly bustling with bed-and-breakfasts, Selicia Fairchild's is one of the most intimate and romantic. The two-story white stucco inn, built in 1919, has a reputation for thoughtful, personalized service. For Selicia, the phone and TV in the parlor are barely tolerable amenities; her idea of relaxation is classical music filling the house as a backdrop for evening hors d'oeuvres and pleasant conversation in front of the fireplace.

There are three distinct bedrooms, all tastefully done with fine period antiques, cutwork linens, European feather beds, down comforters, and prizewinning quilts. One bedroom set is a replica of Abraham Lincoln's purported wedding suite. Fresh flowers and plush Turkish bathrobes are indicative of the care that goes into

everything here, including the elegant champagne breakfasts served in summer in the lacy gazebo in the garden. For special occasions, a romantic breakfast in bed can be arranged with advance notice.

Address: *606 Butler St., Saugatuck, MI 49453, tel. 616/857–5985.*
Accommodations: *3 double rooms share 2 baths.*
Amenities: *Air-conditioning, bathrobes; phone, TV, and fireplace in parlor.*
Rates: *$95; full breakfast. MC, V.*
Restrictions: *No smoking, no pets; 2-night minimum on weekends and May–Oct.*

The Inn at Union Pier

Chicagoans Mark and Joyce Pitts bought the 1910 main house and two cottages in 1993. The lakeside resort, which sits on impeccably landscaped grounds, has a light Scandinavian look, with plenty of comforters, watercolor pictures, and wallpaper patterned in small print. Comfort and thoughtfulness are the buzzwords here. For instance, towels are provided for those who wish to dip into either the hot tub on the back porch or Lake Michigan, 200 feet away.

Hikers, bicyclists, and cross-country skiers all find tree-lined Lakeshore Road an attractive conduit to several interesting shops and galleries in neighboring New Buffalo. This is where orchard country meets the shoreline, so sunset cruises and wine-

tasting are also just a short drive away.

Address: *9708 Berrien St. (Box 222), Union Pier, MI 49129, tel. 616/469–4700, fax 616/469–4720.*
Accommodations: *16 double rooms with baths.*
Amenities: *Air-conditioning, hot tub, sauna, beach towels; cable TV and phone in Great House; fireplaces in 12 rooms.*
Rates: *$105–$175; full breakfast, afternoon and evening refreshments. D, MC, V.*
Restrictions: *No smoking, no pets; 2-night minimum on weekends, 3-night minimum on holidays.*

Maplewood Hotel

This 1860s Greek Revival has been gradually restored since Catherine and Sam Simon bought it in 1990. Part of the hotel's charm is in its combination of formality and hospitality; it's one of the few in the area that truly welcomes children. Each of the 15 antique-filled bedrooms has its own bath (five have whirlpool tubs), and five of the rooms have working fireplaces. Breakfast is served at 14 small, linen-covered tables in the dining room and on the screened porch.

Maplewood's central location puts first-rate shops, galleries, and restaurants within shouting distance—literally—so street noise can be a concern. But the spot has the advantage of nearby golf, tennis, boating, and fishing.

Address: *428 Butler St. (Box 1059), Saugatuck, MI 49453, tel. 616/857–1771, fax 616/857–1773.*
Accommodations: *15 double rooms with baths.*
Amenities: *Air-conditioning, cable TV, phone; fireplace in 5 rooms; whirlpool in 5 rooms; lap pool.*
Rates: *$80–$155; full breakfast. AE, MC, V.*
Restrictions: *No smoking, no pets; 2-night minimum on weekends, 3-night minimum on holidays, closed for 3 days at both Thanksgiving and Christmas.*

Parsonage 1908

Once a parsonage, this stunning two-story, white Queen Anne–style house, adorned with black shutters, geranium-filled window boxes, and tricolor crescent flags, sits on a little rise in an upscale residential section of Holland. Like so many neighborhoods in this heavily Dutch community, there is a palpable sense of order and serenity in the rows of immaculately kept houses, lawns, and gardens.

Bonnie McCoy-Verwys, assisted by her daughters Wendy and Heather, is an outgoing hostess and a very capable gardener and cook. She bought the house in 1974 and 10 years later opened it as Holland's first bed-and-breakfast. Through patience and attention to detail, she has restored the Victorian house over the years. The oak woodwork and leaded-glass windows are supplemented by less obvious touches of authenticity: lined dresser drawers with a sachet in each, for instance; a bedroom closet holding high-button shoes, hatboxes, and other old-fashioned accessories. In the finely landscaped backyard, croquet wickets share space with a fragrant—and rare—mimosa tree.

Address: *6 E. 24th St., Holland, MI 49423, tel. 616/396–1316.*
Accommodations: *3 double rooms share 2 baths.*
Amenities: *Air-conditioning, TV in sitting room, portable phone in hallway, fireplace.*
Rates: *$90–$95; full breakfast, refreshments. No credit cards.*
Restrictions: *No smoking, no pets; closed last week in Feb.*

Pebble House

The American Arts and Crafts movement of the early 1900s is faithfully followed inside this simple 1912 concrete-block and river-rock house. Ed and Jean Lawrence, who own the East Road Gallery in town, have meticulously furnished guest rooms and common areas with distinctive clean-lined Mission-style furniture and accessories, including hand-hammered copper bowls and green cut-glass lamps. Dried flowers and pastel accents help to soften the lines of the style, which is carried over in the nearby Coach and Blueberry houses, connected to the main house by walkways. The Lawrences work hard to make this a true retreat: Phones and children are discouraged, and there's nary a television in sight. Alternatively, some 2,000 books, including volumes of fiction, travel, and design, are tucked all over. Outside, a tennis court and nearby beach beckon.

Address: *15093 Lakeshore Rd., Lakeside, MI 49116, tel. 616/469–1416.*
Accommodations: *3 double rooms with baths, 3-bedroom Coach House with bath, 2-bedroom Blueberry House with bath.*
Amenities: *Air-conditioning, phone in guest room upon request, phone in main lounge, kitchenette and wood-burning stove in Blueberry House.*
Rates: *$90–$136, Blueberry House $200; full breakfast, refreshments. D, MC, V.*
Restrictions: *No smoking indoors, no pets, closed Dec. 24.*

Pine Garth Inn

Guests immediately get a good feeling about this comfortably rumpled summer estate, which is as unpretentious as its owners, Russ and Paula Bulin. The Illinois transplants bought the 90-year-old yellow frame house in 1988 and dressed it up in what Paula calls country eclectic—a blend of striped and floral linens and wallpaper, and family furniture. Russ is a professional woodworker. Samples of his handiwork are everywhere inside the inn and five adjoining contemporary wooden cottages: log beds, twig furniture, distressed pine armoires. The inn sits on a bluff overlooking 200 feet of private beach. All but one of the guest rooms have a full view of the water; four rooms have private decks. The cottages are good for family gatherings; otherwise, the rooms in the house are more desirable.

Address: *15790 Lakeshore Rd., Union Pier, MI 49129, tel. 616/469–1642.*
Accommodations: *7 double rooms with baths, 5 2-bedroom cottages with baths.*
Amenities: *Air-conditioning, TV and VCR in bedrooms, phone in library, hot tubs and fireplaces in cottages.*
Rates: *$110–$145, cottages $195–$225; full breakfast, afternoon refreshments. AE, D, MC, V.*
Restrictions: *Smoking in Great Room only, no pets; 2-night minimum on weekends, 3-night minimum on holidays.*

Victorian Villa Inn

At 13 Ron Gibson was hired to clean out a neighbor's attic—the first step, in a lifetime of collecting antiques, that lead to owning this red brick Victorian mansion. Occupying a tree-shaded corner lot, it was built in 1876 for $12,000 by local big shot L. Smith Hobart. His former bedchamber, now the Renaissance Suite, is the most sumptious guest room in the house. Although Gibson and innkeeper Cindy Coates have maintained the home's opulent integrity, whimsical touches show they're not above having a little fun. Accordingly, the inn regularly stages Sherlock Holmes Mystery Weekends and other Victorian-themed special events.

Gibson, who clearly knows his way around a kitchen, has built a dining room and deck onto the main house.

They blend gracefully with the surrounding gardens, which include a giant flag-bedecked gazebo, fountains, and honeysuckle trees. Hobart's tombstone stands in the shadows of the carriage house, allowing him to keep an eye on his old property. He undoubtedly approves of what he sees.

Address: *601 North Broadway St., Union City, MI 49094, tel. 517/741–7383 or 800/34–VILLA, fax 517/741–4002.*
Accommodations: *7 double rooms with baths, 3 suites.*
Amenities: *Air-conditioning in suites and 4 rooms, fireplace in 1 suite, phone in common area; bicycles.*
Rates: *$75–$125; full breakfast, afternoon tea. D, MC, V.*
Restrictions: *No smoking indoors, no pets.*

Yelton Manor

A pair of self-styled refugees from the corporate world, Elaine Herbert and her husband, Robert Kripaitif, have turned this rambling 1873 Victorian into arguably the finest bed-and-breakfast in South Haven. The house is done in an elegant country style, with most of the furnishings new oak reproductions. The grounds include Elaine's award-winning perennial and rose gardens as well as the recently built guest house, designed for those desiring a more intimate setting. Each room features a fireplace, whirlpool, and TV; upper-level rooms have balconies and panoramic lake views. Patrons in the main house are served a full breakfast featuring homemade pastries; those in the guest house have a Continental breakfast delivered to their door. The fridge in the separate guest kitchen is

kept stocked with juices, homemade cookies, and other goodies.

In the heart of South Haven, The Yelton is only a quarter-block from North Beach access. One mile north is the Kal-Haven Trail, a 38-mile bicycle path that is especially pretty in July when the blueberry fields are in fruit.

Address: *140 N. Shore Dr., South Haven, MI 49090, tel. 616/637–5220, fax 616/637–4957.*
Accommodations: *17 double rooms with baths.*
Amenities: *Air-conditioning, cable TV in rooms, whirlpool bath in 11 rooms, fireplace in 7 rooms, 6 guest phones.*
Rates: *$95–$190; full or Continental breakfast, refreshments. AE, MC, V.*
Restrictions: *No smoking indoors, no pets.*

Upper Peninsula

When Ernest Hemingway was writing "Big Two-Hearted River" in the early 1920s, he kept a map of northern Michigan pinned to the wall of his Paris apartment. Such inspiration is almost superfluous for those who have visited Michigan's Upper Peninsula and treasure mental canvases of the region's rugged natural beauty.

Remote and thinly populated, the U.P. (as it's commonly called) is nearly surrounded by Lakes Superior, Michigan, and Huron. It's larger than Massachusetts, Connecticut, Rhode Island, and Delaware combined, but even its largest city, Marquette, has only 22,000 people. It has more in common with Wisconsin, with which it shares a long western border, than with the lower half of Michigan. The U.P. was awarded to the Wolverine State in 1837 as settlement in a boundary dispute with Ohio, which got Toledo. The progress of the various industries that have since shaped the area—copper and iron mining, lumbering, maritime shipping—can be traced by the various museums, ghost towns, and shipwreck preserves that dot the region. Despite the presence of a healthy commercial fishing industry and several fine colleges and universities, today the U.P. is best known as a visually stunning outdoor paradise.

Natives of the region, who proudly refer to themselves as "Yoopers," have historically reveled in their isolationism. Over the years there have been serious attempts to make the U.P. a separate state, and such names as "Cloverland," "Hiawathaland," and "Superior" have been proposed. When the Mackinac Bridge opened in 1957, finally linking the two dissimilar halves of the state, one noted Yooper suggested bombing it. Those south of the bridge were pretty sure he was kidding.

This is not to say that Yoopers, a good many of whom are retired auto workers from the Lower Peninsula, aren't an affable bunch. If anything, they're too busy enjoying their

*surroundings to worry about a visitor's origin. Spring finds the
rivers teeming with spawning trout, salmon, and steelhead,
and the forests growing shaggy and fragrant. From Memorial
Day through Labor Day the U.P. is filled with vacationers,
although even in the peak months of July and August it's easy
to find solitude in the region's many state parks or on its
numerous lakes. Air-conditioning is unnecessary, as the
warmest days dissolve into cool, even bracing, nights. From
early September to mid-October there is an autumn color show
that rivals anything in New England. With 6 million acres of
land open to hunting, the forests and wetlands are filled with
orange-jacketed men and women pursuing deer, black bear,
ruffed grouse, snowshoe hares, bobcats, raccoons, and coyotes.
The long months of winter are thoroughly enjoyed by skiers,
snowmobilers, ice fishermen, and participants in the never-
ending stream of dogsled races and ice carnivals. Winter is
declared over when students at Lake Superior State University
in Sault Ste. Marie ceremonially burn a snowman in effigy.*

*Although the Upper Peninsula has many finely furnished
places to bed down and to eat in, you may occasionally run
across tacky or threadbare lodgings euphemistically labeled
"rustic." Most of the region's visitors are looking forward to
long evenings discussing trout fishing, not comparing the U.P.
with Newport or Martha's Vineyard; their priority—with
apologies to E.M. Forster—remains a view with a room.*

Places to Go, Sights to See

Isle Royale National Park (tel. 906/482–0984). This island wilderness, in the
northwest corner of Lake Superior, is accessible only by seaplane or boat, and is
as rugged a vacation experience as one can find. You won't find any roads here:
what await you are lots of moose, wolves, and other wildlife, unspoiled forests,
and cold, refreshing lakes. The park's small marina and two lodges are open from
May through October and reservations are a must.

Lighthouses. For more than 150 years, Great Lakes mariners have entrusted
their lives to these beacons. There are more than 40 fully operational lighthouses
along the shores of the Upper Peninsula, many of them unmanned. You can
explore three in the Hiawatha National Forest near Brimley, including the 65-
foot Iroquois Lighthouse (tel. 906/437–5272). Built in 1870, it has a museum that
focuses on the lives of lighthouse keepers and their families.

Soo Locks. A 21-foot drop-off in St. Mary's River near Sault Ste. Marie forced early settlers to portage from Lake Superior to Lake Huron. The discovery of huge copper and iron deposits in the western U.P. prompted the building of two locks and a canal in 1855 to handle deep-draft vessels. Today viewing platforms give an almost overwhelmingly close-up look at ships from many nations, including superfreighters up to 1,000 feet long and 105 feet wide.

Tahquamenon Falls. The most spectacular of the U.P.'s 150 waterfalls is also the second largest east of the Mississippi River. They can be reached via Route 123 from Paradise, the closest community. Tahquamenon's fame was first secured in Longfellow's "Song of Hiawatha," and tourists haven't stopped coming yet. The surrounding country is magnificent in the autumn, by which time the crowds have dwindled, and breathtaking in the winter, when light bouncing off the water turns giant icicles into rainbows of ice sculptures.

Underwater Preserves. Hundreds of shipwrecks can be found in the cold, clear waters of the Great Lakes. They are accessible to divers at several underwater preserves, including the Marquette Underwater Preserve (300 Lakeshore Blvd., Marquette, tel. 906/226–2006 or 800/338–7982), where vessels ranging from iron freighters to wooden schooners sit in the waters of Lake Superior. Dive charters and boat tours are available at the Alger Underwater Preserve (Commercial St., west side of Munising Bay, Munising, tel. 906/387–4477) in Munising Bay, the resting place for shipwrecks dating back to the 1850s. Some are visible from the surface, others are 110 feet under. About 60 miles north of the Mackinac Bridge, Whitefish Bay, a notorious stretch of Lake Superior's navigable waters, has been the site of numerous shipwrecks, including the *Edmund Fitzgerald*, which met its end in 1975. These are commemorated at the Great Lakes Shipwreck Museum (Whitefish Point Rd., tel. 906/293–3392) at Whitefish Point, about 11 miles north of Paradise. The memorial includes an 1849 lighthouse. For those who'd like a closer look, the Whitefish Point Underwater Preserve (tel. 906/492–3445) offers some of the best diving opportunities in North America.

Fishing

Anglers look on the U.P. as nirvana: With its 4,300 inland lakes, 12,000 miles of rivers and streams, and access to three of the Great Lakes, how could it be anything less? Giant Lake Gogebic in the western U.P. and Little Bay de Noc, near Escanaba in the south central part of the region, are famous for their large walleyes. The Sylvania Wilderness and Recreation Area near Watersmeet has a fish population of pike, perch, bass, trout, and walleye. The Great Lakes offer coho, lake trout, steelhead, chinook salmon, yellow perch, northern pike, and small-mouth bass. The shore has numerous marinas and public-access sites from which to launch or charter a boat.

Skiing

Some of the best alpine skiing in the Midwest can be had in the U.P. Vertical drops of 600 feet and runs of 5,000 to 6,000 feet are common at Marquette Mountain (tel. 906/225–1155), a mile south of Marquette on County Road 553, and Big Powderhorn Mountain (tel. 906/932–4838) in Bessemer and Porcupine Mountains State Park (tel. 906/885–5275) near Ontonagon, both in the western corner of the

U.P. Cross-country trails are nearly everywhere, running alongside roads and frozen streams and inside forests and state parks.

Snowmobiling

With annual snowfalls exceeding 200 inches in some areas, snowmobiling has long been a popular recreation in the Upper Peninsula. There are hundreds of miles of trails groomed and marked by the state, many of them passing right through the center of towns and others leading to frozen waterfalls, forests, and other scenic overlooks. Rentals can be arranged through snowmobile dealers in most communities.

Restaurants

Dog Patch (820 E. Superior St., tel. 906/387–9948) and **Robin's Nest** (3520 I–75 Business Spur, tel. 906/632–3200) in Sault Ste. Marie are representative of most restaurants in the U.P.: casual and inexpensive, specializing in seafood dishes such as lake trout and whitefish. **The Harbor Haus** (1 block off U.S. 41, Copper Harbor, tel. 906/289–4502), which overlooks Lake Superior in Calumet, breaks out of the mold somewhat by offering a German menu along with the freshest lake catch.

Tourist Information

The **Upper Peninsula Travel & Recreation Association** (Box 400, Iron Mountain, MI 49801, tel. 906/774–5480 or 800/562–7134 for IL, MI, MN, and WI residents) is the central source for travel information in the region. The **Michigan Department of Natural Resources** (530 W. Allegan St., Lansing, MI 48933, tel. 517/373–1204) can answer questions on boating, fishing, and hunting regulations and opportunities. **The Michigan Travel Bureau** (333 S. Capitol Ave., Lansing, MI 48933, tel. 800/543–2937) has statewide tourist information.

Laurium Manor Inn

Dave and Julie Sprenger were working as engineers in San Jose, California, when, as Julie describes it, they "decided to commit corporate suicide" and trade the Golden State's laid-back charms for the ruggedly isolated Keweenaw Peninsula. They shared a dream of owning a mansion they had visited in Laurium, a former copper boom town. In 1988, they bought the vacant three-story neoclassic house, and after three years of restoration work, which included attaching showers to a half-dozen claw-foot tubs, they reopened its heavy oak doors as a bed-and-breakfast.

The Upper Peninsula's largest and most opulent mansion was built in 1908 by Captain Thomas H. Hoatson, owner of the Calumet & Arizona Mining Company. At a time when miners were toiling 6,000 feet underground for 8¢ an hour, Hoatson spent $50,000 constructing the 40-room mansion, and an additional $35,000 furnishing it. The copper magnate had impeccable taste, as lodgers and afternoon tour groups ($2 a head) quickly learn.

Every room is a marvel. Silver-leaf overlay draws your eye to the ceiling of the music parlor. The dining room boasts stained-glass windows and gilded elephant-hide wall coverings, and the kitchen has a wall-size, built-in icebox made of marble, tile, and oak. And then there are the two cedar closets that are big enough to serve as bedrooms in most bungalows.

The bedrooms were built extra-large. The largest, the Laurium Suite, is a majestic 530 square feet and has a hand-carved oak fireplace and private balcony. All the guest quarters are outfitted with queen- or king-size beds, handmade flannel quilts, and period antiques.

During the buffet breakfast of pastries, cereal, and fruit, you can plan day trips to the historic Calumet Theatre, where Sarah Bernhardt, Lillian Russell, and Douglas Fairbanks, Jr., performed, or to one of the ghost towns sprinkled throughout the copper region. Lake Superior is just 4 miles away; Fort Wilkins State Park, a mid-19th-century army post on the northernmost tip of Keweenaw, is a short drive up U.S. 41.

Address: *320 Tamarack, Laurium, MI 49913, tel. 906/337-2549.*
Accommodations: *8 double rooms with baths, 2 doubles share bath, 2 suites.*
Amenities: *Fireplace in 2 guest rooms, phone and cable TV in den.*
Rates: *$49-$109; Continental breakfast. D, MC, V.*
Restrictions: *No smoking, no pets.*

Michigamme Lake Lodge

Everything about this lodge is larger than life, from its location atop a bluff overlooking Lake Michigamme (a Native American word for "Big Lake") to its massive 2½-story stone fireplace. That's wholly in keeping with the Bunyanesque image of the Upper Peninsula where, according to legend, Babe the Blue Ox's hoofprints created many of the lakes.

The truth is a tad less sensational, but interesting nonetheless. After a prominent fruit wholesaler and banker named Sam Cohodas selected the site for his summer home, a platoon of Finnish woodsmen spent a year felling, cutting, and fitting giant white pines to build the all-log dwelling; the stone for the great room's fireplace was also quarried in the area. The lodge was opened in 1935 and was used for the next 52 years by the Cohodas family. Frank and Linda Stabile, hoteliers in Marquette, bought it in 1988 and reopened it as a bed-and-breakfast.

Barbara Sacks manages the three-person staff. The management's philosophy is to keep the lodge as rustic as it was when it opened, which explains the complete lack of radio or television (although Native American flute music is softly piped in). The range of activities, like the scenery, seems limitless. You can swim along the 1,700-foot private beach, bike along old logging trails, paddle a canoe to explore the giant lake's necklace of jade islands, go fishing for walleye and bass, hike, or look for moose in the nearby 17,000-acre McCormick wilderness preserve.

The cavernous interior is filled with bird's-eye maple furniture. Guest rooms are large and have views of the lake; the beds have down quilts and handcrafted pillows. Arrangements of axes, carpentry tools, and decoys share wall space throughout the lodge with a veritable herd of deer heads and bearskins. The rails of an inside balcony overlooking the main floor are draped with colorful rugs, and a fireplace anchors the large common areas, which have unique cedar chandeliers and a giant 125-year-old mirror. A 40-foot sun porch stuffed with antiques and original Adirondack and twig furniture is a favorite of the guests at any time of the day or night.

Listed in the State and National Registers of Historic Places, this may just be the grandest rustic lodging in an area brimming with them—and that's no tall tale.

Address: *Michigamme Lake Lodge Rd. (Box 97), Champion, MI 49814, tel. 906/339–4400 or 800/358–0058.*
Accommodations: *3 double rooms with baths, 6 doubles share 3 baths.*
Amenities: *Phone on first floor.*
Rates: *$69–$125; Continental breakfast. MC, V.*
Restrictions: *No smoking, no pets; closed Jan. 1–Apr. 30.*

Big Bay Point Lighthouse

his 1896 brick-tower lighthouse, 30 miles north of Marquette at the end of a rocky point, is one of only three in the country operated as a bed and breakfast. Owners Linda and Jeff Ganble were active in historic preservation in Chicago when they purchased the decommissioned but still-operating lighthouse in April 1992. "We emphasize a stress-free environment here," says Linda. To that end, television is banned and the phone is off-limits except for emergencies. After breakfast, guests are encouraged to get out and explore the ruggedly picturesque surroundings. You can climb to the top of the tower, which rises 103 feet above the water, or tramp the 53 acres of hardwoods and meadows and 4,500 feet of Lake Superior shoreline.

One guest room is in the base of the lighthouse and the others are in the former lightkeeper's house attached to the tower. There is plenty of log furniture and a large collection of watercolor paintings, photographs, and other works by local artists. In the living room, guests gather every evening in front of the fireplace to drink wine and listen to Linda and Jeff discuss lighthouse history and local lore.

Address: *3 Lighthouse Rd., Big Bay, MI 49808, tel. 906/345–9957.*
Accommodations: *5 double rooms with baths, 2 doubles share bath.*
Amenities: *Sauna.*
Rates: *$99–$165; full breakfast, evening wine. No credit cards.*
Restrictions: *No smoking, no pets.*

Eagle's Nest Bed & Breakfast

agle's Nest is perched on a 300-foot ridge overlooking Lake Superior and the village of Eagle River on the western edge of the Keweenaw Peninsula. Three-quarters of a mile from the nearest neighbor, the property includes 20 acres of mixed hardwoods and pine, a stocked trout pond, and several hiking trails. Linda La-Motte, a U.P. native who summered here as a child, sold her Atlanta flying school in 1980 and bought the large, two-story cedar-log house, which was built in 1858 at the start of the copper mining boom. She also owns the Eagle River Inn, the sole business in the four-block downtown. Despite the growing presence of snowmobilers and wealthy developers, Eagle River remains a perfect retreat.

The living room, last redone in the 1940s, has mohair furniture, a hardwood floor, stained-glass windows, brass wall lamps, and a hand-carved birch fireplace. In the evening, Popov, Linda's 110-pound half-wolf, half-malamute guardian, plops in front of the 6-foot-tall Royal Oak parlor stove in the adjacent Humboldt Room. The guest rooms' cedar furniture is timeless in design, if not in fact.

Address: *Garden City Rd. (Box 14), Eagle River, MI 49924, tel. 906/337–4441.*
Accommodations: *3 double rooms share 2 baths.*
Amenities: *Phone in hallway.*
Rates: *$55–$65; full breakfast. MC, V.*
Restrictions: *No pets.*

Pinewood Lodge

J erry and Jenny Krieg sold their electronics store in Milwaukee to build this massive three-story log house in 1990. Twenty-seven miles east of Marquette on Route 28, Pinewood Lodge's greatest asset is its enviable location, one of the most coveted in the U.P. It sits on a private beach bordering Lake Superior in an area surrounded by raw natural beauty. There are volleyball nets set up in the sand and plenty of other recreational options, including swimming, and trails for cross-country skiing, snowmobiling, biking, and hiking (the atmosphere, however, is more geared to playful adults than families).

The large, airy public rooms feature pine paneling and the ubiquitous log furniture; the great room features a TV, VCR, stereo, fireplace, and an antique Apollo player piano with 70 rolls of music. A filling breakfast that typically includes waffles, Yorkshire pudding, and baked Finnish pancakes served with fruit is taken in a sun-filled dining room. Of the guest rooms, the upstairs quarters are larger, and the two third-floor rooms offer sweeping views of Lake Superior. A homey loft also overlooks the water and is a favorite gathering spot.

Address: *Rte. 28 (Box 176), Au Train, MI 49806, tel. 906/892–8300.*
Accommodations: *4 double rooms with baths, 3 doubles and 1 single share 2 baths.*
Amenities: *Hot tub and sauna.*
Rates: *$65–$80; full breakfast. D, MC, V.*
Restrictions: *No smoking indoors, no pets.*

Water Street Inn

F or those infatuated with Great Lakes lore, the Water Street Inn is the perfect place to drop anchor. The sprawling, three-story Queen Anne is in the heart of Sault Ste. Marie, the third-oldest city in the United States, and just an hour's drive north of the Mackinac Bridge.

The house, bought by retirees Phyllis and Greg Walker in 1991, has classically elegant accoutrements, including a turret, Tiffany windows, and marble fireplaces. The sometimes whimsical decor is a reflection of the Walkers' travels, with a Colombian sculpture of a rain god sharing space with a Mexican stuffed owl. Phyllis serves "a serious Northern breakfast" of lemon bread, apple butter, oatmeal pancakes, and other delights. The four second-floor guest rooms are comfortable, tidy, and filled with family heirlooms. The front-facing guest rooms have wonderful views of the river and the twinkling lights of Canada. From the wraparound porch or the gazebo, guests can relax and watch freighters slowly pass on the St. Mary's River.

Address: *140 E. Water St., Sault Ste. Marie, MI 49783, tel. 906/632–1900 or 800/236–1904.*
Accommodations: *4 double rooms with baths.*
Amenities: *Portable phone.*
Rates: *$70–$95; full breakfast. D, MC, V.*
Restrictions: *No smoking indoors, no pets.*

Mackinac Island

In 1780, fearful of an American attack during the Revolutionary War, the British moved an entire town from what is now known as Mackinaw City over icy waters to a remote island. The townspeople could never have envisioned that today nearly 1 million visitors flock to Mackinac Island (pronounced "Mac-i-naw, like the city) each year to absorb its rich history and natural beauty.

Mackinac Island is between three of the Great Lakes (Huron, Michigan, and Superior) in the Straits of Mackinac, where Huron and Michigan join. The region played a vital role in the northern frontier beginning in the 1600s, long before the island was settled by the British. The Chippewa supplied the French with furs in exchange for such items as blankets, cooking utensils, and weapons. Originally called Michilimacinac, after a Native American word meaning "great turtle," Mackinac Island, with its rising bluffs, looks like the back of a turtle.

In 1815, after more than 30 years of military struggles, Mackinac Island became a permanent part of U.S. territory, and in 1875 Congress created the nation's second national park on the island. The land, which now comprises more than 80% of the island's 2,200 acres, was later transferred to Michigan and became its first state park.

The island's military history and late-1800s culture come to life inside the walls of Fort Mackinac. This historic fort has been painstakingly restored (14 of its buildings are more than 200 years old), and a tour is one of the best ways to learn about the island. Be forewarned, however; the fort's cannons are fired numerous times throughout the day as part of dramatic reenactments, and although islanders have learned to take this in stride, more than a few visitors have been shaken by the blasts.

Aside from these noises, Mackinac Island has a romantic and timeless tranquility about it, and visiting is akin to traveling

*back about 100 years. As you approach the island, a foghorn
sounds in the distance, and magnificent Victorian homes
overlooking the harbor come into view. The only signs of the
20th century are the five-seater airplanes that fly over from St.
Ignace or the catamaran that ferries you to the island. There
are no bridges leading from the mainland. The beautiful
Mackinac Bridge, an experience in itself to travel over or look
at, connects only Michigan's upper and lower peninsulas.*

*Three different boat companies operate from the towns on
either side of the bridge (Mackinaw City on the Lower
Peninsula and St. Ignace on the Upper Peninsula). The ferry
lines are comparable in schedule and price, and competition is
stiff—so stiff, in fact, that, after exiting I–75, the main
highway leading north from central Michigan, you'll start
seeing individual ticket booths a good 10 minutes before you
get to the docks.*

*Plan to leave your car behind when you board the ferry, since
no motorized vehicles are allowed on Mackinac Island.
(Parking is free for day visits and just a few dollars for
overnight.) Once you've landed, step lightly, since the main
mode of transportation is the horse-drawn carriage; more than
600 horses inhabit the island during the summer months.
Visitors can also rent bikes or walk to almost anywhere on the
island. Bicycle valets will deliver your luggage from the ferry
docks, leaving you to peruse the island at your leisure.*

*Main Street winds along the harbor, and although "downtown"
is not exactly peaceful, the sounds of clomping horses and
bicycle bells add some charm to the noise of the crowds during
peak season (July and August). A wealth of tourist
attractions, such as fudge shops (an island specialty and
source of the name "fudgie," humorously bestowed upon
tourists), souvenir and gift shops, galleries, restaurants, bike
rentals, and carriage companies, makes this the busiest spot
on the island. Watching the hustle and bustle of the ferry
handlers is a fascinating reminder of a bygone era, since most
everything needed on the island (food, supplies, horses, and so*

forth) is brought by ferry from the mainland and then delivered by carriage or bicycle to its destination.

The island is only 8.1 miles in circumference, and a paved road circles the perimeter. A bicycle ride or carriage tour around the island is a popular way to enjoy the natural beauty of Mackinac Island State Park, which provides unique limestone formations and breathtaking views of the Great Lakes.

Mackinac Island has an active year-round community of about 600 residents. The tourist season runs from mid-May to mid-October, and most accommodations are booked far in advance for July and August. Known worldwide for events such as the Lilac Festival in June and Stone Skipping Contest in July, Mackinac attracts an international set. September offers a calmer pace, since crowds have diminished and the weather is still warm during the day but cooler at night, wonderful for sound sleeping. Most of the attractions are only open during the tourist season, and until the whole collegiate work force arrives on the island, don't be surprised to find your innkeeper still finishing up some last-minute details.

Places to Go, Sights to See

Beaumont Memorial (Market St., tel. 906/847–3328). Dr. William Beaumont is renowned for his landmark experiments on the human digestive system in the 1820s. Educational displays tell of his experiments and discoveries, and the conditions under which he worked.

British Landing Nature Center (tel. 906/847–3328). On the northwest side of the island, the center has exhibits that provide information about the night of July 16, 1812, when 36 British soldiers and hundreds of their Native American allies landed and captured Fort Mackinac without firing a single shot.

Colonial Michilimackinac (tel. 906/847–3328). Located in Mackinaw City, this is a reconstruction of the original mainland fort and surrounding frontier fur-trading village, which was founded in 1715.

Fort Mackinac (E. Bluff Rd., tel. 906/847–3328). Costumed interpreters demonstrate 19th-century blacksmithing and stage dramatic reenactments. Also of interest are the exhibits, artifacts, and a Discovery Room for children, where they can try on period clothing and "fire" muskets. Fourteen of the restored buildings are more than 200 years old.

Grand Hotel (Cadotte Ave., tel. 906/847–3331). One of the island's premier land-marks, the Grand Hotel first opened in 1887 and is considered one of the world's finest resorts. Visitors may stroll on its 700-foot veranda, visible from the main-land; partake of afternoon tea; meander through its gardens; peruse the historical photo collection; or even swim in the pool, built especially for the 1946 Esther Williams film *This Time for Keeps*. A special $5 guest pass must be purchased by any visitor who is not a hotel guest.

Indian Dormitory (Main St., tel. 906/847–3328). Native American culture dis-plays and period settings are enhanced by live interpretations of life in the 1800s.

Mackinac Island State Park. A tour of the park, from Arch Rock (a natural limestone arch that stands almost 150 feet above the water and 50 feet across) to Wildflower Trail (a small grove of wildflowers that shows a beautiful array of col-ors) is a must, especially since it encompasses nearly 80% of the island.

Mill Creek (tel. 906/847–3328). Located on the mainland, in Mackinaw City, this is an authentically reconstructed, operating, water-powered sawmill. Founded in 1790, it supplied lumber for many of the buildings on Mackinac Island.

Ste. Anne's Church (Huron St.). Still an active parish, the church is an architec-tural beauty built in 1874.

Stuart House Museum (Market St., tel. 906/847–3328). Housed in John Jacob Astor's American Fur Company warehouse, which was built in 1810, the museum depicts the history of the bygone fur-trading era.

Restaurants

The Pub Oyster Bar (Main St., tel. 906/847–3454) serves up seafood chowder, homemade pizza, and, of course, oysters. The elegant, 100-foot-long lunch buffet served daily at the **Grand Hotel** (Cadotte Ave., tel. 906/847–3331) includes a large selection of entrées and great desserts; dinner is also served, and a $5 dis-count to offset the guest pass is applied to the restaurant bill. In the Iroquois Hotel, **The Carriage House** (Main St., tel. 906/847–3321) offers gourmet dining overlooking the water; a specialty is Great Lakes whitefish. At **Horn's Gaslight Bar** (Main St., tel. 906/847–6154), you can enjoy burgers, steaks, and, at dinner, Mexican food accompanied by a piano player and dancing.

Tourist Information

Mackinac Island Chamber of Commerce (Mackinac Island, MI 49757, tel. 906/847–6418); **Mackinac State Historic Parks Visitors Center** (Main St., Box 370 G, Mackinac Island, MI 49757, tel. 906/847–3328); **Michigan Travel Bureau** (333 S. Capitol, Lansing, MI 48933, tel. 800/543–2937).

Bay View at Mackinac

Owner Doug Yoder's great-great-grandfather, Dr. John R. Bailey, a surgeon at Fort Mackinac, would be pleased. Doug, who works in the music industry in Nashville during the winter, has painstakingly restored this 1890s house, which has been in his family for more than 100 years. The two-year renovation, which cost a half-million dollars, has made the most of the home's elegance.

The sitting room's tin ceiling and fireplace and the refinished wood moldings throughout the house have kept their charm. The wraparound porch is decked out in green and white with skirted, glass-topped tables. Panoramic views of the water and abundant bright begonias and geraniums make this a perfect place to enjoy late afternoon refreshments.

Guest rooms feel more modern than Victorian as a result of the renovation, but bright new fabrics, skirted tables, and flower-garden wallpaper borders mixed with authentic period pieces, such as an antique, inlaid mahogany headboard, create a nice blend of old and new. Marble floors and ceramic tile in the bathrooms add a classic touch. All the curtains and bedspreads have been handmade for the inn, as was the carpeting throughout the hallways and stairs. Three different designs were cut and laid together to create a beautiful rose-colored and flowered carpet.

Newlyweds and chronic romantics will especially enjoy Doug's final additions—three suites, each luxuriously furnished with a whirlpool, television, a CD and video library, wet bar, and private balcony overlooking the harbor. There have already been several weddings on those balconies.

Upon arrival you'll discover a sampling of fudge in your room in true Mackinac Island tradition. In the morning you'll awaken to the aroma of Doug's Bay View Blend Coffee and home-baked pastries. Take your breakfast up to the second-floor balcony snd start your day off right—with a spectacular view of the Straits of Mackinac.

Address: *Summer: Main St. (Box 448), Mackinac Island, MI 49757, tel. 906/847–3295. Winter: 920 Cantrel Ave., Nashville, TN 37215, tel. 615/298–2759.*
Accommodations: *17 double rooms with baths, 3 suites.*
Amenities: *Ceiling fans in rooms, TV in sitting room on request, conference room, gallery and marine supply store; short-term docking facilities.*
Rates: *$95–$165; $285 for suites; Continental breakfast. MC, V.*
Restrictions: *No pets; 2-night minimum on weekends, closed Oct. 15–Apr.*

Haan's 1830 Inn

The charm of Haan's 1830 Inn is not just in its appearance but in the owners themselves. Vernon and Joy Haan share business responsibilities at the inn with their son Nicholas and his wife, Nancy. Even their grandchildren lend a hand by folding napkins before breakfast at the 12-foot harvest table.

The house was built around the foundations of a log cabin that had been dragged over the ice from the mainland during the Revolutionary War. In the mid-1800s, it was the home of Fort Mackinac officer and onetime island mayor Colonel Preston. The white columns in front give evidence that the inn is the oldest Greek Revival home in what was the Northwest Territory; it was also the first B&B on Mackinac Island.

The Haans have turned what could have seemed old and shabby into someplace warm and inviting. Guest rooms are named after figures from the island's past and are tastefully decorated with a variety of antiques, including an elegant burled-walnut headboard. Taller guests should avoid the Reverend William Ferry and Pere Marquette rooms, since the ceilings in that part of the house are unusually low, probably to retain heat in the winter.

A fascinating centerpiece in the sitting room is a large black safe originally used by one of fur trader John Jacob Astor's agents. Original 1830 prints

hang on the wall, and there is a large, dark cherry-wood desk that was built and used in Fort Mackinac. The second-story porch, tucked under the trees, is a great place to hide out and absorb the island's atmosphere; for those looking for more excitement, the island's downtown is a mere three blocks away.

The Haans clearly enjoy running the inn. The marble-top breakfast buffet brims with delicious coffee cakes, muffins, and jams to be enjoyed at your leisure in front of a crackling fire in the dining room. Vernon is a history buff with a special talent for bringing history to life. In fact, you won't need to spend money on any of the island tours; Vernon is far more interesting and lively. The Haan in the inn's name, like the 1830, is clearly not just for effect.

Address: *Summer: Huron St. (Box 123), Mackinac Island, MI 49757, tel. 906/847–6244. Winter: 1134 Geneva St., Lake Geneva, WI 53147, tel. 414/248–9244.*
Accommodations: *4 double rooms with baths, 2 doubles share bath, 1 housekeeping suite.*
Amenities: *Ceiling fans and chocolates in rooms, vouchers for cocktails at local restaurants.*
Rates: *$75–$115; Continental breakfast. No credit cards.*
Restrictions: *No smoking indoors, no pets; closed Nov.–Apr.*

The Inn on Mackinac

Trying to find all 13 colors on the inn's exterior, beyond the purple, pink, green, and peach, is a favorite pastime of guests. Assistant general manager Kelly Irby says that most people can only identify five or six. The bright colors, inspired by Victorian homes like the so-called "painted ladies" of San Francisco, make the Inn on Mackinac one of the more eye-catching houses on the island.

Built in 1867, with the back section added later, the house used to be called the Chateau Beaumont in memory of the fort's famous army surgeon, William Beaumont. In 1988, the inn was remodeled to emphasize its quaint Victorian charm while providing a number of modern amenities.

The larger, more expensive rooms in the front, older section of the house are furnished with charm: cherry armoires, white shutters in the windows overlooking the street, and white lace swags over the beds. Although the rooms in the back section are comfortable and also redecorated, they lack the view and are smaller. Request a room with a bay window (they can be found in both sections) since they add a sense of spaciousness to the room.

Although you are unlikely to meet up with owners Pat and Alice Pulte (they also own the Murray Hotel), a complete staff is on hand to answer any questions you might have about the island or the inn. Because of its size, the inn may lack some of the intimacy of other B&Bs, but it makes up for that in style and convenience. Although not right in the center of town, it is certainly close.

A sense of camaraderie is evident as soon as you step out onto the expansive wraparound porch on the second floor, where guests gather throughout the day. In fact, the outdoor areas at the inn are as enjoyable as the rooms. At street level, a lattice-covered arch leads to a charming brick patio surrounded by gardens. This level, which includes the lobby and dining room, was created during remodeling by digging out the home's basement and adding French doors all the way around. You can eat breakfast inside or on the patio or sample some of the Pultes' homemade fudge, made fresh daily and sold in the lobby.

Address: *Summer: Main St., Mackinac Island, MI 49757, tel. 906/847–6348 or 800/462–2546. Winter: Box 7706, Ann Arbor, MI 48107, tel. 313/665–5750.*
Accommodations: *44 double rooms with baths.*
Amenities: *Air-conditioning, TV in rooms, wheelchair accessible.*
Rates: *$88–$160; Continental breakfast. MC, V.*
Restrictions: *No pets; closed Oct. 15–Apr.*

Metivier Inn

Y ou can't miss the Metivier Inn, located on a quiet section of Market Street one block from the hustle and bustle of Main Street. Beautiful landscaping and a white picket fence along the sidewalk in front of the house make this inn a standout.

The house, built in 1877, was a single-family home until 1984, when it opened as a B&B. Originally it had only 13 guest rooms, but recent renovations have added more on the third floor. The back deck off that floor, overlooking the magnificent Grand Hotel and golf course, is very peaceful and popular for weddings. A side porch, accessible from four rooms on the second floor, is perfect for a group of people looking for some shared privacy. The front porch runs the full width of the house and is nicely furnished with the owners' personal collection of antique white wicker. In fact, soft colors and antique-style furniture throughout give the inn a simple, clean, and tasteful look.

Various names from Mackinac Island's past adorn the doors to each guest room. Because of its larger size and unique view, the John Jacob Astor Room, in the turret at the front of the house, is one of the nicest. An antique sleigh bed adorns one of the main-floor rooms, or, for a romantic night, try one of the four rooms outfitted with a four-poster canopy bed.

A Continental breakfast, brought in from a local bakery each morning, is served in the lobby, which, although somewhat sparse, is nonetheless comfortable; it is furnished with couches, chairs, and a wood-burning stove that adds atmosphere when stoked up on cooler days or in the evenings.

Metivier is efficiently run and quiet, but it lacks some of the personal touches that can make for a unique stay. Although it is owned by two couples, Ken and Diane Neyer and Mike and Jane Bacon, the inn is professionally managed by Roger and Pam Spaven, who live on the premises and seem very responsive to their guests' needs without being intrusive.

Guests can also enjoy a visit to Biddle House, a restored turn-of-the century home, right next door.

Address: *Summer: Market St. (Box 285), Mackinac Island, MI 49757, tel. 906/847–6234. Winter: tel. 616/627–2055.*
Accommodations: *20 double rooms with baths, 1 housekeeping suite.*
Amenities: *Wood-burning stove and cable TV in sitting room, conference room.*
Rates: *$115–$175; $240 for suite; Continental breakfast. D, MC, V.*
Restrictions: *No pets; closed Nov.–Apr.*

Bogan Lane Inn

Trish Martin grew up in this home on Bogan Lane, and, even though the house shows its age in some areas (it was built around 1850), she has made it so cozy that her guests will feel at home as well. The location just off Huron Street, three blocks from downtown, is close enough for visitors to enjoy the island and far enough for them to hear only the foghorns at night.

Of the guest rooms, the Porch Room, with charming quilts and curtains, offers a cozy retreat, although it has only twin beds. The Yellow Room, next door, is furnished with a comfortable antique double bed.

As the only year-round B&B on Mackinac Island, Bogan Lane Inn is perfect for a cross-country-ski weekend or midwinter getaway, and Trish's home-baked pastries warm up even the coldest morning. Whether enjoying a fire in the living room, playing one of the many board games kept on hand, or getting the scoop from Trish on the island's secret spots, you'll feel like you're staying at your grandmother's cottage.

Address: *Bogan La. (Box 482), Mackinac Island, MI 49757, tel. 906/847–3439.*
Accommodations: *4 double rooms share 2 baths.*
Amenities: *Ceiling fans in guest rooms.*
Rates: *$55–$60; Continental breakfast. No credit cards.*
Restrictions: *No smoking indoors, no pets.*

Cloghaun Bed & Breakfast

Baskets of bright red begonias adorning both balconies are the first things you see at this Market Street B&B. Inside, century-old family treasures, beamed ceilings, arched windows and doors, the butter churn by the fireplace, and rosebud china set out for breakfast create the relaxed and charming atmosphere at the Cloghaun (pronounced "Clawhahn").

The original owners, Thomas and Bridgett Donnelly, left Cloghaun in Ireland during the great famine of 1848 and settled here. The house, built in 1884 for their growing family, is still owned by descendants James Bond and his wife. The property is managed by Chris and Ray Clark, who run it in such an inviting manner that you'd think it was their own.

All the rooms interconnect and can be turned into suites if desired. Even those without private baths have sinks. The sitting room is full of books, historical tidbits, jigsaw puzzles, games, and even a box of toys for the younger set.

Address: *Summer: Market St. (Box 203), Mackinac Island, MI 49757, tel. 906/847–3885. Winter: 15355 Windmill Point Dr., Grosse Pointe Park, MI 48230, tel. 313/331–7110.*
Accommodations: *8 double rooms with baths, 2 doubles share bath.*
Amenities: *TV with VCR in sitting room.*
Rates: *$75–$105; Continental breakfast. No credit cards.*
Restrictions: *No smoking indoors, no pets; closed Oct. 15–May 15.*

Murray Hotel

The Murray Hotel, dubbed the "centennial bed-and-breakfast inn," has been providing hospitality to visitors for more than 100 years. Owned by islanders Pat and Alice Pulte (they also own the Inn on Mackinac), it has a distinctly Victorian air, enhanced by the wide balustrade staircase and wicker-filled lobby. The guest rooms are clean but simply decorated with floral wallpaper borders, wicker furniture, and a few antique dressers and headboards.

The Murray is on Main Street, in the heart of Mackinac Island's downtown. This means noise from morning to night during the summer season, but it's a great spot for people-watching and for being at the heart of the comings and goings.

With a professional staff running the daily operations, dining rooms, delicatessen, cocktail lounge, and a more formal check-in procedure, the Murray feels somewhat more like a quaint 19th-century hotel than a B&B retreat.

Address: *Summer: Main St. (Box 476), Mackinac Island, MI 49757, tel. 906/847–3361 or 800/462–2546. Winter: Box 7706, Ann Arbor, MI 48107, tel. 313/665–5750.*
Accommodations: *69 double rooms with baths.*
Amenities: *Air-conditioning and TV in rooms, whirlpool bath in 2 rooms.*
Rates: *$75–$160; Continental breakfast. MC, V.*
Restrictions: *No pets; closed Oct. 15–Apr.*

1900 Market Street Inn

Facing Marquette Park, this recently renovated turn-of-the-century house was formerly a private home owned by the Triskett family. Island residents and sisters Sandra and Deborah Orr teamed up to convert it into a B&B in 1991.

The downstairs guest room is elegant and romantic, with high ceilings, a fireplace, a piano, and a beautiful four-poster bed. The woodwork up the wide staircase leading to the second-floor rooms was beautifully restored, and each room, from the chintz to the wallpaper, carefully adheres to coordinated color schemes, from soft pastels in one to deep burgundy and green in another.

Although very clean and modern, the inn itself is relatively small, with only

a sparse lobby and tiny front porch to gather in. Coffee and pastries are served in the lobby each morning; there's also a complimentary Continental breakfast two blocks away at the Pub Oyster Bar that offers more variety.

Address: *Market St. (Box 315), Mackinac Island, MI 49757, tel. 906/847–3811.*
Accommodations: *7 double rooms with baths.*
Amenities: *Ceiling fans, cable TV in rooms, wheelchair accessible.*
Rates: *$85–130; Continental breakfast. MC, V.*
Restrictions: *No pets; 3-night minimum during boat races, closed Nov.–April.*

Grand Traverse Region
Including Traverse City

The Traverse City Convention and Visitors Bureau promotes Traverse City as "a Great Lakes paradise," a statement that may not be far from the truth. More than 250 miles of Lake Michigan shoreline and numerous inland lakes contribute to this area's natural beauty and recreational opportunities. The region that Chicago businessman Perry Hannah built as a lumber empire in the late 1800s has long been a popular vacation destination for Midwesterners. Over the past 10 years, it has gained national prominence as a convention area. It is also host to the National Cherry Festival.

Its popularity is most obvious during the summer (May through Labor Day), when the population swells from just under 30,000 to 200,000. Traffic jams can be annoying, and reservations for weekend lodging are a must. Winter also attracts visitors, since the terrain is perfect for cross-country skiers, and four of the Midwest's top downhill ski resorts are within an hour's drive. Luckily, winter crowds are not overwhelming. Fall, which brings the brilliant foliage to the hardwood trees, and spring, when cherry orchards are in full blossom, also offer a special beauty, and crowds are not as intense.

Three counties—Leelanau, Grand Traverse, and Benzie— make up what Michiganders refer to as the Grand Traverse region. It stretches north from Frankfort, up the east side of Lake Michigan to the tip of Leelanau Peninsula, back down to Traverse City, and east through a town with the unlikely name of Acme. The Old Mission Peninsula juts north from Traverse City, dividing the waters of Grand Traverse Bay into the East and West bays. Although East Bay is home to a wide variety of chain motels and restaurants, it also claims some of the cleanest beaches in the area. The growth of West Bay has been more carefully monitored, so there are numerous public beaches, marinas, parks, and a bike path that stretches the full width of the harbor.

Traverse City, at the foot of West Bay, is considered the metropolitan hub of northwestern Michigan and is the area's central destination point. With a year-round population of just under 20,000, it offers an unusually strong mix of cultural activities, and a huge selection of shops for a town its size. Among the city's entertainment offerings are a fine-arts museum, professional theater, symphony orchestra, zoo, steam-power passenger train, ski area, active arts council and community playhouse, and public recreational center (complete with lighted walking and biking paths, an indoor ice rink, a swimming pool, and tennis courts); it also has a college. Traverse City, however, has maintained an appealing small-town feel: Tree-lined historic neighborhoods, a downtown waterfront, regularly held open-air block parties and street sales, and people with a well-deserved reputation for friendliness help to keep the city bustling, but accessible.

Myriad opportunities for fun are not confined to Traverse City. Touring Old Mission and Leelanau peninsulas is a perfect way to spend a day. Acres of generations-old farms and wineries mingle with art galleries, restaurants, shops, antiques stores, parks, and beaches. The climate is favorable for farming, and the area boasts abundant orchards and six excellent wineries offering free tastings and tours. Visitors can also play golf in the Grand Traverse area, on courses designed by Jack Nicklaus and Arnold Palmer. The nationally renowned Interlochen Center for the Arts, just south of Traverse City, hosts a variety of entertainment, which includes the Canadian Brass, the Tokyo String Quartet, the Red Star Red Army Chorus and Dance Ensemble, and Peter, Paul, and Mary.

Places to Go, Sights to See

Dennos Museum Center (1701 E. Front St., Traverse City, tel. 616/922–1055), built in 1991, contains three galleries that hold exhibits from around the country and displays a permanent collection of Inuit art, said to be one of the largest in the United States. There are also hands-on exhibits for children, a small theater, and a 367-seat auditorium, home to the summer stock Michigan Ensemble Theatre.

Grand Traverse Lighthouse (M201, just north of Northport on Leelanau Peninsula, tel. 616/386–5503) was built in 1858, has been restored, and is now a living museum. Descendants of the former lighthouse keeper live in the front half of the building; the remaining space is devoted to pictures and displays—including a Fresnel lens used in the lighthouse—testifying to the rugged life of a keeper.

Gwen Frostic Prints (5140 River Rd., Benzonia, tel. 616/882–5505) is on a 280-acre nature preserve 30 minutes southwest of Traverse City. The stone studio, library, and printing facility were created by popular naturalist, author, and artist Gwen Frostic. Frostic's beautifully simple nature prints and poetry are reproduced in books, stationery, and other paper products and shipped around the world. Visitors may find it fascinating to watch the press at work or take delight in wandering around the grounds.

Interlochen Center for the Arts (Rte. 137, tel. 616/276–9221) has earned international recognition as a leading center for the development and training of talented and gifted students and as an advocate of the arts. It operates as a private high school during the school year, with students from around the world, and hosts a music camp for all ages during the summer. Throughout the year, student and faculty exhibits and performances are held along with those of internationally acclaimed artists. The 1,200 acres of scenic forest that make up the campus are on the edge of Green Lake in Interlochen, just south of Traverse City. The campus is open to visitors year-round.

Leelanau Sands Casino and **Grand Traverse Band Bingo Palace** (Rte. 22, just north of Suttons Bay, Peshawbestown, tel. 616/271–3538) are operated by the Grand Traverse Band of Ottawa and Chippewa Indians. Under the provisions of an agreement with the federal government concerning the sovereignty of Native American reservations, the tribe offers the only legal gambling in the region. Visitors can try their luck at anything from blackjack and poker to slot machines and bingo, where stakes can run as high as $25,000.

The **Manitou Islands,** off the coast of Lake Michigan near Leland, offer hiking and camping made enjoyable by the enchanting scenery. Motorized tours are also available. Both North and South Manitou islands are under the jurisdiction of the National Park Service. For information on day trips and evening cocktail cruises leaving from Fishtown, in Leland, call Manitou Island Transit (tel. 616/256–9061).

The **Music House** (Rte. 31, 2 mi north of Acme, tel. 616/938–9300) is an emporium and museum offering a magical experience. Wander through replica villages and listen to the working displays of automated music machines, pipe organs, and jukeboxes as well as to the Amaryllis, a 30-foot-wide dance organ from the Victoria Palace Ballroom in Belgium. Exhibits of record collections, early radios, television sets, and phonographs provide an amusing and lively history of the sounds of music.

Sleeping Bear Dunes National Lakeshore (tel. 616/326–5134), one of the world's largest moving sand dunes, towers over the waters of Lake Michigan and Glen Lakes. The area is part of the National Lakeshore Park and also includes the Manitou Islands. A scenic drive through the park provides spectacular views of the dunes, Lake Michigan, and the Glen Lakes. There's a dune climb, for hearty visitors, and plenty of other areas to explore on foot. The Philip A. Hart Visitors

Center on Route 72 in Empire offers park information, a minimuseum, and an excellent multimedia presentation.

Traverse City Opera House (112½ E. Front St., tel. 616/941–8082), built in 1891, is one of only 18 opera houses remaining of the 127 built in Michigan. This Victorian landmark is listed on both the National and the State Registers of Historic Sites. Architecture lovers will appreciate the meticulously restored vaulted ceiling and elaborate decorative moldings. The original curtain is still in place, and vintage advertisements and a landscape mural add considerably to the Victorian ambience. There is no charge to tour the opera house, which is host to a variety of community events.

Beaches

In this region known for its attractive shoreline, the beaches are too numerous to list, but rest assured that there is a beach for everyone and no charge for enjoying it. Such city beaches as **Clinch Park** and **West End,** within walking distance of downtown Traverse City, come complete with lifeguards and refreshment stands, marinas, and nearby establishments renting out boats. At the remote **Pyramid Point** and **Good Harbor** beaches (off Route 22, on the southwest side of the Leelanau Peninsula), you can enjoy building a fire while watching the sunset on Lake Michigan. Parks with beaches include **Interlochen State Park** (Rte. 137 via U.S. 31, tel. 616/775–9727) and **Traverse City State Park** (Munson Ave., tel. 616/775–9727).

Restaurants

On the Old Mission Peninsula are two very different restaurants in the same big house: **The Bowery** (13512 Peninsula Dr., tel. 616/223–4333), the more casual of the two, is known for its barbecued ribs and large beer selection, and **Bowers Harbor Inn** (13512 Peninsula Dr., tel. 616/223–4222) offers romantic dining overlooking the bay. Visitors may want to inquire about the resident ghost. **Old Mission Tavern** (17015 Center Rd., tel. 616/223–7280) is filled with an eclectic collection of works by local artists, which are for sale. In Traverse City, two elegant restaurants that serve regional cuisine with views of the bay are **Top of the Park** (300 E. State St., tel. 616/946–5000), on the 10th floor of the Park Place Hotel, and **Windows** (7677 W. Bayshore Dr., tel. 616/941–0100), 2 miles north of town. For a taste of the old lumbering era, try **Dill's Olde Towne Saloon** (423 S. Union St., tel. 616/947–7534), home in the summer to the musical Golden Garter Revue, or **Sleder's Tavern** (71 Randolph St., tel. 616/947–9213), in Slabtown, where you are presented a gift if you kiss the moose head. On the Leelanau Peninsula, the **Riverside Inn** (302 River St., tel. 616/256–9971), overlooking the Leland River in Leland, offers fresh whitefish, French cuisine, and an extensive wine selection. In Suttons Bay, you can try cozy **Boone's Prime Time** (102 St. Joseph's St., tel. 616/271–6688) for steak, fish, or burgers, or the gourmet **Hattie's Bar and Grille** (111 St. Joseph's St., tel. 616/271–6222), where diners can enjoy an eclectic menu ranging from risotto to veal chops while sitting amidst an art exhibit that changes monthly.

Tourist Information

Traverse City Area Chamber of Commerce (202 E. Grandview Pkwy., Traverse City, MI 49684, tel. 616/947–5075); **Traverse City Convention and Visitors Bureau** (415 Munson Ave., Suite 200, Traverse City, MI 49684, tel. 800/872–8377, fax 616/947–2621).

Centennial Inn

The Centennial Inn, in the heart of Leelanau County's rolling farmland, was designated a Michigan Centennial Farm by the state's Historical Commission. In the same family for more than 100 years, the farm got its first new owners when Karl and JoAnne Smith bought it four years ago.

The Smiths have carefully restored the two-story clapboard farmhouse, built in 1865. The original barn and two outbuildings are still in excellent condition. The smaller one has been turned into a gift shop, featuring antiques and folk art created by local artisans, as well as JoAnne's baskets and Karl's reproduction furniture. Since the inn is about 6 miles from the small town of Lake Leelanau, guests will need to drive a short way to find restaurants and shops.

As you approach the house, you'll come across a glistening sundial. The lettering around it reads, "Grow old along with me, the best is yet to be." The Centennial Inn is proof that what is old can also be very good. On the front porch, pots of red-blossomed geraniums are placed around a white bench, creating a colorful frame for the entrance.

The Smiths have decorated the farm in Shaker style, yet their loving attention makes what could seem sparse feel warm and inviting. A scattering of Oriental rugs complement the glow of the refinished, original hardwood floors. A candle chandelier hangs over the rough-hewn pine table in the dining room, and an elaborate pewter collection is displayed above the buffet. The parlor, one of the coziest spots, is perfect for reading, watching TV, or just enjoying the country fireplace.

The guest rooms continue the Shaker theme. The front room downstairs has a four-poster bed with a white lace canopy and homemade white quilt. Every detail harmonizes, down to the blue-and-white checkered curtains in the window and the old crockery on the tables.

A deluxe Continental breakfast is more than enough to fill you up. In the cooler months, breakfast can be enjoyed in the cozy dining room, but during the summer, either of two outside areas makes a perfect eating spot: The deck on the west side overlooks a big birch tree and apple orchards, and, on the east side, there's a redbrick patio with twig furniture. A swing in the back overlooks acres of unspoiled rolling land: The peaceful sight can take you back 100 years.

Address: *7251 E. Alpers Rd., Lake Leelanau, MI 49653, tel. 616/271–6460.*
Accommodations: *3 doubles share bath.*
Amenities: *Nordic ski trails, bicycling trails.*
Rates: *$60; Continental breakfast. MC, V.*
Restrictions: *No smoking, no pets.*

Linden Lea

A small and enchanting spot on the shore of a crystal-clear inland lake, Linden Lea is, as one of its owners describes it, reminiscent of scenes in the movie *On Golden Pond.* Country roads wind their way to the bed-and-breakfast, and, once you've found it, you won't want to leave.

In 1979, Jim and Vicky McDonnell bought a small summer cottage built around the turn of the century by three Civil War veterans. Vicky remembers, "The original cottage was a mess—rotting floors and everything—but I just kept looking at the view and saying, 'This is it. This is the place.'" Since then, Jim, a former teacher, has skillfully renovated the building and tacked on an addition; five years ago the couple opened their multilevel, contemporary home as a B&B.

The living room, complete with a marble and cherry-wood fireplace from the late 1800s, expansive picture windows, high ceilings, and a large, comfortable sectional sofa, is an inviting place to unwind and enjoy the view. With that in mind, the guest rooms have cushioned window seats that overlook the lake. The rooms, separate from the family quarters, also offer a measure of privacy.

The mix of antiques and treasures creates a warm, eclectic atmosphere. Jim began collecting unusual paperweights on a trip to Scotland, and now more than 30 of the colorful glass pieces

adorn a table near the stairway. The handmade dolls and the decorative plates scattered throughout the house are gifts Vicky's mother received while serving as an army nurse. A player piano dating from 1871 is a favorite of guests.

The McDonnells and their daughter, Audrey, are a congenial family. They've been known to offer baby-sitting services and to invite guests to join the family for dinner on cold winter nights when the prospect of curling up in front of the fireplace seems more appealing than braving the elements to find a restaurant.

The breakfast menu varies, and guests may be treated to such delights as quiches, freshly baked peach puffs, chocolate-chip banana muffins, and stuffed French toast. After breakfast, guests can take the rowboat to explore one of Long Lake's many islands.

Address: *279 S. Long Lake Rd., Traverse City, MI 49684, tel. 616/943–9182.*
Accommodations: *2 double rooms share bath.*
Amenities: *TV and VCR in living room; private sand beach, rowboat available.*
Rates: *$65–$75; full breakfast. No credit cards.*
Restrictions: *No smoking, no pets; 2-night minimum May–Oct.*

North Shore Inn

Originally part of an estate, this rambling, colonial-style home was built in 1946. Sue Hammersley, who has lived in the area for 22 years, bought the house in 1983, remodeled it, and turned it into her family home. Sue was a preschool teacher at the time, but a few years later, with her family's support, she left her job to convert the home on the shores of picturesque West Bay into a luxurious retreat.

The sit-down gourmet breakfast (Continental buffet if you miss the 9 AM meal) is an experience. Sue varies the menu according to the season, and the portions are generous. There is always a selection of muffins, coffee cake or cobblers, fresh fruit and juice, and a main dish such as pancakes, eggs, or a sausage casserole. Many of the herbs she uses in cooking and the fresh flowers found throughout the house are grown in Sue's English garden, whose colorful accent can be seen from the Wedgwood Suite.

The common room is filled floor to ceiling with books, games, and a collection of old movies for the VCR. A bay window stretches the full height of the room and looks out over the lawn and the beach. The musically inclined can tinkle on a grand piano and a Hammond organ. At the south end of the house, a screened-in porch is a marvelous place to enjoy the outdoors, even on an overcast or rainy day.

All the guest rooms are large; the popular Heritage Room, on the main floor, has a private entrance and a kitchen. Another favorite is the Country Rose Room, which has a pink marble fireplace and a private balcony overlooking the beach. Sue made the Whig Rose quilt that adorns the brass bed. All the guest rooms except the Bayshore Room, which is the smallest, have separate sitting rooms with sofa beds, so two couples may comfortably share a suite. The fireplace in each room has wood laid, ready to light when you arrive.

There is much to enjoy on the premises, but a bonus is the inn's location: only a few minutes' drive from either the restaurants and shopping in the quaint town of Northport or the rugged beauty of Northport State Park.

Address: *12271 N. Northport Point Rd., Northport, MI 49670, tel. 616/386–7111.*
Accommodations: *1 double room with bath, 2 suites, 1 housekeeping suite.*
Amenities: *Morning coffee and tea baskets left outside guest rooms.*
Rates: *$125; full breakfast, afternoon refreshments. MC, V.*
Restrictions: *No smoking, no pets; closed March and April.*

Birch Brook

A fieldstone walkway leads to this charming brick ranch, nestled in 2 acres of pastoral land with a brook running through it. Guests fall asleep to the soothing sounds of water just outside their windows. To relax, you may choose among three decks and patios, each with its own view of the woods.

The living room overlooks the back woods and is tastefully decorated with wing chairs, fresh flowers, art, and a collection of Hummel figurines. Books and old photos of logging days in the area adorn the rooms. The guest rooms, although small, are warmly furnished with patchwork quilts, a walnut washstand, rocking chairs, and candles. On summer mornings, the greenhouse is a cheery spot to enjoy breakfast.

Owners George and Lynn Anderson have been Northport residents for many years and are happy to give tips on the best restaurants, places to visit, and fine beaches. The house is within walking distance of Northport, so guests can peruse its shops and galleries and then return easily to the peaceful bed-and-breakfast.

Address: *310 W. 3rd St., Northport, MI 49670, tel. 616/386–5188.*
Accommodations: *1 double room with bath, 2 doubles share bath.*
Amenities: *Fireplace in living room.*
Rates: *$50–$65; Continental breakfast. No credit cards.*
Restrictions: *No smoking, no pets.*

Bowers Harbor Bed & Breakfast

T his 1870 farmhouse in the heart of the Old Mission Peninsula's cherry country is on 200 feet of private sandy beach on the West Bay. Owners Gary and Mary Ann Verbanic named each guest room in the two-story house after the view seen from its windows: The Harbor View Room looks down on Bowers Harbor; the Pine View Room overlooks 100-year-old white pines. Each is decorated in a classic country style, with brass beds, goose-down pillows, and comforters. The living room, which also has a view of the water, contains a large stone fireplace and is a peaceful place to enjoy quiet conversation or a good book.

The house has a wraparound fieldstone porch, a perfect spot to watch northern Michigan's dramatic sunsets or the

morning mist as it rises off the water. You might go for a swim at the beach, though the water can be on the chilly side. For a surer bet, play a game at the tennis courts or have a meal at one of the area's best restaurants, Bowers Harbor Inn, both within walking distance.

Address: *13972 Peninsula Dr., Traverse City, MI 49684, tel. 616/223–7869.*
Accommodations: *3 double rooms with baths.*
Amenities: *Off-street parking.*
Rates: *$85–$110; full breakfast. No credit cards.*
Restrictions: *No smoking, no pets; 2-night minimum on weekends July–Sept. 15.*

Brookside Inn

Owners Pam and Kirk Lorenz have created a private haven perfect for romantic getaways, and they even promote a couples-only policy to ensure quiet and privacy for their guests.

The guest rooms contain king-size waterbeds, TVs, wood-burning stoves, and whirlpool baths for two. Each also has a different theme: The Garden Room has colorful flowered wallpaper, and the New Orleans Room has wrought-iron window trim and flower boxes.

A full-service restaurant on the main floor of the contemporary, cedar-sided structure offers a large selection of unique dishes, including the popular "stone dinner." Delivered to the table on marble warmed by a square stone heated to 900°, this delicious dish consists of beef or veal, boneless chicken breast, shrimp, and three homemade sauces. A full breakfast is also served in the dining room. The Lorenzes cook all food from scratch, using herbs from their garden and wine from their cellar. Guests are invited to partake in some wine tasting, but alcoholic beverages are not included in the room rate.

Address: *115 N. Michigan Ave., Beulah, MI 49617, tel. 616/882–7271.*
Accommodations: *20 double rooms with baths.*
Amenities: *Saunas, steam baths, and tanning solariums in some rooms.*
Rates: *$185–$240, including full breakfast and dinner for two. AE, MC, V.*
Restrictions: *No pets.*

Chateau Chantal

Located atop 65 acres of rolling countryside, Chateau Chantal (named after the owners' daughter, Marie Chantal) easily boasts the most spectacular vista of any area B&B. The inn has views of both the east and west arms of Grand Traverse Bay, which surrounds this unique spit of land known as Old Mission Peninsula.

Owners Robert and Nadine Begin have created, as one guest described it, "the ambience of an exclusive European estate." Their primary business is the on-site winery, which was founded in 1983 and now produces 7,000 cases of wine and champagne annually, but the property's wine-related features coexist happily with the inn.

The two downstairs suites—done in French Country decor—have a private entrance off the main floor. Also downstairs are the public area of the winery and the great room, which has a fireplace, cushioned window seats, and a circular picture window in the ceiling. Stained-glass French doors lead to the bricked veranda overlooking the vineyard—a perfect spot to enjoy sunsets, wine tastings, or a quiet country moment.

Address: *15900 Rue de Vin, Traverse City, MI 49684, tel. and fax 616/223–4110.*
Accommodations: *1 double room with bath, 2 suites.*
Amenities: *TV, phone, individual heat and air controls in rooms, winery tours and wine tastings.*
Rates: *$85–$115; full breakfast. MC, V.*
Restrictions: *No smoking indoors, no pets, 2-night minimum June 15–Oct.*

Cherry Knoll Farm

Dorothy and Percy Cump recently remodeled this 1885 Victorian farmhouse on 115 acres of beautiful rolling farmland a few minutes from Traverse City. The interior is decorated in true country fashion; older furnishings are mixed with authentic antiques.

The family room, with a fireplace, is shared by guests and the Cump family, and the guest rooms are large enough to provide a comfortable upstairs escape if you need some privacy. The bedrooms may not be elegant, but they are comfortably furnished and include such special touches as a bedspread crocheted by Dorothy's grandmother and several patchwork quilts that are family heirlooms.

An old-fashioned porch runs across the front of the house and is a great place to watch the sun rise or to unwind at the end of the day. Guests are free to walk around the property and pick cherries from the orchard during the summer or look for morel mushrooms in the spring.

Address: *2856 Hammond Rd. E, Traverse City, MI 49684, tel. 616/947–9806 or 800/847–9806.*
Accommodations: *3 double rooms share 2 baths.*
Amenities: *Air-conditioning, restricted-diet breakfasts on request.*
Rates: *$60–$65; full breakfast. MC, V.*
Restrictions: *No smoking indoors, no pets, closed Nov.–Apr.*

Lee Point Inn

Nestled in the woods at the tip of Lee Point on the picturesque Leelanau Peninsula is the home that Fred and Patty Kilbourn built in 1979 and opened as a bed-and-breakfast three years ago. They manage to blend their family life (they have two school-age children) and their business quite well. Guest rooms, one of which has a king-size water bed (great for a bad back), are upstairs with the family bedrooms. To provide privacy, some areas of the house are designated for guests only, but Patty reports that many a visitor ends up curled up on the couch in the Kilbourns' family room off the kitchen, and that's fine with them. The living room, on the south side, has a woodstove and classic country decor.

The dining room leads out onto a multilevel deck, which runs across the back of this large, contemporary home and offers a wonderful view of West Bay. Steps lead down to the private beach, which guests are welcome to use. Cross-country trails start outside the front door, making the inn a great place for beach lovers and ski enthusiasts alike.

Address: *2885 S. Lee Point La. (Rte. 2, Box 374B), Suttons Bay, MI 49682, tel. 616/271–6770.*
Accommodations: *1 double room with bath, 2 doubles share bath.*
Amenities: *Ceiling fans in guest rooms; picnic table, canoe.*
Rates: *$85–$115; full breakfast. MC, V.*
Restrictions: *No smoking indoors, no pets.*

Leelanau Country Inn

John and Linda Sisson opened the Leelanau Country Inn in the spring of 1984, placing more of an emphasis on cuisine than on accommodations. The excellent restaurant features a varying menu, drawn from at least 20 appetizers and nearly 50 entrées, ranging from fresh seafood flown in from both coasts to homemade linguine. There's a Continental breakfast, but guests may want to pay a little extra for the elaborate daily brunch, voted "best in the region" by a local magazine.

The inn is across the street from Little Traverse Lake, in the heart of the Leelanau County countryside. The spacious, two-story clapboard house was built in 1891, and an addition was put on four years later. The guest rooms are small but nicely decorated in country style with fresh flowers, plants, quilts, and pine furniture. Request any of the four rooms that are a bit larger than the rest. This is not always the quietest bed-and-breakfast, since you can often hear the restaurant and bar well into the night, but memories of your meals may well make up for it.

Address: *149 E. Harbor Hwy., Maple City, MI 49664, tel. 616/228–5060.*
Accommodations: *6 double rooms share 2 baths.*
Amenities: *Off-street parking.*
Rates: *$45–$55; Continental breakfast. AE, MC, V.*
Restrictions: *Smoking in restaurant only, no pets.*

Neahtawanta Inn

In the early 1980s the Neahtawanta Inn started to establish itself as a center for peace research and now houses the nonprofit Neahtawanta Research and Education Center, focusing on "peace, community, sustainable use of resources, and personal-growth issues." Innkeepers Sally Van Vleck and Bob Russell maintain a healthy and quiet environment for the inn's guests. Sally leads a weekly yoga class, where guests are welcome.

The three-story inn was built around the turn of the century as a summer hotel called the Sunrise Inn. Antique beds and dressers from the hotel's early days are still used to furnish the guest rooms, and original washbasins with marble counters are found in two of the rooms. The common area on the first floor is open and airy but almost cluttered with books, newspapers, magazines, and tapes. The room's centerpiece is a sunken fieldstone fireplace.

The inn sits on a bluff overlooking Bowers Harbor on Old Mission Peninsula, about 12 miles north of Traverse City. Lush woods add to its natural, peaceful appeal.

Address: *1308 Neahtawanta Rd., Traverse City, MI 49684, tel. 616/223–7315.*
Accommodations: *4 double rooms share bath, 1 double suite.*
Amenities: *Sauna; private beach.*
Rates: *$55–$70, double suite $140; Continental breakfast. MC, V.*
Restrictions: *No smoking, inquire about pets.*

Old Mill Pond Inn

Michigander David Chrobak has spent his winters running a florist business in the Virgin Islands for more than 20 years, but in the summers he heads back north to live in and operate the Old Mill Pond Inn. Built in 1895, the three-story wooden house is tucked away in a beautiful setting and accented by gardens galore, all of them designed by David. The biggest is the side garden, which displays several larger-than-life statues. There is also a thriving rose garden.

A delightful eclectic collection of David's treasures makes up the interior decor. In one room you might find Marilyn Monroe memorabilia mingled with fine crystal; in another, South American tapestries hang next to original 20th-century masterpieces. Even the guest rooms have a relaxed personality all their own. Since David believes that most guests seldom use dressers, he has replaced them with comfortable chairs to give each room a cozy sitting area.

David, an excellent cook, serves a wide variety of food: vegetable quiche, eggs with herbs and mushrooms, crêpes, and fresh fruit.

Address: *202 W. 3rd St., Northport, MI 49670, tel. 616/386–7341.*
Accommodations: *5 double rooms share 2½ baths.*
Amenities: *Bicycles.*
Rates: *$70–$90; full breakfast. MC, V.*
Restrictions: *No pets; closed Nov.–May.*

The Victoriana 1898

Although the name dates this gracious Victorian home, innkeepers Flo and Bob Schermerhorn provide the intimate elegance. Before opening the B&B in 1987, they enjoyed, as Flo describes it, "people professions"—she was a teacher and he a hospital administrator. Their love of people carries through in their hospitality and lively conversations at breakfast—a big affair offering anything from Flo's Norwegian pastries to waffles with strawberry-rhubarb sauce.

The house, which sits in a historic neighborhood just two blocks from downtown and public beaches, displays its magnificent craftsmanship with two ceramic-tile fireplaces, an oak staircase, and original fretwork throughout. The parlor and library are furnished with an eclectic mix of antiques and family heirlooms, including a framed wreath made with pieces of hair from members of Flo's family. A functional 1912 Seybold Pipe Organ, salvaged from a Catholic Mission Church, sits in the library. An artesian well, drilled in 1898, is still flowing in the back of the house; the gazebo was originally the bell tower for the area's first high school.

Address: *622 Washington St., Traverse City, MI 49684, tel. 616/929–1009.*
Accommodations: *2 double rooms with baths, 1 suite.*
Amenities: *Air-conditioning, fireplace in parlor.*
Rates: *$60–$75; full breakfast, evening refreshments. MC, V.*
Restrictions: *Smoking on porch only, no pets.*

Little Traverse Bay Region

About five hours north of Detroit and seven hours from Chicago lies the small but lively area around Little Traverse Bay. The two-lane highway running through the region (U.S. 31) winds along the rugged Lake Michigan shoreline, providing constant glimpses of the water. The towns of Charlevoix, Petoskey, and Harbor Springs dominate the area, largely made up of rolling terrain, picturesque farms and orchards, numerous inland lakes, and sleepy summer-resort towns with names like Walloon Lake and Boyne City.

The region has had a varied history. Since the late 1800s, it has served as a lumbering mecca, as an escape from law and order for the likes of Al Capone, and as a playground for elite families from Chicago and Detroit. Ernest Hemingway spent most of his childhood summers at a family home on Walloon Lake and in the small town of Horton Bay, which provided the background for some of his early short stories, most notably the Nick Adams stories and "Up in Michigan."

Today the region has evolved into one of northern Michigan's finest resort areas. Visitors enjoy beaches, golf, and culture galore during the summer months, and crackling fireplaces, magical winter landscapes, and some of the Midwest's best Alpine and Nordic skiing in the winter. Nearby ski areas include Boyne Highlands, Schuss Mountain–Shanty Creek Resort, Nubs Nob, and Boyne Mountain. A variety of annual festivals and art fairs are held throughout the year as well.

From Memorial Day weekend through Labor Day, the area is crowded with tourists from all over the country and around the world. Art galleries and exclusive shops mix comfortably with the delights of small-town Americana: Petoskey's concerts in the park; Charlevoix's colorful Petunia Mile, a stretch of Main Street lined with flowers planted by residents each spring; and evening strolls in town parks and along beaches. Harbor Springs, often referred to as the "Newport of the Midwest," boasts a deep natural harbor and attracts a world-class boating community as well as a growing colony of artists.

Places to Go, Sights to See

The **Bay View Association,** founded by the Methodist Church in 1875, is a well-preserved summer community occupying 400 acres just north of Petoskey. Beautiful turn-of-the-century cottages are part of this historical landmark, where resort life is still enjoyed. Excellent cultural and musical programs abound during the summer months and are open to the public; a full schedule is available at the Petoskey Chamber of Commerce (tel. 616/347–4150).

Beaver Island, settled by descendants of Irish fishermen, is a rustic island with 400 year-round residents. Its claim to fame is that it was once a kingdom. Mormon leader King James Jesse Strang broke away from the church in the 1850s and took some 2,000 followers with him to the island. He was later assassinated by one of his own dissatisfied followers. For information on the two-hour ferry ride from Charlevoix, contact Beaver Island Boat Company (tel. 616/547–2311).

The **Earl Young Houses** were designed and built by a Charlevoix real-estate agent and self-taught architect. These eccentric homes, made of natural stone and cedar shakes, have an almost magical look. Their mushroom cap–shaped roofs, low ceilings, and tiny doorways belie conventional construction methods and make them look like houses for gnomes. Most are now privately owned, but you can obtain a map showing their location from the Chamber of Commerce (tel. 616/547–2101).

The **Gaslight District,** named after the gaslights that line the streets of Petoskey's renovated downtown, has more than 75 distinctive shops and art galleries, most of them open year-round.

Little Traverse Historical Museum (100 Depot Ct., Petoskey, tel. 616/347–2620) occupies the now-defunct 1892 Chicago and West Michigan Railroad depot. Converted into a delightful museum, it features 100-year-old handcrafted Ottawa quill boxes, a passenger-pigeon display, and information on Ernest Hemingway's ties to the region. It is open from May to November.

Petoskey Stones are pieces of fossilized coral from millions of years ago, now in the form of greenish gray stones. Their distinctive designs can be seen only when held underwater. You can buy these popular stones in stores or search for them along the beach, which can be the most satisfying way to obtain this souvenir unique to northern Michigan.

Thorn Swift Nature Preserve and Beach (Rte. 119, just north of Harbor Springs, tel. 616/526–6401) is 30 acres of beach, dunes, and fragrant cedar swamp offering hiking trails and panoramic views of Little Traverse Bay. Naturalist-rangers give guided tours from Memorial Day through October, but you can call ahead for permission to enter during the rest of the year.

Beaches

Visitors will discover many beautiful beaches along this stretch of Lake Michigan and Little Traverse Bay. Two state parks, **Petoskey State Park** (Rte. 119, 1½ mi. north of U.S. 31, tel. 616/347–2311) and **Fisherman Island State Park** (U.S. 31, outside Charlevoix), offer larger beaches and rugged shoreline. Smaller downtown beaches include **Michigan Avenue** and **Lake Michigan beaches** (off Grant St., Charlevoix); **Pennsylvania Park** (off U.S. 31, Petoskey), complete with an old-fashioned band shell used throughout the summer for free concerts; and **Zorn** and **Ford parks** (1 block east of Main St., Harbor Springs). These town beaches offer calmer water in protected bays and may provide picnic areas and playgrounds. A drive through neighboring Antrim County will reveal the small public beaches and boat launches of northern Michigan's pristine **Chain of Lakes** (including Torch Lake). It encompasses 163 miles of shoreline and includes a 65-mile inland waterway.

Restaurants

In the town of Ellsworth, about 10 miles southeast of Charlevoix, are two of Michigan's finest restaurants: the **Rowe Inn** (603 E. Jordan Rd., tel. 616/588–7351) and **Tapawingo** (9502 Lake St., tel. 616/588–7971). They are recognized nationally for their gourmet regional cuisine and use of such local delectables as whitefish and morel mushrooms. At the **Arboretum** (7075 S. Lakeside Dr., tel. 616/526–6291), in Petoskey, you can enjoy good steaks, chops, and seafood, and get your car washed at the same time. In Harbor Springs, **Juillerett's** (131 8th St., tel. 616/526–2821) is known for its whitefish dinners, and **Stafford's Pier** (102 Bay St., tel. 616/526–6201), overlooking the bay, offers elegant Continental cuisine. Charlevoix's **Great Lakes Whitefish Company** (411 Bridge St., tel. 616/547–4374) serves Michigan's most popular catch in classic fish-and-chips style, while **Willie's Up North** (1273 S. Advance Rd., tel. 616/536–2666), 2 miles north of East Jordan, may have the best barbecued ribs in the region.

Tourist Information

Boyne Country Convention and Visitor Bureau (Box 694, Petoskey, MI 49770, tel. 800/845–2828); **Charlevoix Area Chamber of Commerce** (408 Bridge St., Charlevoix, MI 49720, tel. 616/547–2101); **Michigan Travel Bureau** (333 S. Capitol, Lansing, MI 48933, tel. 800/543–2937); **Petoskey Regional Chamber of Commerce** (Main St., Petoskey, MI 49770, tel. 616/347–4150).

Belvedere Inn

After 22 years of marriage, Tim and Karen Wattersthey felt the time was right to act on what began as Karen's dream—to own an inn on the west shore of Michigan. Following a two-year search, they discovered this stately Victorian home, built in 1887 as a "cottage" in Charlevoix's elite summer colony; later it was operated as a hotel and a boarding house. The couple completely restored the house in three months—everything from porcelain faucets and dual showerheads to new tile, carpet, and Victorian furniture—before opening in March of 1994. They have more plans for the indoors as well as out, where they envision a multitiered flower garden and picnic area.

Their love of antiques is evident throughout the house. The upright grand piano in the parlor belonged to Tim's great-grandmother, and Karen's grandmother received the curved mahogany shelf, now holding brochures of area attractions and restaurant menus, as payment for cleaning rooms when she was 16 years old. A dining-room shelf sparkles with an eclectic collection of crystal and glassware that Karen purchased at auctions over the years. Tim laughingly explains, "I kept asking Karen why she was always buying this stuff, but now I realize that she had a plan."

Romantics will enjoy the king-size canopy bed in the Spring Room; it is completely surrounded by a white lace curtain from floor to ceiling. One guest delightedly recalled, "It was like waking up in a cloud." Bathrooms for guests in the Spring and Autumn Rooms are located off the hallway, but bathrobes have been thoughtfully provided. The Rose Room has twin beds and is located on the main floor. The noisiest room is probably the Winter Room; it faces the street and the Grey Gables Inn, a restaurant next door (where Belvedere Inn guests receive a special discount). The efficiency apartment boasts a private entrance and full kitchen, but it is the only area not decorated in the crisp, fresh style of the rest of the house.

Guests are served a complete breakfast that includes such specialties of Karen's as praline- or blueberry-stuffed French toast and sausage, or a strata of baked egg, ham, and cheese. An extra treat is the homemade dessert—which could be anything from cherry pie to strawberry shortcake to warm peanut-butter cookies—that is served each evening in the parlor or living room or, on warm nights, on the spacious front porch.

Address: *306 Belvedere Ave., Charlevoix, MI 49720, tel. 616/547–2251.*
Accommodations: *5 double rooms with baths, 1 suite, 1 efficiency.*
Amenities: *Ceiling fans in rooms, fireplace and cable TV in parlor.*
Rates: *$85–$115; full breakfast. MC, V.*
Restrictions: *Smoking on porch only, no pets.*

The Benson House

As a former Chamber of Commerce executive transplanted from downstate, Rod Benson knows how to make people comfortable; he and his charming wife, Carol, make an unbeatable team when it comes to hosting a bed-and-breakfast. The Bensons go out of their way to help you enjoy your stay by providing area restaurant menus, a travel planner, and chocolates in each guest room.

Set in a quiet, tree-filled neighborhood in Petoskey, the Benson House has an enviable location. As the locals tell it, when it opened in 1879 as the Ozark Hotel, people were aghast that anyone would put such an establishment so far from downtown. Nowadays, however, guests are only a few blocks' walk from the shopping and entertainment of the Gaslight District and minutes by car from first-class golf and skiing, but they still feel miles away.

The two-story wood-frame house has been thoroughly renovated to provide modern amenities while still retaining elements of its Victorian history: high ceilings, wood moldings, pocket doors, old gas fixtures, floral prints, hardwood floors, and area rugs. The spacious guest rooms have individual themes, from the cathedral ceiling, dark wood, and fruitwood four-poster bed of the Grand Master Suite to the white wicker and original wooden water closet in the bathroom of the Wicker Room.

Adjacent to the large living room is a game room, complete with an elegant parquet floor, entertainment center, backgammon and cribbage boards, puzzles, books, and a cozy couch, where the Bensons say they often discover guests relaxing with a short nap.

The most popular gathering spot is the 80-foot veranda, which wraps around two sides of the house and overlooks Little Traverse Bay. Furnished with white wicker and ablaze with colorful hanging plants, it is the perfect place to enjoy Carol's hearty breakfasts during the warmer months. Her menu varies and includes a shrimp quiche she calls Neptune's Delight, Irish Cream bread, and sticky-bun French toast. And, after a long day of shopping or recreating, you can return to the veranda, where the Bensons' afternoon hors d'oeuvres quell those hunger pangs and make you feel at home once again.

Address: *618 E. Lake St., Petoskey, MI 49770, tel. 616/347–1338.*
Accommodations: *4 double rooms with baths.*
Amenities: *Fireplace in living room, turn-down service with chocolates.*
Rates: *$78–$112; full breakfast. MC, V.*
Restrictions: *No smoking indoors, no pets; 2-night minimum on weekends, 3-night minimum on holidays.*

The House on the Hill

As part of their early retirement plan, lifelong Texans Buster and Julie Arnim considered opening an art gallery in the Southwest, but after a tour of New England bed-and-breakfasts, they decided to open their own. Selling their Houston suitcase business in 1984, the Arnims moved north to see the turn-of-the-century farmhouse they had purchased, sight unseen, after an eight-state hunt for the perfect rural setting. A real-estate ad stated it was "near a gourmet restaurant"; Julie was convinced their B&B would be a success if good food was near at hand. Indeed, two of northern Michigan's finest restaurants, Tapawingo and the Rowe Inn, are within two blocks.

After some hard work during the renovation process, the Arnims have made the House on the Hill a successful and elegant B&B. The carefully restored gray and white Victorian (including an addition used as their private quarters) sits on a hill near the little village of Ellsworth, overlooking 53 acres of countryside and the St. Clair Lake. Guests are free to hike or ski cross-country around the property and even borrow the boat docked at the lake. A spacious veranda wraps the house and is filled with white wicker furniture and rocking chairs.

Inside, a curved staircase leads to the guest rooms upstairs. They are all spacious, immaculate, and pleasantly decorated. Each has its own thermostat, fresh flowers, candy, ice water, and bedside lights. A favorite is the Pine Room, with its cathedral ceiling, custom-built four-poster bed draped in white lace, and peaceful view of the woods behind the house. Antiques and such touches as a 200-year-old hand-carved ebony Oriental desk, Julie's rose-colored glass collection, and Japanese-style porcelain could make you nervous about kicking back and really relaxing, but the Arnims make you feel at home with a perfect blend of friendliness and reserve.

Julie and Buster serve a marvelous hearty breakfast on their large oak table, complete with fine china and silver. A culinary whiz, Julie rotates 65 different breakfast menus; for early risers, she puts out a basket filled with home-baked muffins, juice, and coffee. The delicious breakfasts are the cornerstone of Julie's management theory: a B&B is a success when good food is near at hand.

Address: *Lake St. (Box 206), Ellsworth, MI 49729, tel. 616/588–6304.*
Accommodations: *5 double rooms with baths.*
Amenities: *Ceiling fans in rooms, cable TV in parlor.*
Rates: *$85–$135; full breakfast. MC, V.*
Restrictions: *Smoking on porch only, no pets.*

Kimberly Country Estate

The Greek Revival architecture and the gracious hospitality of the Kimberly Country Estate recall the genteel era of the Old South, but the interior is an elegant, gracious re-creation of an English country estate. Regardless of either impression, it's a treat to discover this 8,000-square-foot house in the heart of northern Michigan.

Owners Billie and Ronn Kimberly spent more than a year carefully remodeling this 30-year-old home in an effort to enhance its architecture while adding some modern conveniences. They put in new fireplaces, an updated kitchen, recessed lighting, and traditional mullion-style windows to take the place of the modern casements. In the living room, they replaced the sliding glass doors leading to the terrace with more graceful French doors. This attention to detail is evident throughout the house.

The Kimberlys moved from the Detroit area to Harbor Springs in the early 1980s, after owning a flower shop as well as restoring and decorating three homes together. Once in Harbor Springs, they first opened the shop Kimberly's Nest; the bed-and-breakfast followed in 1989. Throughout their 40-year marriage, they have been avid antiques collectors, acquiring such treasures as a Dutch pin armoire, a cast-iron chandelier, four-poster beds, and numerous chairs and accessories.

Floral chintz mixed with stripes and plaids creates a warm, romantic look, as do the fresh flowers, overstuffed sofas and chairs, Oriental rugs, and Battenburg lace spreads in the guest rooms. The B&B has become a very popular place for weddings; the entire house is often rented out on these occasions (or for the occasional executive retreat).

All the guest rooms are very spacious. The two largest rooms are the Lexington, with a fireplace, sitting area, and separate study, and the Verandah, which opens to a private terrace and has a fireplace and whirlpool bath. Guests are free to use the main-floor library, which, with its North Carolina black walnut paneling, fireplace, English-style armchairs, and paisley fabric–covered ceiling, has the feel of an old club—an old club founded on the grounds of a stately southern plantation.

Address: *2287 Bester Rd., Harbor Springs, MI 49740, tel. 616/526–7646.*
Accommodations: *5 double rooms with baths, 1 suite.*
Amenities: *Baby-grand piano in living room; swimming pool.*
Rates: *$135–$250; Continental breakfast, afternoon tea. MC, V.*
Restrictions: *No smoking, no pets; 2-night minimum weekends, 3-night minimum holidays.*

Stafford's Bay View Inn

It's hard to miss Stafford's Bay View Inn, set just off the main road running through Petoskey's historic Bay View district. A popular dining spot for both tourists and residents as well as a bustling inn, the imposing three-story Victorian was built in 1886; it served as lodging for summer visitors coming north via the now-defunct railroad to enjoy Bay View's cultural programs.

Owners Stafford and Janice Smith met and fell in love while working at the inn for the previous owner. They purchased it during the early 1960s and have now been joined in running the inn by their son and daughter-in-law, Reg and Lori, who are the day-to-day innkeepers. Over time, they have redecorated, and added onto the inn—including five new suites—while retaining its comfortable charm. Furnishings in the second- and third-floor guest rooms include canopy and four-poster beds, richly colored wallpapers, antique dressers, wicker furniture, and such details as handmade eyelet and ribbon pillows.

The third floor was renovated in 1987, and the Smiths, keeping in mind that the house should remain a place for young families to visit, added a third-floor sitting room so parents could enjoy stepping out without venturing too far away from sleeping children. Children can often be seen happily romping in the first-floor common areas while parents finish their meal at a leisurely pace.

What the Bay View Inn may sometimes lack in quiet, it makes up for in its delicious food and the unending hospitality of its hosts. Open and airy, the main dining room is decorated with chandeliers, draped tables with fan-backed chairs, fresh flowers and plants, and white lattice dividers between booths. Sometimes it may feel as though the restaurant crowd has taken over the inn, but a trip to the third floor or a stroll down to the water offers a good escape for overnight guests. The menus include such specialties as steaming bread pudding with raisins and cream. A splendid buffet awaits guests for Sunday brunch; selections may include ham, turkey, whitefish, chicken, biscuits, and scrumptious desserts. Although the inn does not serve alcoholic beverages, guests are invited to bring their own wine to dinner.

Address: *613 Woodland Ave., U.S. 31, Petoskey, MI 49770, tel. 616/347–2771.*
Accommodations: *24 double rooms with baths, 7 suites.*
Amenities: *Air-conditioning, gas fireplace and whirlpool bath in 5 suites, cable TV in sun room and library.*
Rates: *$88–$160; full breakfast. MC, V.*
Restriction: *No pets, no smoking in third-floor guest rooms.*

Bear River Valley

Russ and Sandra Barkman, avid bicyclists and cross-country skiers, moved north a few years ago and created a marvelous, year-round, rustic retreat. Sandra used to manage the VIP Guest House at the University of Michigan, and her experience contributes to the private, relaxed aura at Bear River Valley. Sitting on 2 acres of natural woodlands south of Petoskey, the contemporary cedar-sided home is nestled among birches, maples, and pines. Skiing and boating are just minutes away, and the country roads are perfect for cycling.

Porches and decks surround three sides of the home. The open living room has vaulted ceilings, lots of windows, and a fireplace, ideal for the Barkmans' cozy après-ski refreshments. Guest rooms are not large, but they are clean and comfortably decorated in a Scandinavian/country motif. A wood-fired Finnish sauna will relax you instantly.

Freshly squeezed juices and whole-grain cereals are standard breakfast fare, but Sandra's signature recipe is wild blackberry oatmeal muffins.

Address: *03636 Bear River Rd., Petoskey, MI 49770, tel. 616/348–2046.*
Accommodations: *3 double rooms share 2 baths.*
Amenities: *Terry-cloth robes, TV and VCR in common room.*
Rates: *$60–$75; Continental breakfast. No credit cards.*
Restrictions: *No smoking, no pets, 2-night minimum on weekends.*

The Bridge Street Inn

Although just a block from downtown on Charlevoix's busy main street, this three-story, 1895 Colonial revival house, with a tulip-lined walkway and a wraparound porch, has a cozy, calm air. John and Vera McKown moved from California three years ago to run the inn. John has been in the hotel business for 25 years.

Maple floors and artistic touches—a Renoir reproduction over the living-room fireplace and stained glass in the front window—lend an elegance to the inn. Guest rooms vary, however. Some look worn and in need of refurbishing, while others like the Bridal Suite and Garden View offer a pleasant Victorian getaway, complete with four-poster beds, lace curtains, washstands, floral carpets, and, in the case of Evening Glow, a beautiful view of the sunset.

Belgian waffles, homemade strawberry bread, and raspberries from his garden are a few of John's breakfast specialties.

Address: *113 Michigan Ave., Charlevoix, MI 49720, tel. 616/547–6606.*
Accommodations: *3 double rooms with baths, 6 doubles share 3 baths.*
Amenities: *Ceiling fans in some rooms, baby-grand piano in common area.*
Rates: *$90–$113; full breakfast, afternoon and evening refreshments. MC, V.*
Restrictions: *No smoking, no pets; 2-night minimum on weekends July–mid-Oct.*

The Gingerbread House

Sisters Mary Gruler and Margaret Perry have avoided making this pink-and-white, turn-of-the-century Victorian home too cute, despite what the name implies. Surrounded by hedge roses, morning glories, and a new English garden, the cottage is right in Bay View, enabling guests to take advantage of all its activities.

Inside are spacious rooms, like Country Blues, with a hand-painted iron bed and white wicker; Classic Rose, whose ruffled, rosebud-patterned window seat offers a view of Little Traverse Bay. The Victoria, decorated in the style of an English rose garden with floral fabrics and more wicker, has a sitting area, day bed, and French doors leading to a private balcony. The large dining and sitting area downstairs provides a welcome place for guests to gather, peruse its bookshelves, or enjoy their breakfast.

Mary and Margaret are delightful hostesses who share a marvelous sense of humor and a sincere interest in their guests' well-being, but who operate with a nice respect for privacy.

Address: *205 Bluff St. (Box 1273), Bay View, MI 49770, tel. 616/347–3538.*
Accommodations: *3 double rooms with baths, 1 housekeeping double with bath, 1 housekeeping suite.*
Amenities: *Private outside entrances to guest rooms.*
Rates: *$55–$100; Continental breakfast. MC, V.*
Restrictions: *No smoking, no pets; closed Nov.–Apr.*

Main Street Bed & Breakfast

Donna and Jerry Karson's restored, two-story, wood-frame home is indeed located on Harbor Springs's Main Street, but it is a far cry from the big city of Detroit, which they left four years ago.

The most popular gathering spot is an enclosed wraparound porch in a blue-and-white country motif: white-wicker flower baskets and blue-patterned cushions on wicker furniture. The Karsons' tasteful decorations are found throughout the home, including a blue-and-white Delft collection in the kitchen. Guest rooms are large, immaculate, and quiet.

Donna is a marvelous cook, who, with Jerry's friendly assistance, serves a delicious assortment of her own creations, including cinnamon-bread French toast, cornmeal pancakes, and lemon-poppyseed waffles. Breakfast can be enjoyed on cooler days in the dining room or, in summer, on the porch, with a view of Main Street and Little Traverse Bay.

Address: *403 E. Main St., Harbor Springs, MI 49740, tel. 616/526–7782.*
Accommodations: *4 double rooms with baths.*
Amenities: *Air-conditioning, TV in common room, complimentary wine on anniversaries and honeymoons.*
Rates: *$90–$100; full breakfast. MC, V.*
Restrictions: *No smoking, no pets; 2-night minimum on weekends May–Oct.*

Torch Lake Bed & Breakfast

Situated with a full view of—and only a short walk from—Torch Lake (once named one of the world's most beautiful lakes by *National Geographic*), this turn-of-the-century clapboard house has been lovingly restored by its owners, Patti and Jack Findlay.

An oak staircase, handcrafted by a local carpenter, leads to the second-floor guest rooms. The Violet Room has a private bath and overlooks the lake; crisp white linens of lace and eyelet on the brass-and-iron bed make it clean and fresh. Stained-glass windows and Australian-sheepskin rugs add to the room's distinct personality.

The parlor, which has lace curtains and bright prints, has a country feel; and the front porch, which of course has a

view of the lake, is outfitted with rocking chairs for friendly, Alden-style relaxation. Patti is an excellent cook; her breakfast specialties include sausage-filled crepes, raisin scones, French toast with pecan-praline syrup, and locally made fruit preserves.

Address: *10601 Coy St., Alden, MI 49612, tel. 616/331–6424.*
Accommodations: *1 double room with bath, 2 doubles share bath.*
Amenities: *Ceiling fans in guest rooms.*
Rates: *$65–$80; full breakfast. No credit cards.*
Restrictions: *No smoking indoors, no pets, closed mid-Sept.–Memorial Day weekend.*

Walloon Lake Inn

Some inns are recognized for their ambience or their hosts, and, while Walloon Lake Inn is up to snuff in both areas, it is the food that's truly remarkable here.

Innkeeper David Beier is an accomplished chef, and, even though a delicious Continental breakfast is included with a guest room, dinner is the most popular meal. Regional specialties include fillet of brook trout smoked on the premises; venison covered with a sauce of prosciutto, Madeira, and thyme; morel sauce over breast of chicken; strawberry-almond duck; and daily veal specials. That's not to mention the desserts, which include homemade ice cream and pastries. A special children's menu makes for perfect family dining.

The two-story, cottage-style home was built nearly 100 years ago, and the guest rooms were completely renovated in 1986. They are clean and comfortable, although at times noise from the restaurant can be disruptive. No worry, just head to the common area that overlooks Walloon Lake or down to the dock to dangle your feet in the water.

Address: *4178 West Rd. (Box 85), Walloon Lake Village, MI 49796, tel. 616/535–2999.*
Accommodations: *5 double rooms with baths.*
Amenities: *Beach and dock access on lake, restaurant.*
Rates: *$50–$70; Continental breakfast. MC, V.*
Restrictions: *No pets.*

Minnesota

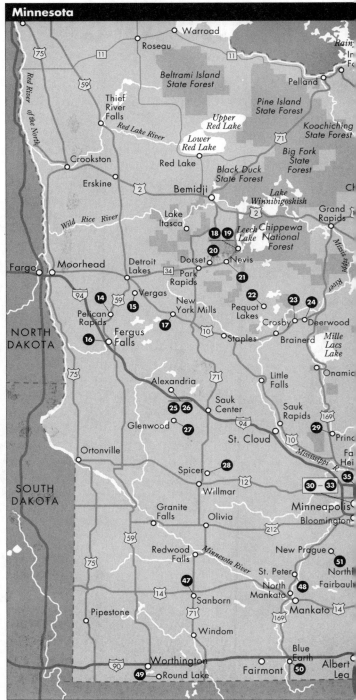

Minnesota

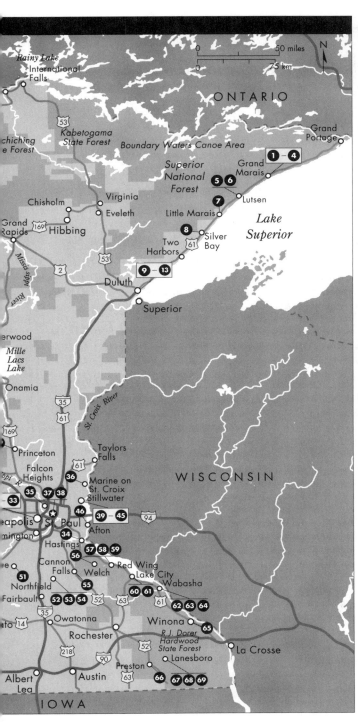

Park Row
Bed & Breakfast, **48**

Park Street Inn, **21**

Peace Cliff, **18**

Peters' Sunset
Beach, **27**

Pincushion Mountain
Bed & Breakfast, **3**

Prairie House on
Round Lake, **49**

Prairie View
Estate, **14**

Pratt-Taber Inn, **59**

Quill & Quilt, **55**

Red Gables Inn, **61**

Rivertown Inn, **44**

Robards House, **25**

Rose Bed &
Breakfast, **35**

St. James Hotel, **57**

Schumacher's New
Prague Hotel, **51**

Sod House on the
Prairie, **47**

Spicer Castle, **28**

Stone Hearth Inn
Bed & Breakfast, **7**

Stonehouse
Bed & Breakfast, **22**

Superior Overlook
B & B, **4**

Thorwood Historic
Inns, **34**

Tianna Farms, **19**

Victorian Bed &
Breakfast, **60**

Walden Woods, **24**

Whistle Stop Inn, **17**

William Sauntry
Mansion, **45**

Twin Cities Area

*Hollywood certainly knew what it was doing when it placed
Mary Tyler Moore's fictional television character, Mary
Richards, here. Like Mary, the twin cities of Minneapolis and
St. Paul can be cosmopolitan while still wearing sensible
shoes. A good example of this blend of style and practicality is
the area's clean and efficient mass-transit system, which
includes an extensive network of climate-controlled glass
skyways that allows citizens to spend an entire day downtown
without once setting their galoshes outdoors.*

*Minneapolis was formed in 1872 when the lumbering village
of St. Anthony, which sat on the east bank of the Mississippi,
joined hands with a hamlet on the west bank. Its name derives
from a Sioux word for water ("minne") and the Greek suffix
for city ("polis"). St. Paul, on the other hand, had an
uproarious past. The original settlement was called Pig's Eye,
a tribute to a French trader named Pierre "Pig's Eye"
Parrant, an evil-eyed villain who sold whiskey to the Native
Americans. Presumably as an act of repentance, the name
was changed in 1841 to honor a log chapel dedicated to St.
Paul.*

*Over time, railroad and steamboat traffic transformed St.
Paul into a booming transportation center. Meanwhile, flour
mills in Minneapolis grew into giant international
corporations, such as General Mills, Pillsbury, and Cargill.
As a result, hundreds of thousands of immigrants settled
hereabouts in the 19th and early 20th centuries.*

*Like a long-married couple, these geographical partners are
beginning to look more and more alike, although St. Paul is
still considered the more conservative of the two. It's typical of
the cities' differing styles that the flamboyant rock star
formerly known as Prince hails from Minneapolis. The entire
metro area, however, enjoys a rich and varied popular music
scene and has evolved into the cultural center of the Upper
Great Lakes. Besides many thriving music and dance groups,*

the Twin Cities have the Walker Art Center; the country's first and only full-time chamber orchestra, the St. Paul Chamber Orchestra; more than 90 theaters, including the Guthrie Theater; and a large gallery district in Minneapolis.

Both communities have masterfully blended the old with the new. State-of-the-art research facilities and glass-walled skyscrapers tastefully co-exist with turn-of-the-century neighborhoods and historic commercial districts. Summit Street in St. Paul, for instance, has a 5-mile stretch of Victorian homes that includes the house where F. Scott Fitzgerald wrote This Side of Paradise.

For a metropolitan area of some 2 million people, the cities remain delightfully small-town in character, due in no small part to the Minneapolis park system, thoughtfully designed by farsighted urban planners of an earlier era and unusual in its proximity to the city. You can stroll or bicycle along the river or a lake just blocks from the center of downtown. Minneapolis alone has 22 lakes and 153 parks, giving it a lush appearance in summer and a romantic Dr. Zhivago setting when the snow falls. And the winters here are not nearly as severe as legend and the popular St. Paul Winter Carnival might have you believe. The average daily temperature in February is 26 degrees, certainly comfortable enough to enjoy the cross-country skiing and ice-skating available right in the cities.

Although it's easy to get around the Twin Cities, it's also easy to get turned around. To the frustration of outsiders, the interlocking grid of highways and streets often appears to be as organized as a spilled bag of pretzels. Blame it on the mighty Mississippi, which not only divides the cities but also cuts through sections of each, including the center of St. Paul. The Big Muddy actually takes several turns, forcing streets to run on a diagonal and baffling tourists hoping to use the river as a north–south compass. Make sure you carry a good street map. Inconvenience aside, generations of locals, from Pig's Eye Parrant to Mary Richards, would undoubtedly attest that there is hardly a more pleasant place to get lost.

Places to Go, Sights to See

Mall of America (I–494 and Rte. 77, Bloomington, tel. 612/883–8800), dubbed the Mega Mall, is the nation's largest shopping and entertainment complex. Twenty minutes south of downtown Minneapolis, it features 416 stores, Knott's Camp Snoopy indoor amusement park, restaurants, and nightclubs.

Minneapolis's Parks and Lakes. Minneapolis has an extensive park system with bike and walking paths that meander past and along Minnehaha Creek, the Mississippi River, and six lakes (Cedar Lake, Lake of the Isles, Lake Calhoun, Lake Harriet, Lake Hiawatha, and Lake Nokomis). At Lake Harriet (W. Lake Harriet Pkwy., tel. 612/661–4800), be sure to catch a free summer concert at the bandshell, visit the rose garden, take a boat ride, or ride the old streetcar line between Lake Harriet and Lake Calhoun.

Minnesota State Capitol (Cedar and Aurora Sts., St. Paul, tel. 612/296–2881), built on a hill overlooking downtown, was designed by renowned St. Paul architect Cass Gilbert in 1905 and contains more than 25 varieties of marble, sandstone, limestone, and granite. Near the south entry are cases displaying Minnesota's two constitutions and artifacts from early statehood years. Take time to walk around the exceptionally beautiful grounds. Free 45-minute tours are given daily.

A half-hour south of the Twin Cities, the **Minnesota Zoo** (13000 Zoo Blvd., Apple Valley, tel. 612/431–9200) was built to resemble the natural habitat of the wild animals that reside there. The zoo contains some 1,700 animals and more than 2,000 plant varieties. Other features include a zoo lab, bird and animal shows, camel rides in summer, and daily film and slide shows. Among the amenities are eating facilities, picnic areas, rest areas, and stroller rentals.

Mississippi River Cruises (Padelford Packet Boat Co., tel. 612/227–1100). Daily sightseeing tours, Sunday brunch, and weekday and weekend dinner tours of the Mississippi from both St. Paul and Minneapolis are offered aboard the *Anson and Betsey Northrop, Josiah Snelling,* and *Jonathan Padelford,* modern stern-wheelers modeled after 19th-century Mississippi riverboats. Excursions last 1¾ hours and leave from Harriet Island, St. Paul, or Boom Island Park, Minneapolis.

Riverplace (43 Main St. SE, tel. 612/378–1969) and **St. Anthony Main** (125 Main St. SE, tel. 612/378–1226), neighbors on the historic east bank of the Mississippi, are complexes with horse-drawn carriage rides, stores, movies, and waterfront restaurants. There are river walkways and a bridge linking the area to Nicollet Island, which has outdoor concerts in its park. This area is especially popular in the summer months.

Summit Avenue, long one of St. Paul's most prestigious addresses, runs 4½ miles from the Cathedral of St. Paul, built in 1915, to the Mississippi, and is the nation's longest row of intact residential Victorian architecture. F. Scott Fitzgerald lived at number 599 in 1918 while writing *This Side of Paradise.* Mount Zion Temple, home of the oldest Jewish congregation in Minnesota (founded in 1856), is at number 1300. Number 240 is the James J. Hill House (tel. 612/297–2555), the 19th-century mansion home of the famous railroad baron; tours include a skylit art gallery with changing exhibits.

Walker Art Center (725 Vineland Pl., Minneapolis, tel. 612/375–7600) was founded in 1879 by Thomas Barlow Walker and was established at its current location in

1927. It has been described by *The New York Times* as "one of the best contemporary art exhibition facilities in the world." The permanent collections are strong on 20th-century American and European art, especially paintings, sculpture, prints, and photography from the past two decades. The center offers regular programs of dance, theater, music, and films. In autumn 1988, the Walker opened the Minneapolis Sculpture Garden, the largest urban sculpture garden in the nation. The garden has recently been expanded from 40 works to almost twice that many. The adjoining Guthrie Theater (tel. 612/347–1111), known for its balance of classics and more avant-garde productions, offers tours that include dressing rooms, prop rooms, backstage, and other areas. Reservations are not necessary; meet the tour guide at the ticket office in the lobby on Saturday mornings at 10.

Warehouse District (call the MC Gallery, tel. 612/339–1480, for dates and gallery guides). More than a dozen art galleries, cafés, eclectic shops, and avant-garde theater companies are clustered in Minneapolis's 3-block Warehouse District, just north of downtown.

Restaurants

Thanks to an influx of immigrants, restaurants in Minneapolis and St. Paul offer a diverse range of cuisines—including Thai, Vietnamese, and Sri Lankan—that belie the stereotype of bland Midwestern cooking.

In Minneapolis, the bohemian **Loring Cafe** (1624 Harmon Pl., tel. 612/332–1617), which overlooks Loring Park, is near the Guthrie Theater and Walker Art Center on the edge of downtown Minneapolis. It features pastas and fish with creative sauces, and salads; in the summer, you can relax and dine on an unusual alley patio accompanied by the sounds of a saxophone player. **The Nicollet Island Inn** (95 Merriam St., tel. 612/331–1800), with large windows that overlook the Mississippi River, specializes in regional cuisine that uses such local produce as walleyed pike and wild rice. The more elegant **Yvette** (65 Main St. SE, tel. 612/379–1111) is a French restaurant on the river at Riverplace.

If you're looking for elegant dining in St. Paul, try the **St. Paul Grill** (350 Market St., tel. 612/224–7455) in the newly restored St. Paul Hotel. For a more casual meal, check out **W. A. Frost & Co.** (374 Selby Ave., tel. 612/224–5715), a restored turn-of-the-century landmark. American-style food is served by the fireplaces or out on a large patio. The newer **Café Latté** (850 Grand Ave., tel. 612/224–5687) is a modern restaurant serving sandwiches, salads, and coffee cafeteria-style in the heart of the popular Grand Avenue shopping area.

Tourist Information

Greater Minneapolis Convention and Visitors Association (4000 Multifoods Tower, 33 6th St. S, Minneapolis, MN 55402, tel. 612/661–4700); **Minneapolis Park and Recreation Board** (100 Metro Square, 121 7th Pl. E, Minneapolis, MN 55101—2112, tel. 612/661–4800 or 612/661–4875); **Minnesota Office of Tourism** (400 4th St. S, Suite 200, Grain Exchange, St. Paul, MN 55415–1400, tel. 612/296–5029 or 800/657–3700); **St. Paul Convention and Visitors Bureau** (101 Norwest Center, 55 E. 5th St., St. Paul, MN 55101, tel. 612/297–6985).

The Ann Bean House

The Ann Bean House was an eight-unit apartment building when proprietors Victoria and Bruce Brillhart bought it. Converting it to a country inn was a challenge, but they had a lot to work with. Their 1880 Victorian Stick—style house is a graceful one, with many bay windows and towers and turrets of varying heights. The interior of the house is filled with woodwork that reflects Minnesota's lumbering past, including a beautiful carved oak banister and cherry, oak, and walnut parquet flooring in the vestibule. The abundance of large windows makes the house light and airy.

Two of the five bedrooms, the Guest Room and Ann and Albert's Room, measure a luxurious 20 feet square. The Guest Room has a brass sleigh bed, an enormous bay window, and a working fireplace with a carved oak mantel. Ann and Albert's Room has an east-facing bay window, as well as a new bath with a tempting whirlpool that fits into the shorter of the building's towers. Cynthia's Room has a 6-foot-diameter whirlpool and a fireplace embedded with turquoise-colored marble tiles.

Even more impressive, perhaps, is the whimsical pink Tower Room with a slanted ceiling and a white cast-iron bed. A few stairs up, you'll find a delightful white wicker table for two, perfect for morning coffee or wine in the evening. Up another flight of stairs at the top of the tower is the star attraction—a 7-foot-square aerie with windows on four sides, offering spectacular views of hilly Stillwater and the St. Croix River.

The house's charm is accentuated by the Brillharts' hospitality, especially Victoria's cooking. When you check in here, you're offered homemade herb bread, cheeses, and hot artichoke dip, with a glass of wine. Breakfast is a mélange of four or five of Victoria's fruit-and-yeast breads, fresh fruit, sausage rolls, and hot dishes such as eggs Florentine. After breakfast, your hosts can tell you about paddleboat trips, hot-air ballooning, and antiques hunting in the area.

Address: *319 W. Pine St., Stillwater, MN 55082, tel. 612/430–0355.*
Accommodations: *4 double rooms with baths.*
Amenities: *Fireplace in 2 rooms, whirlpool tubs in 3 rooms.*
Rates: *$95–$149; full breakfast, afternoon refreshments. AE, D, MC, V.*
Restrictions: *Smoking on porch only, no pets.*

Asa Parker House

On a rainy day, the Asa Parker House, in the tiny historic village of Marine on St. Croix, looks like something out of a British miniseries. Extensive grounds, elaborate flower gardens, a tennis court, and a gazebo make the setting of this Greek Revival B&B one of the finest in Minnesota. The house, built in 1856 by lumber-industry pioneer Asa Parker, was distinctive enough to tempt owner and innkeeper Marjorie Bush not to retire; she had previously owned two other Minnesota B&Bs.

The public and guest rooms are all airy, bright, and extremely floral. The parlors, painted pink, have white wicker, chintz, and lots of doilies and dried-flower wreaths.

If you can get past the frills, the guest rooms can be lovely. The rose and dusty green Isabella Parker Room, with white wicker furniture and a claw-foot tub, offers spectacular river valley views from its corner spot. The Alice O'Brien Suite, tucked under the eaves, has gabled windows, a large bath with a whirlpool tub, and a private deck with white Adirondack chairs and views of the flowering lawns. A screened porch downstairs overlooks Marjorie's attractive herb garden.

Marjorie uses Minnesota products to make her delicious and very caloric breakfasts, such as wild rice and bacon-and-egg casserole. She'll also pack picnic baskets for guests to take

to the screened gazebo or on a hike in William O'Brien State Park, just down the road. The park has miles of hiking, biking, and cross-country ski paths. There's also a marina a couple of blocks away where you can rent canoes. But the sweeping views of the St. Croix River are so beautiful—particularly once the leaves begin to fall—that guests may just want to relax on the lawn.

Address: *17500 St. Croix Trail N, Marine on St. Croix, MN 55047, tel. 612/433–5248.*
Accommodations: *3 double rooms with baths, 1 suite.*
Amenities: *Air-conditioning, down comforters, whirlpool bath in suite, stove in 1 bedroom; tennis court, screened gazebo.*
Rates: *$99–$135; full breakfast, afternoon refreshments. AE, D, MC, V.*
Restrictions: *No smoking, no pets; 2-night minimum on holiday weekends and on weekends when the leaves are changing color (usually October).*

Le Blanc House

Le Blanc House is an elegant piece of the 19th century tucked into a modest and modern Minneapolis neighborhood. The 1896 Queen Anne is a striking structure with a delicate lavender exterior. In summer, its banks of petunias and walls of morning glories and nasturtiums are famous in the neighborhood. Add sparkling stained-glass windows and inviting front and back porches—the latter with the traditional swing—and you could be back in the days when the original owner, William Le Blanc, returned home each evening from the grain mills of the Mississippi.

Current owners Barb Zahasky and Bob Schulstad, a retired salesman who now runs the inn full time, have kept the decor faithful to the inn's period, and named the three guest rooms after the daughters of its former owners. Both Zofie's and Amelia's rooms have great views of the city skyline. Zofie's Room, a corner room with a bay window and a private bath—perfect for weekday business travelers—is furnished with a 19th-century high-topped walnut bed and matching marble-top dresser. Marissa's Room, the smallest of the three, is invitingly cozy. It has an antique brass bed, oak furnishings, handmade quilts and linens, and an unusual porthole window. All rooms have colorfully patterned Victorian reproduction wallpaper.

You'll awaken to the aroma of Bob's homemade breakfasts wafting from the dining room. Dishes include "heavenly" Belgian waffles, spinach-pistachio quiche, French toast stuffed with jelly and cream cheese, and filled crêpes. Barb's sister owns a St. Paul bakery, and many mornings she brings over fresh muffins and pastries.

Le Blanc House is just blocks away from the many attractions of the Minneapolis riverfront, where you'll find the exclusive shops of St. Anthony Main and Riverplace, as well as Boom Island Park, which offers paddleboat cruises and a riverfront walk. The area is quite culturally diverse, so you'll also find a wide variety of restaurants—Japanese, French, Lebanese, and Polish—within walking distance.

Address: *302 University Ave. NE, Minneapolis, MN 55413, tel. 612/379–2570.*
Accommodations: *1 double room with bath, 2 doubles share bath.*
Amenities: *Air-conditioning, phone in rooms, TV available; off-street parking.*
Rates: *$75–$95; full breakfast. AE, MC, V.*
Restrictions: *Smoking on front porch only, no pets.*

The Rivertown Inn

John O'Brien, a wealthy Stillwater lumber baron, built what is now the Rivertown Inn in 1882. In 1987, Chuck and Judy Dougherty were searching for a change. They considered opening a restaurant, but after seeing the imposing Queen Anne Victorian, they found their calling: Although the mansion was designed as a stylish home for the O'Brien family, the Doughertys thought its wraparound porch and site on a hill near the St. Croix River would be perfect for a B&B. After major renovations—seven bathrooms were added—the Rivertown Inn opened for business.

The downstairs has kept a turn-of-the-century character, with four-wood parquet floors, stained-glass windows, and ball-and-stick wooded archways. There are many impressive antiques, as well as smaller knickknacks reminiscent of the Victorian flair for detail. The most notable of the larger furnishings, a matching dining-room table and buffet, came all the way from a castle in England. There is also an ornate Ben Franklin stove, which serves as the centerpiece of the parlor. In the summer, guests can relax in the gazebo or on a screened porch with a wicker swing.

The guest rooms are named after former residents. Julie's Room, done in blues, has a high walnut bed and dresser and, once the leaves have fallen, a lovely view of the river. Faith's Room, in peach and blue, has

an enormous black-walnut half-tester bed, a fireplace, and a double whirlpool bath. The rooms on the third floor are smaller, some under dormered eaves, but pleasantly cozy nonetheless. All of the floors have sitting areas with books, games, and plush reading couches.

Breakfast is either served downstairs, or brought up to the rooms, and consists of an assortment of homemade pastries, flans, an egg dish, and sometimes even champagne. The Doughertys now also run the Cover Park Manor across town, which offers more modern accommodations.

Address: *306 Olive St. W, Stillwater, MN 55082, tel. 612/430–2955 or 800/562–3632, fax 612/430–9292.*
Accommodations: *8 double rooms with baths (1 bath is nonadjoining).*
Amenities: *Ceiling fans, whirlpool baths in 4 rooms.*
Rates: *$69–$149; full breakfast, afternoon wine, hors d'oeuvres. AE, D, MC.*
Restrictions: *No smoking, no pets. Two-night minimum stay on fall and holiday weekends.*

The William Sauntry Mansion

The William Sauntry Mansion is a meticulous restoration of an enormous 1890 Queen Anne home. The work done in the parlor—which was re-created down to wall beading and corner ornaments—was so accurate that a former resident who came to visit remarked to owners Duane and Martha Hubbs on how well the wallpaper had held up. Some things are original: the parquet flooring laid in four woods and the parlor's oil-on-canvas ceiling, as well as light fixtures, fireplaces, and special stained-glass windows.

The Hubbses have restored houses in both Chicago and St. Louis. When they moved to Stillwater in 1988, they found the 25-room mansion converted to apartments and deteriorating. In 1991, after a two-year restoration in which the second floor was stripped down to the studs, they opened it as a bed-and-breakfast.

Aiming to remain true to the period not only in architecture and design, but in mood as well, the Hubbses provide such authentic touches as a five-course Victorian meal and piano playing in the parlor during the social hour. The bedrooms, which have large windows and fireplaces, are also done in a Victorian style, with Oriental and floral motifs and the rich-hued paints favored by 19th-century builders.

Beltram's Room, with its south-facing tower bay window overlooking the gardens, green-tiled fireplace, spoon-carved cherry bedroom set and private bath, is especially pleasant. For a Japanese ambience, try William's Room, which has crown dentil molding and is papered with in exotic pattern of gold, blue, and rust. Eunice's Room, in rose and blue, has an antique headboard, parquet floor, and a delicate oak fireplace ringed by the original rose-and-cream ceramic tiles. Its private bath, down the hall, has a galvanized tin tub dating from the 1860s.

Sauntry, an Irish immigrant turned lumber baron, had maverick ideas about home construction: He sent his architects as far as the Alhambra Palace in Spain to gather details. Behind his home he built a recreation facility complete with ballroom, bowling alley, and swimming pool, and connected it to the house with Minnesota's first skywalk. The skywalk is gone and the building is owned by another family, but Sauntry's spirit lives on in his enormous house.

Address: *626 N. 4th St., Stillwater, MN 55082, tel. 612/430–2653 or 800/828–2653.*
Accommodations: *6 double rooms with baths (2 nonadjoining).*
Amenities: *Bathrobes, fireplace, double whirlpool in 2 rooms.*
Rates: *$89–$149; full breakfast, early morning coffee, afternoon refreshments. AE, D, DC, MC, V.*
Restrictions: *No smoking, no pets, weekend stay requires dinner package on one evening ($29.95 per person).*

The Afton House Inn

This 1867 hotel, just a few miles south of I–94 in the old town of Afton, stands on the edge of the St. Croix River.

The hotel's guest rooms, all rather dark, have a reproduction country look, with print wallpaper, carpeting, pine furniture, bedspreads patterned to look like patchwork quilts, and lots of ducks. Rooms 44, 45, and 46, recently added on the first floor, are the nicest, with pine four-poster beds, whirlpool baths, gas fireplaces, tiny skylights over the beds, and sliding glass doors leading to small patios.

Hotel owners Gordy and Kathy Jarvis offer dinners and Sunday brunches in the Wheel Room, which is accented by wood carvings from local artists and has a view of the river. The bar, which serves more casual lunches and dinners, specializes in catfish caught just out the back door in the St. Croix.

Address: *3291 St. Croix Trail S (Box 326), St. Croix Trail, MN 55001, tel. 612/436–8883.*
Accommodations: *15 double rooms with baths, 1 guest cottage with 2 bedrooms.*
Amenities: *Air-conditioning, TV, phone in all bedrooms, gas fireplace in 8 rooms, double whirlpool bath in 10 rooms, private balcony in 4 rooms, restaurant, bar.*
Rates: *$60–$135; Continental breakfast. AE, D, MC, V.*
Restrictions: *No smoking in some bedrooms, no pets.*

Battle Hollow Bed and Breakfast

Battle Hollow, on a 2-acre hilltop with a St. Croix River view, was built in 1890 by Stillwater's founder for his daughter. Beth and Jeff Griffith, B&B devotees for 18 years, opened the Queen Anne–style house as an inn in 1991, following three years of remodeling.

Filled with elegant period furniture, the downstairs is stunning but not at all pretentious. Original pale pink stained- and leaded-glass windows and pocket doors, as well as an unusual Art Nouveau–style morning-glory frieze in the sitting room, are the attention getters. There's also a baby grand piano in the music parlor. Guests can relax on a wraparound front porch furnished in white wicker.

From the balcony off George's Room, decorated in teal and rose, guests can enjoy the St. Croix river valley views. Ella's Room, in mauve and pink, doesn't have the same view but does have a huge bay window, a gas fireplace, and a pale pink fainting couch.

Address: *903 N. 4th St., Stillwater, MN 55082, tel. 612/439–0449.*
Accommodations: *2 double rooms with baths.*
Amenities: *Imported herbal soap, fresh flowers, TV/VCR in library.*
Rates: *$95–$105; full breakfast, afternoon refreshments. No credit cards.*
Restrictions: *No smoking, no pets; primarily open weekends only in winter—please inquire.*

The Brunswick Inn

Owners Duane and Martha Hubbs had so many requests for fireplaces and whirlpool baths at the William Sauntry Mansion that they immediately had them installed in the three guest rooms of their latest venture, The Brunswick Inn. Located in busy downtown Stillwater, the Brunswick shouldn't be taken for a retreat from civilization—rather it's the perfect spot from which to explore Stillwater's many notable antiques shops and restaurants.

Inside the simple 1848 Greek Revival, everything is geared toward romance and relaxation. Amelia's room, the Brunswick's most popular accommodation, has a matching baroque mahogany bedframe and mantel from the 1880s. The Amish-style quilt, handcrafted by Martha, lends a tasteful

sense of balance to the room. The sunken bathroom sits under pleasantly wallpapered dormered eaves.

The elegant downstairs area, open to both the public and guests, consists of formal dining chambers where high tea and fixed-price, five-course Victorian dinners are served.

Address: *114 E. Chestnut St., Stillwater, MN 55082, tel. 612/430–2653.*
Accommodations: *3 double rooms with baths.*
Amenities: *Double whirlpools and fireplaces in rooms, phone and sherry decanter on upstairs landing.*
Rates: *$129–$139; full breakfast. AE, D, DC, MC, V. Weekend stays require dinner on one evening ($29.95 per person).*
Restrictions: *No smoking, no pets.*

Chatsworth B&B

This may be the only bed-and-breakfast in the world with a yoga studio in the basement: Owner Donna Gustafson is an enthusiast. She runs the B&B with her husband, Earl, in the turn-of-the-century Victorian home where they raised eight children.

The first floor has leaded-glass windows and glowing birch woodwork with an especially lovely birch buffet in the dining room, though the overall effect is somewhat marred by the emerald green shag carpeting.

Each of the five guest rooms has a theme. The Victorian Room has an antique carved-walnut dresser and bed, and large bay windows with table and chairs. The corner Scandinavian Room is done in soothing rose and

blues with pine furniture. The African-Asian Room—with African knick-knacks, beaded curtains, and modern black-and-peach whirlpool bath—strikes an unusual decorating note, but has the advantage of a private deck.

Address: *984 Ashland Ave., St. Paul, MN 55104, tel. 612/227–4288.*
Accommodations: *3 double rooms with baths, 2 doubles share bath.*
Amenities: *Air-conditioning in 1 room, whirlpool tub in 2 rooms, private deck in 1 room, guest phone in foyer; off-street parking.*
Rates: *$60–$115; generous Continental breakfast. No credit cards.*
Restrictions: *No smoking, no pets.*

Evelo's Bed & Breakfast

Opening their inn in 1979 made David and Sheryl Evelo the Twin Cities bed-and-breakfast pioneers. They picked a convenient location and managed to keep the prices reasonable. "We try to be the affordable alternative," says David.

Even with a front screened porch with white wicker furniture, their 1897 neo-classical Victorian house looks fairly modest. Inside, it's a different story: The first-floor parlor and dining/sun room are full of distinguished ball-and-stick woodwork, walnut and oak parquet floors, a cozy fireplace, and gorgeous Art Nouveau glassware and lamps.

The three third-floor guest rooms, accessible by a second stairway, are under the eaves in the former ser-vants' quarters. The cozy rooms have slanted ceilings and painted wood floors with rag rugs.

As testimony to the Evelo's comfortable atmosphere, many visitors are repeat or long-term guests.

Address: *2301 Bryant Ave. S, Minneapolis, MN 55405, tel. 612/374–9656.*
Accommodations: *3 double rooms share bath.*
Amenities: *Clock radio in rooms, refrigerator, coffeemaker, and phone on third floor landing, additional single bed in 2 rooms.*
Rates: *$50; Continental breakfast. AE, MC, V.*
Restrictions: *Smoking on porch only, no pets.*

The Garden Gate Bed and Breakfast

Charming hosts Miles and Mary Conway are happy to socialize with their guests, but if you prefer solitude, it's easy to find in this unusual duplex-style Victorian house built in 1906. The Conways live in one half, while in the other the guests share their own dining room, first-floor half bath, and living room with television. Mary is a massage therapist, however, so you may want to make an appointment, rather than making yourself scarce.

Lots of white woodwork, refinished oak and maple floors, and a wide, inviting front porch make the Garden Gate bright and comfortable. Upstairs, the vividly painted guest rooms are named after appropriate flowers: The Delphinium is a purplish blue, the Gladiola a rich yellow, and the Rose a deep pink. The Delphinium has floral bedspreads, twin beds, a table and chairs, and two large, south-facing windows. They've recently added a third-floor suite done in light peach tones, which lends itself to a contemplative mood.

On a quiet block just south of St. Paul's historic district and busiest shopping area, the inn is quite convenient.

Address: *925 Goodrich Ave., St. Paul, MN 55105, tel. 612/227–8430 or 800/967–2703.*
Accommodations: *3 double rooms and 1 suite share bath.*
Amenities: New York Times *delivered daily, fresh flowers.*
Rates: *$50–$85; Continental breakfast. No credit cards.*
Restrictions: *Smoking on porch only.*

The Heirloom Inn

Here, small is beautiful. Stillwater's Heirloom Inn, a simple
1860s Italianate house built by
Swedish craftsmen, has seen few alter-
ations in its century-plus lifespan.

Owners Sandy and Mark Brown have
made their inn reasonably priced and
quite comfortable for guests. Even
with its fireplace, oak parquet floors,
baby grand piano, and big bay window,
this is not a luxurious place to stay, but
it is a restful one.

The two upstairs guest rooms are light
and airy, especially Annie's Room (so
named because "Annie" was seen pen-
ciled on plaster uncovered during some
restoration work), a blue-and-white
corner room with pine floors, four windows, and lots of southwest sun.

Guests will appreciate the antique
quilts on display, the large perennial
garden, and the inn's proximity to both
downtown Stillwater and the bluff
overlooking the St. Croix River. The
three- or four-course breakfast is
served in the dining room or on the
screened porch.

Address: *1103 S. 3rd St., Stillwater,
MN 55082, tel. 612/430–2289.*
Accommodations: *2 double rooms
with baths.*
Amenities: *Air-conditioning, fresh
flowers, and candy.*
Rates: *$85; full breakfast, afternoon
refreshments. No credit cards.*
Restrictions: *Smoking on porch only,
no pets; closed Dec. 24–25.*

James A. Mulvey Residence Inn

When avid collectors of pottery Truett and Jill Lawson
entered the Mulvey Inn and
saw a magnificent Grueby tile fireplace
in the living room, they knew they had
to buy the beautiful little 1878 Italianate house. In 1905, owner and prosperous lumberman James A. Mulvey
bought the fireplace (one of only two in
Minnesota) from the Grueby Tile Co. of
Boston, and then added the dining
room's heavy oak beams and wainscoting, and the gold and green tulip-
design stained-glass windows
bordering the front door. Indicative of
the Italianate style, huge windows
make the house light, airy, and seem-
ingly larger than it is.

The Lawsons' pottery collection is
spread throughout the house, and each
guest room, named after a pottery

style, includes a book describing the
specific technique. The nicest guest
room is the Rookwood Room, in gold,
black, and maroon with Renaissance
Revival furniture, inlaid oak and walnut floors, cranberry glass lamps, and
huge corner windows.

Address: *622 W. Churchill St., Stillwater, MN 55082, tel. 612/430–8008.*
Accommodations: *5 double rooms
with baths.*
Amenities: *Air-conditioning, fireplace
in 3 rooms, whirlpool bath in 2 rooms;
mountain bikes.*
Rates: *$95–$139; full breakfast, afternoon refreshments, picnic lunches
available. MC, V.*
Restrictions: *No smoking, no pets.*

Nicollet Island Inn

This 1893 limestone building, on a small island in the middle of the Mississippi River, was formerly the Island Sash and Door Company. In the late-1980s, the building was gutted, leaving only maple floors and a few exposed-brick and limestone walls, and converted into the Nicollet Island Inn.

The first floor is occupied by a restaurant where you can dine on regional cuisine at tables overlooking the river. There's also a pleasant, sunny bar with equally good views, and a lounge with a fireplace.

Guest rooms, on the second and third floors, have Early American and country-style reproduction furniture. The rooms aren't large, but they are quite comfortable, and half have river views.

The best rooms are corner rooms 209 and 309, which overlook the river and the park, where free concerts are held on summer evenings.

Address: *95 Merriam St., Minneapolis, MN 55401, tel. 612/331–1800, fax 612/331–6528.*
Accommodations: *24 double rooms with baths.*
Amenities: *Cable TV, VCRs, phones, hair dryers, mineral water, cookies, newspapers; whirlpool tubs in 2 rooms; restaurant and bar, 3 meeting rooms, movies for rent; off-street parking.*
Rates: *$110–$145; breakfast extra. AE, D, DC, MC, V.*
Restrictions: *No smoking in some rooms, pets upon request only.*

1900 Dupont

This B&B in the prosperous, tree-lined Kenwood/Lowry Hill neighborhood is the best-located B&B in Minneapolis. It's just blocks from downtown, the Guthrie Theater, Walker Art Center, and Lake of the Isles.

Location is only the beginning of what this 5,000-square-foot 1896 Colonial Revival house has to offer. The unusual library—you enter through leaded-glass doors on the landing between the first and second floors—is a wonderful mahogany-lined retreat of leather sofas, built-in bookcases, and a huge fireplace. In contrast to the masculine library is a lovely small solarium with a glass table and chairs. Owner Chris Viken's background is in museum curation, so there are well-kept antiques throughout.

Three of the guest quarters are corner rooms with bay windows. Joseph's Room, the largest, shares a bath with Elliott's Room. Leslie's Room, the nicest of the three, has a bay window, a queen-size bed, sunny exposure, and a private blue-and-white tiled bath. Margeret's room, the newest addition, combines antiques with contemporary art.

Address: *1900 Dupont Ave. S, Minneapolis, MN 55403, tel. 612/374–1973.*
Accommodations: *2 double rooms with baths, 2 doubles share bath.*
Amenities: *Air-conditioning, TV in den.*
Rates: *$69–$89; generous Continental breakfast. No credit cards.*
Restrictions: *No smoking, no pets.*

The Rose Bed and Breakfast

he Rose Bed and Breakfast is a charming 1925 English Tudor brick house set on 1.6 acres. Owners Carol Kindschi and Larry Greenberg's tastes are quite eclectic: There's a built-in buffet in the dining room, Oriental rugs, leather furniture, lots of ethnic wall hangings, and some very modern purple barrel chairs. Even more unusual are the Welsh deacon's bench from the 19th century and the turn-of-the-century dental cabinet (complete with tools) in the living room.

Both suites overlook the University of Minnesota's golf course and the house's tennis court. The third-floor Rosepointe Suite has the best views of the grounds and the most privacy. Its large, carpeted bedroom has Scandinavian furniture, a sitting area has a wicker chaise longue, a new black and white bathroom centers around a large deep bathtub, and sliding glass doors lead to a private deck. The less private second-floor suite, with bedroom, bath, and a corner study, opens onto the same hallway as the master bedroom.

Address: *2129 Larpenteur Ave. W, Falcon Heights, MN 55113, tel. 612/642–9417 or 800/966–2728.*
Accommodations: *2 suites.*
Amenities: *Air-conditioning, phone, TV, VCR, clock radio in both suites, down comforter, fresh flowers, bedtime snacks, refrigerator in 3rd floor suite; tennis court.*
Rates: *$75–$85; full breakfast. No credit cards.*
Restrictions: *No smoking, no pets.*

Schumacher's New Prague Hotel

chumacher's New Prague Hotel was originally the Broz Hotel, established in 1898 and designed by Cass Gilbert, the architect who also designed the Minnesota State Capitol and the Library of Congress. Although the exterior, which is listed in the National Register of Historic Places, was restored in 1974, the interior was essentially gutted by owner John Schumacher, and remodeled into an immaculate Bavarian-style inn. Now managed by John and his wife, Kathleen, the hotel is well run and eclectic in decor. The guest rooms, each with a German feather bed, are a comfortable, elegant, and colorful mixture of modern amenities, European antiques, and handmade Bavarian-style furniture.

John, a former chef for the Marriott Hotel Corporation, has brought his culinary talent to the hotel's well-respected Central European Restaurant. Especially popular are the baked goods, such as the home-baked *kolaches* (sweet rolls).

Address: *212 W. Main St., New Prague, MN 56071, tel. 612/758–2133, fax 612/758–2400.*
Accommodations: *11 double rooms with baths.*
Amenities: *Air-conditioning, half-bottle of wine, chocolates, phones, sound systems, and whirlpool tubs; gas fireplace in 7 rooms; restaurant.*
Rates: *$105–$155; breakfast extra. AE, D, MC, V.*
Restrictions: *No pets.*

Mississippi River Valley and Bluff Country
Including Red Wing, Wabasha, and Lanesboro

The glaciers that steamrollered Minnesota eons ago somehow missed shearing off the high points in the southeastern part of the state. The result is a sawtooth collection of bluffs and valleys known as Bluff Country.

Bluff Country is farm country, but it's also heavily wooded with oaks and maples. Here you'll find soaring hills and plunging valleys marbled with gently flowing streams and top-notch bike and Nordic ski trails. Scattered about are drowsy little towns, some that bear few signs of modern times. One is the almost impossibly picturesque town of Lanesboro, nestled in the bluffs just east of the intersection of U.S. 16 and Route 52. This isolated community of 900 or so souls is so unspoiled that its entire downtown district has been placed on the National Register of Historic Places.

The Mississippi River is the headline act in this region, of course. There's no better way to view it than from U.S. 61 between Red Wing and Winona. This is a dramatic drive. The road unravels past towers of limestone that at times stretch 500 feet into the sky. According to legend, a despondent Native American maiden named We-No-Nah jumped to her death from these bluffs, giving Winona its name. Today, falcons and eagles can occasionally be spotted circling in the sky where We-No-Nah made her fatal plunge.

Once lumber and shipping centers, the river towns that populate the banks of the Mississippi now vacillate between maintaining their character and giving in totally to the tourist trade.

Popular as destinations for folks from Rochester and the Twin Cities, places like Wabasha, Frontenac, and Lake City are still

largely uncrowded and pleasant. Unlike in Red Wing, which
is particularly frenzied on autumn Saturdays, it's still
possible to quietly enjoy river scenes in these communities.

Places to Go, Sights to See

Cannon Valley Trail (306 W. Mill St., Cannon Falls, tel. 507/263–3954). Bike, hike, or ski along the 19.7-mile asphalt and crushed-limestone Cannon Valley Trail, which follows the Cannon River from Cannon Falls to Red Wing along the Cannon Valley Line's abandoned railbed. The trains ran from 1883 until 1976; bicyclists and skiers can be found there almost year-round now.

Frontenac State Park (Rte. 2, Box 134, Lake City, tel. 612/345–3401), 10 miles southeast of Red Wing along the Mississippi River's Lake Pepin, comprises more than 1,700 acres, including 13.4 miles of hiking trails, 6 miles of cross-country skiing trails, rustic and semimodern campsites, and picnic grounds. It's also a premier site for watching the migration of birds, including warblers, bald and golden eagles, and peregrine falcons.

Northfield, home to both St. Olaf and Carleton colleges, is just 45 minutes south of the Twin Cities. On September 7, 1876, eight members of the infamous James-Younger band of outlaws rode into this community with the intent of robbing the First National Bank. The gang, thwarted midway through their crime by alarmed townspeople, didn't get a dime. Only Frank and Jesse James escaped. Northfield holds a "Defeat of Jesse James Celebration," reenacting the seven-minute bank raid and shoot-out, on the weekend after Labor Day. The bank is now the Northfield Historical Society Museum (408 Division St., Northfield, tel. 507/645–9268).

Red Wing. A historic limestone-bluffed river port and former grain-milling and -shipping town, Red Wing is just an hour south of the Twin Cities. Partake of three self-guided walking tours of the town's historic districts by picking up maps at the Red Wing Heritage Preservation Commission (City Hall, 315 W. 4th St., Red Wing, tel. 612/388–6734). On your tour check out what's playing at the recently restored T. B. Sheldon Auditorium Theatre (3rd St. at East Ave., tel. 612/388–2806), which hosts everything from dramas to country-western concerts. Golfers will love the 27-hole course at the new world-class Mississippi National Golf Links (409 Golf Links Dr., tel. 612/388–1874). Observe pottery being made at the Red Wing Stoneware Company (U.S. 61, 4 mi west of Red Wing, tel. 612/388–4610). The newly established Goodhue County Museum (1166 Oak St., tel. 612/388–6024) remembers the area's history from its geological sculpting to its colonization to recent developments. Red Wing has many lovely and historic homes and buildings, and from May through October you can enjoy a narrated ride through these historic sections of town aboard Red Wing Trolley's "Spirit of Red Wing" (604 Bush St., tel. 612/388–3300).

Winona. The River City Carriage Company (601 Winona St., tel. 507/452–4221) offers horse-drawn carriage tours of this historic river town, as well as package rides that include a picnic, dinner, and lodging. History buffs will also enjoy the Juluis C. Wilkie Steamboat Center (in Levee Park on Main St. at the river, tel.

507/454–1254), a full-scale replica of an old-time steamboat. The first deck contains a museum of the river's history, steamboat artifacts, and a slide presentation prepared by Winona State University. The Polish Cultural Institute of Winona (102 Liberty St., tel. 507/454–3431) houses Kashubian artifacts, family heirlooms, religious articles, and folk art. Garvin Heights Park (straight south on Huff St. past U.S. 14 and U.S. 61) offers hiking trails, a scenic drive, and a 500-foot overlook, all with splendid views of the city, the Mississippi, and Wisconsin on the opposite shore.

Restaurants

In Lanesboro there are two pricey places and an alternative noted for its traditional home-cooked meals. The **Victorian House** (709 Parkway Ave. S, Lanesboro, tel. 507/467–3457), a French restaurant in a house setting, offers lamb Provençal and filet mignon. **Mrs. B's** (101 Parkway Ave., Lanesboro, tel. 507/467–2154) serves multiple-course meals table d'hôte style using such Minnesota products as wild rice and berries. The lower-priced **Chat and Chew Cafe** (701 Parkway Ave. S, Lanesboro, tel. 507/467–3444) stands out for home-baked rolls and homemade soups. The American-style dining is good at the St. James Hotel's **Port of Red Wing** (406 Main St., Red Wing, tel. 612/388–2846 or 800/252–1875). In Wabasha stop in at **The Anderson House** (333 W. Main St., Wabasha, tel. 612/565–4524 or 800/862–9702), where the country-style cooking is hearty and the breads and pastries home-baked. Many people staying in Wabasha, Lake City, and even Winona cross Lake Pepin to Pepin, Wisconsin, to have dinner at the justifiably famous **Harbor View Cafe** (1st and Main Sts., Pepin, tel. 715/442–3893), to savor its superb breads, creative cookery, and equally creative wine list.

Tourist Information

Minnesota Office of Tourism, Southern Regional Office (Box 286, Mankato, MN 56001, tel. 507/389–2683 or 800/657–3700); **Red Wing Area Chamber of Commerce** (Box 133–B, Red Wing, MN 55066, tel. 612/388–4719 or 800/762–9516); **Winona Convention and Visitors Bureau** (67 Main St., Winona, MN 55987, tel. 507/452–2272); **Northfield Area Chamber of Commerce** (Box 198, Northfield, MN 55057, tel. 507/645–5604 or 800/658–2548).

JailHouse Inn

Law abiding citizens of the past century hurried past this 1869 Italianate redbrick building, which served as the Fillmore County Jail for more than 100 years. After then sitting empty for 15 years, the jail and the adjacent sheriff's quarters and offices were turned into a 13-room inn, having been so extensively remodeled in 1985 that it is almost impossible to guess the structure's original use. Almost. One room provides an unforgettable reminder: The Cell Block Room still has its bars. Otherwise, it is much more comfortable than any inmate could have dreamed. Two queen-size beds with tufted bedspreads occupy separate cells and are fitted with rag rugs, a whirlpool bath big enough for two, a sitting area, and the original toilet and basin.

Rest assured that you won't feel the least bit incarcerated in the other bedrooms, all of which have beautiful pine or oak floors, and many of which are decorated with Eastlake furniture. The blue-and-rose Master Bedroom has a crocheted bedspread, large windows, and a huge old 1,000-pound china tub. The Oriental Room has a purple-and-black marble fireplace and a large, comfortable bathroom with a claw-foot tub. The pine-floored, maroon-and-rust Detention Room has access to the south-facing second-floor porch. The newest room, once the drunk tank, has the original over-sized sheriff's tub. Even some of the JailHouse's smaller rooms—such as the bright yellow and white Sun Room or the blue and white Amish Room—are just as light and clean as the larger rooms.

There are plenty of public spaces, including the front parlor, which has a pine floor, marble fireplace, and grandfather clock; the larger and brighter oak-floored kitchen; and the first- and second-floor porches. Breakfast is served in a sunny, spacious basement dining area.

Owners Jeanne and Marc Sather, former restaurant designers from San Francisco, are accomplished cooks and veteran hosts, happy to lend their premises and their talents to special events or even to impromptu trout dinners if you should find yourself lucky enough to catch one in the nearby Root River.

Address: *109 Houston 3 NW (Box 422), Preston, MN 55965, tel. 507/765–2181, fax 507/765–2558.*
Accommodations: *12 double rooms with baths, 1 2-bedroom suite.*
Amenities: *Air-conditioning, fireplace in 4 rooms, whirlpool bath in 3 rooms, ceiling fans in 8 rooms; breakfast room and parlor, meeting room, audio-visual equipment; near Root River trailhead.*
Rates: *$40–$140; Continental breakfast weekdays, full breakfast weekends, afternoon refreshments. D, MC, V.*
Restrictions: *No smoking, no pets.*

Mrs. B's Historic Lanesboro Inn

A cheery, four-story 1870 limestone structure on the Root River in downtown Lanesboro, this inn spent part of its 120-year history as a combination retail furniture company and funeral home. No vestige of its former use can be found today: Mrs. B's is bright, light, and bursting with the energy of the outdoorsy people who make up much of its clientele.

Lanesboro is a picturesque small town in the heart of the bluffs. The 35-mile asphalt recreation trail for hiking, biking, and cross-country skiing that follows the Root River runs right by Mrs. B's. You can rent bikes and canoes just down the street, or enjoy the view of the river from the two side decks or the backyard garden patio that faces it.

Inside, Mrs. B's is cozy if not historically significant. Before opening as an inn in 1984, it was essentially gutted—and rooms and baths added. The bathrooms are jarringly modern, but the guest rooms are much more creatively decorated, with most of the furniture (including sleigh and cupboard-style beds) locally made, some of it reflecting the Scandinavian heritage of the town's residents. The nicest rooms are the two back corner ones, which have river views. Also desirable are the three rooms with direct access to the inn's wooden side decks, furnished with large, comfortable, wooden rocking chairs.

The inn's only common area is a rather small but comfortable lobby, equipped with a piano, warmed by a fireplace, and brightened by huge arched windows facing the street. In summer, guests can use the two-story side porch and the riverfront patio.

"Our goal is to make guests comfortable," says owner Bill Sermeus and his wife, Mimi Abell, who bought the inn in early 1991. "We don't have antiques but we do have good beds, soft chairs, and good food."

Indeed, Mrs. B's is well known for its dinners, which are five-course table d'hôte affairs that take advantage of local products. Dinners are available by reservation only and include such specialties as wildflower salad, corn and wild-rice chowder, and wild-berry sorbet.

Address: *101 Parkway Ave. (Box 411), Lanesboro, MN 55949, tel. 507/467-2154.*
Accommodations: *10 double rooms with baths.*
Amenities: *Air-conditioning, gas fireplace in 2 rooms; restaurant.*
Rates: *$58–$68 weekdays, $85–$95 Fri.–Sat.; full breakfast, afternoon tea Fri.–Sat. No credit cards.*
Restrictions: *Smoking on porches only, no pets.*

Pratt-Taber Inn

I f you're still a little sleepy at breakfast and you see a woman in Victorian clothes serving the fruit salad, don't be alarmed. Owner Jane Molander likes to serve breakfast wearing antique hats and dresses from her large collection, all while telling stories the history of her B&B and its former owners.

Jane and her husband, Dick, are innkeepers of a white-trimmed brick Italianate Victorian house in Red Wing, a historic Mississippi River town. Jane, who was born and grew up in Red Wing, named the inn after banker A. W. Pratt, who built it for his family, and for Robert Taber, his son-in-law, who bought it in 1905.

The house, which is listed in the National Register of Historic Places, was restored in 1984. Old photographs guided much of the exterior work, including the replacement of the porches; one of them is embellished with an detailed star pattern that honors the United States' Centennial in 1876, the year the inn was built. Inside there are parquet floors, butternut and walnut woodwork, glass chandeliers, feather-painted slate fireplaces, and in the dining room, a large bay window. Throughout the house you'll find antique furniture that dates from 1860 to 1880, including a 112-year-old Murphy bed housed in a Victorian buffet and a stereopticon with a rare and complete *Tour the World* collection.

Three of the four upstairs rooms are corner rooms, and all are large and full of antiques. Polly's Room is particularly nice, with its queen-size brass bed, soft blue-and-ecru decor, and black marble fireplace. Jane proudly tells guests that radio personality and author Garrison Keillor stayed in antique-filled Mary Lu's Room, which has views of Barns Bluff, while he was in Red Wing to perform at the T. B. Sheldon Theatre.

Breakfast is served in the dining room, on the porches, or in the guest bedrooms, all of which contain tables for two. Jane usually uses her collection of original 1932 Orleans patterned Red Wing pottery.

Being a native and a bit of a town booster, she's also glad to provide guests with information on local activities, especially the summer trolley tours that stop right at the inn's front door.

Address: *706 W. 4th St., Red Wing, MN 55066, tel. 612/388–5945.*
Accommodations: *2 double rooms with baths, 4 doubles share 2 baths; the 2 downstairs rooms, library, and bath can be rented as a suite.*
Amenities: *Air-conditioning, clock radio in rooms, fireplace in 1 room; pickup service at airport, dock, or train station; bicycles.*
Rates: *$69–$110; full breakfast, afternoon refreshments. MC, V.*
Restrictions: *No smoking in bedrooms.*

Thorwood Historic Inns

If you want a luxurious bed-and-breakfast visit, as so many of the repeat guests do, the Thorwood Historic Inns—the 1880 Queen Anne Rosewood and the 1880 Second Empire–style Thorwood—are for you.

Pam and Dick Thorsen, a down-to-earth and friendly couple, fell in love with the river town of Hastings, 20 miles south of St. Paul, and opened Thorwood in 1983. The 6,600-square-foot house was built by a local lumber baron, William Thompson, and his wife, Sara, as their family home. Then, in 1989, the Thorsens opened the 10,000-square-foot Rosewood, six blocks away.

Interestingly, both inns were hospitals at one time, and occasionally people who were born in the buildings come back as guests to celebrate their birthdays.

Thorwood and Rosewood are not cozy, family-style bed-and-breakfasts. Thorwood has retained more of its original rooms and fixtures, and because the Thorsens live there, is the homier of the two inns. It has a bay window and a fireplace in its main parlor, an interesting square bay in the front parlor, and maple floors throughout.

Rosewood has a grand piano, a large fireplace, large ornate public rooms, and several bay windows big enough to park a Volkswagen in. Dark green wallpaper and carpet, and white and oak woodwork, along with the build-

ing's great size, make Rosewood almost overwhelmingly formal.

Remodeling has given fireplaces and whirlpool baths to both inns' guest rooms. The largest and most ornate is a 1,200-foot suite called Mississippi Under the Stars, which has a baby grand piano, a fireplace, a double whirlpool tub under a skylight, a round shower, a copper soaking tub, and a queen-size bed.

Thorwood's most elaborate rooms are Sara's Suite, a purple and white three-level arrangement with a skylight over the bed, a double whirlpool tub, and the best view; and the Steeple Room, with a built-in whirlpool bath set right into the steeple and a glass-domed fireplace dividing the bath area from the bedroom. Any of the other third floor rooms at either inn are also bound to both intrigue and spoil even the hardest-to-please of people.

The Thorsens have taken to offering breakfast either in the public rooms or in baskets at your door.

Address: *315 Pine St., Hastings, MN 55033, tel. 612/437–3297.*
Accommodations: *12 double rooms with baths, 3 suites.*
Amenities: *Air-conditioning, fireplace in 9 rooms, whirlpool bath in 11 rooms, gift shop.*
Rates: *$75–$195; full breakfast, afternoon refreshments, dinners available. AE, D, MC, V.*
Restrictions: *No smoking, no pets.*

The Victorian Bed & Breakfast

Wonderful views of Lake Pepin from each guest room make Lake City's Victorian Bed & Breakfast special. The lake, which many people claim is the most beautiful spot on the Mississippi, also dominates the perspective from the large windows in the downstairs public rooms.

Owners Sandy and Joel Grettenberg are teachers in Rochester, Minnesota, some 35 miles to the west of Lake City. They came to town one fall Saturday to buy apples and ended up buying the inn.

The building, although an 1896 Stick-style Victorian, has a refreshing simplicity inside. Butternut wood on the staircase banisters and elsewhere is carved, but not elaborately so; small and simple stained-glass windows, in rose, amber, and blue, are set atop larger plain-glass windows.

Decorated in antiques, modern sofas, and German and Japanese furniture acquired by Sandy's military family, the Victorian B&B is eclectic and comfortable, but not overstuffed. The most interesting items are the 19th-century German music boxes, one of which plays a variety of tunes including, strangely enough, "The Marseillaise."

Juliette's Room (named after the wife of Thomas Morrow, the local bank director for whom the house was built) is the best one, with sweeping lake views from the huge bay window and a private bath with wide-plank pine floor and rare antique pillbox toilet.

Teresa's and Kari's rooms (named after the Grettenbergs' grown daughters) share a full bath downstairs, but each has its own private half-bath. Teresa's Room is a large corner room at the front of the house with wonderful lake views, a sitting area with white wicker furniture, and a king-size bed that can be divided into two twin beds.

An elaborate Continental breakfast of fresh fruit compote and home-baked breads and muffins is served either in the sunny dining room, which also overlooks the lake, or in guest rooms.

Address: *620 S. High St., Lake City, MN 55041, tel. 612/345-2167.*
Accommodations: *1 double room with bath, 2 doubles with half-baths share downstairs bath.*
Amenities: *Air-conditioning, TV in sitting room.*
Rates: *$60–$75; Continental breakfast, afternoon refreshments. No credit cards.*
Restrictions: *Smoking on porch only, no pets; closed Christmas and Thanksgiving.*

The Anderson House

Minnesota's oldest operating hotel, The Anderson House was built in 1856, two years before Minnesota became a state, and was purchased in the early 1900s by the Anderson family. Except for 12 years in the 1960s and '70s, it's been run by Andersons and their heirs ever since.

Owner John Hall, who has been remodeling the hotel in stages since 1976, has taken care to leave some of the things that give character to an old lodging. Thus, although the baths are modern, the floors slant, the halls are crooked, and the doors occasionally stick.

Guest rooms are furnished with a mixture of antiques, reproductions, and new pieces.

The Anderson House is justly famous for two things: the 15 resident cats that guests can "check out" for the night (complete with food and litter box), and the Pennsylvania Dutch–style food served in its first-floor restaurant, where all baking is done from scratch.

Address: *333 W. Main St., Wabasha, MN 55981, tel. 612/565–4524, fax 612/565—4003.*
Accommodations: *12 double rooms with baths, 7 doubles share 2 baths, 6 suites.*
Amenities: *Air-conditioning, whirlpool bath in 3 suites, 17 rooms have river views, banquet/conference room, restaurant, bar.*
Rates: *$45–$115; breakfast extra. D, MC, V.*
Restrictions: *Closed Mon.–Thurs. Nov. 2–Mar. 31.*

The Archer House

Owner Dallas Haas and his wife are constantly adding to or renovating the 1877 Second Empire–style hotel and the block of adjacent buildings he bought in 1981. The Haases have figured out what appeals to the historic hotel aficionado and, with the constant college trade in Northfield, they have a busy establishment on their hands.

The hallways and guest rooms, heavy on dried flowers, crocheted bedspreads, and wallpaper, are mostly small and dark, for this was originally a modest tradesman's hotel. Hence, the smaller rooms seem right but the larger ones with whirlpool baths seem a bit out of place.

The lobby is cluttered with bric-a-brac, but there's a nice restaurant on the riverfront level that's especially cozy on a winter's day. In summer, have dinner outdoors on a patio overlooking the river.

Address: *212 Division St., Northfield, MN 55057, tel. 507/645–5661, fax 507/645–4295.*
Accommodations: *17 double rooms with baths, 19 suites with whirlpool baths.*
Amenities: *Air-conditioning, TV, phone in rooms; complimentary champagne for rooms with whirlpool baths; ice and soft-drink machines, restaurants, shops, 3 conference rooms.*
Rates: *$45–$150; breakfast extra. AE, D, MC, V.*
Restrictions: *Pets upon approval.*

Bridgewaters Bed and Breakfast

Bill and Carole Moore's B&B, situated just a block from tiny Wabasha's main street and the Mississippi River, is an ideal spot for those seeking a country-style inn in town. A wraparound porch outlines two sides of the blue and white home, and rest of the house is hardly less sunny. Four picture windows, accented with stained glass, light the common area's sitting room, the formal and casual living rooms—neatly furnished with plenty of couches and chairs and such interesting items as a 1920s icebox turned liquor cabinet—and the dining room, which has oak paneling, a built-in buffet, and large oak table.

The five guest rooms, named after bridges on the Mississippi, are all on the second level. The largest is the Wabasha Bridge Room, which has floors of original yellow pine, a hand-carved walnut bed, walnut bureau with marble top, and antique washpan and sink. Three other rooms share two baths, but are all sunny and tastefully furnished with unique antique dressers and down-filled quilts. The final room, not quite completed at press time, will include a two-sided gas fireplace, dormer ceilings, and a double whirlpool bath tucked under a west window.

Address: *136 Bridge Ave., Wabasha, MN 55981, tel. 612/565–4208.*
Accommodations: *2 double rooms with baths, 3 doubles share 2 baths.*
Amenities: *Air-conditioning, stereo with CD player in common area.*
Rates: *$60–$90; full breakfast. MC, V.*
Restrictions: *Smoking on porches only, no pets.*

The Candle Light Inn

This 1877 Victorian was built by Horace Rich, who once managed the Red Wing Stoneware Company. Purchased recently by Mary Jaeb (a former caterer) and her husband, Bud, the home retains its original grandeur.

Much of the woodwork, including the grand staircase, is of walnut, although oak, cherry, and butternut accent the cabinetry, parquet floors, and trim. There are five fireplaces, including a feather-painted one in the parlor and another in the cherry cabinet–lined library. Unusual rose, blue, and orange beveled stained-glass windows mark the entryway, and over 30 Quesale globes, the first lights installed with the advent of electricity, are still found throughout the house. Given all this, it's not surprising that the inn is listed on the Minnesota Register of Historical Places.

The Butternut Suite, a spacious room with a gas fireplace, period sofa, and double whirlpool bath, is the best of the four second-level rooms. The Rose Garden Room, done in green, rose, and white, is also especially charming with its sunny corner location, white woodwork, fireplace, whirlpool bath, and large bay window.

Address: *818 W. 3rd St., Red Wing, MN 55066, tel. 612/388–8034.*
Accommodations: *3 double rooms with baths, 1 suite.*
Amenities: *Air-conditioning, fireplace in 2 rooms, whirlpool bath in 3 rooms.*
Rates: *$75–$135; full breakfast, afternoon refreshments. MC, V.*
Restrictions: *No smoking, no pets.*

Carriage House Bed & Breakfast

This 1870 carriage house is the largest remaining in a river city that once had many such buildings. The three-story structure, white with green shutters, lies behind a matching Italianate house, the home of bed-and-breakfast proprietors Deb and Don Salyards. Both houses are directly across the street from the Winona State University campus, where Don works as an economics professor.

All four guest rooms are on the second floor of the carriage house. Two are expanded versions of the former stable boys' quarters, which retain their original windows and woodwork; the other two are somewhat larger with high ceilings and windows. The best guest room is the Village Loft, which has a small table and chairs and a large bathroom with a skylight over the miniature claw-foot tub.

Guests can have tea and coffee on the first floor in a sunny, four-season porch. Breakfast is delivered to the porch at a time arranged by guests. Deb can direct guests to bike trails, golf courses, and other local activities.

Address: *420 Main St., Winona, MN 55987, tel. 507/452–8256.*
Accommodations: *4 double rooms with baths.*
Amenities: *Air-conditioning; bicycles, shuttle service from boat docks or train station.*
Rates: *$70–$90; Continental breakfast. MC, V.*
Restrictions: *No smoking, no pets.*

Carrolton Country Inn

Half the fun of staying at this 100-year-old farmhouse is getting to it. From Lanesboro follow an old oxcart trail for 3 miles, crossing the Root River and the historic Scanlon-Ford Bridge, as the trail winds along a narrow valley. At the end, you'll reach the Carrolton Country Inn, a nine-room farmhouse built by a Norwegian immigrant family in 1880. Owners Gloria and Charles Ruen opened it as a bed-and-breakfast in 1987 when they moved to a nearby farm (guests pick up the keys there).

The charm of the modest and rather inexpensively decorated house lies in its bucolic setting on 389 cow-dotted acres. In keeping with the rustic mood, guests prepare their own breakfast each morning, helping themselves to the things in the well-stocked refrigerator.

The guest rooms are on the dark side, with a mix of antiques and modern furniture. The best one by far is the Carrolton Room, a large corner room facing north and east with a small private balcony and views of the beautiful farm and dramatic bluffs beyond.

Address: *RR 2 (Box 139), Lanesboro, MN 55949, tel. 507/467–2257.*
Accommodations: *2 double rooms with baths, 2 doubles share bath.*
Amenities: *Air-conditioning, clock radios, piano, TV in parlor, phones in 2 rooms; picnic table.*
Rates: *$60–$90; full breakfast. MC, V.*
Restrictions: *No smoking, no pets.*

Cottonwood Inn

The Cottonwood Inn was moved when the new interstate bridge over the Mississippi River was built. A handsome 1872 Italianate house, built as the Congregational church's parsonage, the inn is across U.S. 61 from Wabasha and the river and set among the bluffs that line the Mississippi here.

The decor is French provincial, and the original oak and maple floors and walnut-and-mahogany banister remain as fine as ever. The best bedrooms are the three upstairs, which are light, with views of the surrounding bluffs and countryside. The Paisley Room, which has a private bath with a claw-foot tub, is especially nice. The other two, which share a bath, also have their own half-baths; the Rose Room, decorated, of course, in pinks and reds, has a partic-

ularly beautiful view. The two downstairs rooms are comparatively darker, but the adjoining family room is a warm spot to relax after a day of skiing at the Coffee Mill Chalet just down the road. Alice Bach-Johnson, who bought the inn in 1991, serves a full breakfast in the dining room or in the three-season garden room, which has plenty of light and country air.

Address: *100 Coulee Way, Wabasha, MN 55981, tel. and fax 612/565–2466.*
Accommodations: *3 double rooms with baths, 2 doubles share bath.*
Amenities: *Air-conditioning in 1 room, VCR/TV in library and family room, fireplace in back parlor.*
Rates: *$50–$80; full breakfast, picnic lunches available upon request. No credit cards.*
Restrictions: *No smoking, no pets.*

Dr. Joseph Moses House

This 1929 Cape Cod house is the first, and as yet the only, bed-and-breakfast in busy, charming Northfield, the home of two well-respected liberal-arts colleges, St. Olaf and Carleton. On a pleasant, tree-lined street four blocks from downtown, the Moses House is a cozy, quiet alternative to the much larger Archer House Hotel or the city's several motels.

Although it's not an ornate house, owners Ron Halversen and Kathleen Murphy have made it quite a pleasant one; they've often served as hosts to parents of students and will even rent out the entire house at a discount for graduations, weddings, recitals, and other events.

Maple floors, slanted ceilings, gabled windows, and distinctive 1930s tiled

bathrooms make the upstairs far more charming than the carpeted, rather sparsely furnished first floor.

Address: *1100 S. Division St., Northfield, MN 55057, tel. 507/663–1563.*
Accommodations: *3 double rooms and 1 single share 2 baths.*
Amenities: *Air-conditioning, clock radios, fireplace in 1 room, cedar-lined closets; cable TV, stereo, and VCR on 4-season porch.*
Rates: *$45–$89; full breakfast. MC, V.*
Restrictions: *No smoking, no pets.*

Historic Scanlan House

All of downtown Lanesboro is on the National Register of Historic Places. At the quiet end of the main street, the Scanlan House is an architectural gem, with its whimsically painted 1889 Queen Anne exterior and balconied, onion-dome turret. It's also just a few blocks from the Root River and the popular 35-mile-long bike-ski trail.

The public areas and bedrooms of the Scanlan House are true to the tradition of Victorian clutter. The rose-and-blue parlor with its three-windowed turret provides an attractive contrast to the adjoining, darker library, which has rich green wallpaper and antique lamps; the dining room contains a large table and classic oak buffet. The small porch outside provides a relaxing spot for two.

Most of the guest rooms are sunny, and several (including the Masquerade and Grandma Bell's rooms) are spacious corner rooms. The Masquerade Room also has the best view of the neighboring bluffs from its second-floor balcony.

Address: *708 Parkway Ave. S, Lanesboro, MN 55949, tel. 507/467–2158 or 800/944–2158.*
Accommodations: *5 double rooms with baths.*
Amenities: *Air-conditioning, chocolates, minibottle of champagne, cable TV in rooms, whirlpool bath in 2 rooms; bicycles and cross-country ski rentals, off-street parking.*
Rates: *$55–$125; full breakfast, coffee and baked goods all day. AE, MC, V.*
Restrictions: *No smoking, no pets.*

Hungry Point Inn

As you drive up the road to the Hungry Point Inn you may feel you've been transported to the 18th century. The inn is part of an unusual 1960 development where all the houses' exteriors were made to look as if they had been built before 1820—in other words, before Minnesota was even settled. The atmosphere continues inside Merriam Carroll Last's inn, with its wide-plank pine floors, beamed ceilings, giant fireplace with copper kettle, and cast-iron candle chandelier. Rooms are furnished with quilts, rag rugs, and antique beds and chests, but most popular is a separate little house—an authentic 1870s log cabin restored to hold a kitchen, two bedrooms (with two beds in each), a small parlor with a Vermont casting fireplace, and a whirlpool tub. A hearty breakfast is delivered to the door.

Guests can roam the Inn's secluded grounds, which also host chickens and Jacob sheep. Hiking trails cut through the wild prairie grasses and forests, and you can also ski, bike, or canoe in the Cannon River Valley (boat rentals are available in nearby Welch).

Address: *1 Old Deerfield Rd., Welch, MN 55089, tel. 612/437–3660 or 612/388–7857.*
Accommodations: *4 double rooms share 1½ baths, 1 2-bedroom log cabin with bath.*
Amenities: *Air-conditioning, fireplace in 2 rooms and cabin, whirlpool bath in cabin.*
Rates: *$69–$135; full breakfast, afternoon herbal tea and cookies. D, MC, V.*
Restrictions: *No smoking, no pets.*

Martin Oaks

Martin Oaks stands out not for opulence but for its lovely simplicity, quiet setting, and the great charm of its proprietors. Frank and Marie Gery's 1869 Victorian Italianate bed-and-breakfast is in tiny Dundas, near where Frank teaches economics at St. Olaf College. Marie works as a professional storyteller and is an accomplished cook. Lovely multiple-course breakfasts of fresh fruit, homemade breads, herbed French toast, or Belgian waffles are served in the dining room, on the screened porch near a flower bed frequented by hummingbirds, or on the reconstructed front porch, which has a gazebo-shaped corner section and a fine view of a new, flower-surrounded fountain.

Guest rooms overlook the trees and gardens, and all three have original wide-board pine floors. The largest, William's Room, has an extra single bed and a sitting area. Sara Etta's Room, which may be the most attractive, has a hand-stenciled ivy pattern along the tops of the walls. Marie changes the rooms' decor seasonally, with cozy handmade quilts and warm draperies in winter and white chenille spreads and airy sheer curtains in summer.

Address: *107 1st St., Box 207, Dundas, MN 55019, tel. 507/645–4644.*
Accommodations: *2 double rooms and 1 single share 2 baths.*
Amenities: *Air-conditioning, grand piano in living room.*
Rates: *$54–$69; full breakfast, evening dessert, bedtime snacks in room. MC, V.*
Restrictions: *No smoking, no pets.*

Quill & Quilt

New owners Dennis and Marcia Flom had been looking for the ideal home for a B&B, and they recently discovered this 1897 Colonial Revival home in serene Cannon Falls. On a warm summer day, guests can relax on one of the house's several porches, or wander down the street to Minnieska Park. In the winter, the parlor's oak-and-marble fireplace and oak, cedar, and hemlock woodwork make it a cozy spot. Breakfast is served in the sunny dining room or on a chosen porch, or is brought to guests' rooms, all of which have handmade quilts and curtains.

The Colvill Suite is probably the nicest room: It has a bedroom, sitting room, a great airy bathroom with a double whirlpool bath, and a private deck overlooking the busy town baseball diamond, where Dennis coaches the Cannon Falls varsity baseball team. Avoid the Quilters' Room unless you don't mind a downstairs room right by the front door, and a bath adjacent to the dining room.

Address: *615 W. Hoffman St., Cannon Falls, MN 55009, tel. 507/263–5507 or 800/488–3849.*
Accommodations: *3 double rooms with baths (2 nonadjoining), 1 suite.*
Amenities: *Air-conditioning, coffeemakers, clock radios; biking, hiking, cross-country skiing on nearby Cannon Valley Trail.*
Rates: *$55–$120; full breakfast, evening dessert and coffee. MC, V.*
Restrictions: *No smoking, no pets; closed Thanksgiving weekend, Dec. 24 and 25.*

Red Gables Inn

Douglas DeRoos, a lifetime military man, traveled with his wife, Mary, throughout Europe, staying in bed-and-breakfasts. The DeRoos decided to buy the already-operating 1865 Italianate Red Gables Inn as their "retirement project."

On a summer afternoon, the most pleasant place to sit at the Red Gables is on the screened porch, where Mary serves appetizers and beverages. The home, built from the trees found on the site, is unusual in that it doesn't have hardwood floors, but rather painted fir floors, which Mary has overlaid with Oriental rugs.

The best room is the large, bright Cotton Blossom, a white, rose, and blue corner guest room that faces east and south but stays cool even on the

hottest summer days. Its large, sunny bathroom has a huge comfortable claw-foot tub (furnished with plenty of bubble bath), a pedestal sink, cheerful pink wainscoting, pink and yellow wallpaper, and a large west-facing window.

Address: *403 N. High St., Lake City, MN 55041, tel. 612/345-2605.*
Accommodations: *5 double rooms with baths.*
Amenities: *Sherry in room; bicycles, antiques store.*
Rates: *$75–$95; full breakfast, picnic boxes, dinner if renting whole house. MC, V.*
Restrictions: *No smoking indoors, no pets.*

St. James Hotel

In 1875, when the St. James Hotel was built by 11 local businessmen, Red Wing was a bustling river town and the largest wheat market in the world. Today what remains (besides the facade) are the black walnut–paneled library and the lobby with its grand staircase, tin ceiling, and 106-year-old Steinway. The guest rooms, about half of which have river views, have mostly reproduction Victorian furniture and modern baths, although there's one antique in every room and a handmade quilt on every bed. Stay in the hotel's original section; a newer wing built in 1979 has lower ceilings, narrower corridors, and generally less charm, although the large, horizontal bay windows do look over the Mississippi River.

The St. James is a hotel, restaurant, shopping area, and meeting complex of

a size that belies its Main Street facade. If you're looking for a quiet spot, try the library on the main floor; in the afternoons stop in at Jimmy's, the elegant top-floor English-style pub.

Address: *406 Main St., Red Wing, MN 55066, tel. 612/388-2846 or 800/252-1875, fax 612/388-5226.*
Accommodations: *60 double rooms with baths.*
Amenities: *Air-conditioning, newspapers, phones, cable TV, and clock radio, whirlpool bath in 6 rooms, 11 meeting and banquet rooms, 2 restaurants, 2 bars, 11 shops; shuttle service from airport and dock.*
Rates: *$75–$155; breakfast extra, complimentary champagne, coffee. AE, D, MC, V.*
Restrictions: *No pets.*

Duluth and the North Shore

For many outdoorsy types, the Upper Great Lakes' most ruggedly handsome wilderness isn't in Michigan's Upper Peninsula or northern Wisconsin. It's to be found in this arrowhead-shaped section of northeastern Minnesota, squeezed between Lake Superior to the east and Canada to the north. Because of its size and distance from most large urban areas, the region is never really crowded—good news for those in dogged pursuit of solitude and pristine settings.

The most intimate way to explore the area is the Superior Hiking Trail. The wilderness trail, which is still being developed, will offer nearly 250 miles of continuous hiking between Duluth and Canada when it is completed. You can take day hikes or overnight backpacking trips on sections between Castle Danger and Little Marais and between Schroeder and Grand Marais.

If chance encounters with moose aren't your style, hit the asphalt on U.S. 61, which runs along the lakeshore from Duluth to the Canadian border, 183 miles away. This highway has consistently been named one of the country's top 10 scenic drives by travel magazines. Sometimes creeping to within yards of the clear, cold waters of Lake Superior, the road winds past waterfalls, streams, secluded harbors, rocky overlooks, ancient bridges, and, in fall, brilliantly colored foliage. Alternate routes include well-groomed hiking trails and the North Shore Scenic Railroad, which offers three-hour round-trip excursions between downtown Duluth and the state's first iron port, Two Harbors.

The north shore was only spottily settled until the highway was built in the 1920s, and the towns between Duluth and Thunder Bay, Ontario, are still little more than flyspecks. Duluth, however, is the state's fourth-largest city. Along with its sister city, Superior, Wisconsin, it remains a major seaport. More than 300 years old, Duluth has several museums and neighborhoods that call to mind the glory days of the late 19th

century, when the iron and steel industries made it a harbor
city of great wealth.

Lake breezes have a moderating influence on temperatures in
the region. Winters are surprisingly mild, while summer
temperatures rarely top 80°. This accounts for the wild beauty
visitors enjoy year-round. Yellow marsh marigold, hawkweed,
and stands of purple and pink lupine share space with wild
strawberries, gooseberries, and blueberries during the
summer. In autumn the hardwood forests are ablaze with red,
gold, and orange, while in the winter the pines poke holes in
the lumpy gray clouds, releasing snowflakes as fat and lazy as
feathers. Despite the growing number of Nordic ski trails,
tourists are rare this time of year. On a weekday in the middle
of January you can stop in the woods, break open a bag of trail
mix, and feel as if you have the entire world to yourself. It's a
bit of selfishness that's understood by anyone who has ever
been here.

Places to Go, Sights to See

Canal Park Marine Museum (1st Ave. at the foot of Main St., Duluth, tel.
218/727–2497). This museum, adjoining Duluth's famous Aerial Lift Bridge and
Lighthouse, exhibits shipwreck relics, reconstructed ships' cabins, and other
artifacts relating to Lake Superior and its history.

Glensheen (3300 London Rd., Duluth, tel. 218/724–8864). The restored 39-room
Jacobean-style mansion of attorney, mining entrepreneur, and state legislator
Chester Congdon, Glensheen is furnished with period pieces and antiques, some
original furnishings. Seven and a half acres of lawns and formal gardens overlook
Lake Superior. For Minnesotans, the mansion holds dark allure as the site of the
1977 double murder of Chester's daughter, Elizabeth Congdon, and her nurse;
you won't hear much about the murder on the tour, however.

Gooseberry Falls State Park (17 mi north of Two Harbors on U.S. 61, tel.
218/834–3855, fax 218/834–3855). This 1,600-acre park 40 miles north of Duluth
has picnic tables and 12 miles of trails for hiking and cross-country skiing. There
is also a nature trail. The Gooseberry River enters the park at a height of 240
feet, creating five waterfalls, two of which are 30 feet high. Interesting igneous
volcanic rock outcroppings are common in the second-growth forest of birch,
poplar, alder, and black spruce.

Grand Marais is a village of 1,300 located at a natural harbor. It's a bustling little
town, and one of the jumping-off places for trips to the Superior National Forest
and Boundary Waters Canoe Area (U.S. 61, Grand Marais, tel. 218/387–2451). The

Gunflint Trail, a 57-mile hiking and cross-country ski trail that runs northwest to Saganaga Lake on the Canadian border, begins in the forest. Many outdoor lovers consider this area to be the greatest canoe country in the world.

Judge C.R. Magney State Park (15 mi north of Grand Marais on U.S. 61, tel. 218/387–2929). In this state park waterfalls and turbulent rapids of the Arrowhead River have carved unusual designs into the hardened lava. There are picnic areas, hiking trails, and fishing spots. It's directly across the highway from Naniboujou Lodge.

The Kayak and Canoe Institute (University of Minnesota, Duluth, tel. 218/726–6258), part of University of Minnesota-Duluth Outdoors Program, offers weekend and day kayak trips as well as longer excursions. The package includes three days of instruction and kayaking along the north shore of Lake Superior, meals, and three nights of lodging at local resorts and bed-and-breakfasts.

Lutsen Mountains Resort (90 mi northeast of Duluth on U.S. 61, tel. 218/663–7281) is the area's largest downhill ski resort, with 27 runs and an average annual snowfall of 9½ feet. Mountain gondola and chair-lift rides operate year-round, and are especially popular during the fall foliage season. Lutsen Resort (tel. 218/663–7212 or 800/346–1467) offers lodging on the lake, while Lutsen Village Inn and Resort (tel. 218/663–7241 or 800/642–6036) offers lodging on the mountain. Area activities include horseback riding, cross-country skiing, tennis, stream fishing, hiking, and an 18-hole championship golf course that stretches along the lake and the Poplar River.

Split Rock Lighthouse State Park (18 mi northwest of Two Harbors on U.S. 61, tel. 218/226–3065, fax 218/226–3065). Perched on a cliff that juts up 170 feet over the water, this 54-foot octagonal lighthouse was built in 1910 to help to prevent iron-ore ships from wrecking on the rocky reefs because of fog. The lighthouse is no longer in use and is now open to tourists, as is the lighthouse keeper's home. A new interpretive center is on the sight. Also in the park are 12 miles of hiking trails, 5 miles of cross-country ski trails, and 6 miles of mountain-biking trails.

The **St. Louis County Heritage and Arts Center,** better known as the **Depot** (506 W. Michigan St., Duluth, tel. 218/727–8025), is in the restored 1892 Duluth Union Depot and houses a wide array of cultural organizations, as well as a historical museum and art gallery.

Vista Fleet (610 Missabe Bldg., Duluth, tel. 218/722–6218) has narrated sightseeing boat tours of Duluth-Superior Harbor. Lunch, dinner, or moonlight cruises are offered from May through October.

Wolf Ridge Environmental Learning Center (230 Cranberry Rd., Finland, tel. 218/353–7414 or 800/523–2733, fax 218/353—7762). A few miles west of Little Marais, the center offers classes on astronomy, birds, nature photography, cross-country skiing, rock climbing, and more for adults, kids, and family groups.

Restaurants

Duluth, a sizable city, has many fine restaurants. If you crave something spicy, go down to the tiny **Hacienda Del Sol** (319 E. Superior St., Duluth, tel.

218/722–7296), which has what some consider to be the best Mexican food in the state. All-American steak-and-seafood meals are offered at the **Pickwick Restaurant** (508 E. Superior St., Duluth, tel. 218/727–8901). Sandwiches and salads are offered at **Grandma's** (522 Lake Ave. S, Duluth, tel. 218/727–4192), a waterfront landmark.

Restaurants are harder to find as you make your way up the north shore so don't miss **Betty's Pies** (on U.S. 61, 4 mi north of Two Harbors, tel. 218/834–3367). If you get as far north as Grand Marais, try the **Birch Terrace** (W. 6th Ave. and Wisconsin St., Grand Marais, tel. 218/387–2215), a log cabin with a view of the lake and a menu of great steaks and fish. Right on the water is the smaller and more casual **Angry Trout Cafe** (U.S. 61, Grand Marais, tel. 218/387–1265), whose specialty is coal-grilled lake trout. A further 14 miles north along the lake, the **Naniboujou Lodge and Restaurant** (U.S. 61, 15 mi east of Grand Marais, tel. 218/387–2688) serves a Sunday brunch that is a favorite with the locals.

Tourist Information

Minnesota Office of Tourism's Northeastern Minnesota Regional Office (320 W. 2nd St., Suite 707, Duluth, MN 55802, tel. 218/723–4692); **Duluth Convention and Visitors Bureau** (100 Lake Place Dr., Duluth, MN 55802, tel. 218/722–4011); **Grand Marais Chamber of Commerce** (Box 1048, Grand Marais, MN 55604, tel. 218/387–2524 or 800/622–4014).

Barnum House Bed & Breakfast

Dick and Dorothy Humes brought up their nine children in this 1910 brick Arts and Crafts–style home. After their children moved out, they opened it as a B&B and named it after the original builder, George G. Barnum, who ran the Duluth Grain Exchange. Nonetheless, the inn has retained the warmth of a well-lived-in, much-loved family home.

Quarter-sawn oak, a reminder of the city's past as a center of the lumber industry, panels the main-floor hall, the staircase, the dining room, and the upstairs hallway. The staircase has a lovely carved-oak newel post.

The Mission-style influence makes itself felt on the first floor in the huge oak beams, light fixtures (all original to the house), and the spare design of the leaded-glass window at the landing. The staircase hall has a seating area with an arched fireplace.

Guest quarters are upstairs. The Barnum Suite, a large, masculine corner room, is decorated in browns and tans, with heavy, dark furniture. It shares a deck that overlooks the ravine and Oregon Creek (and, in winter, the lake) with the large Humes Suite, perhaps the best room of the four. It is done in peach, muted gray-greens, and cream, and has a huge bay window, gas fireplace, and marvelous fainting couch. The only incongruous note is the 1970s-style brown ceramic bathroom vanity.

Fresh-ground coffee or tea, which you may have delivered to your room, make a fine beginning for the elegant and filling breakfast of fruit and entreés such as hash brown–crusted quiche or caraway-seed French toast, served in the formal dining room at the ornate, intricately carved 1880s table.

Because the Barnum House is at the end of a dead-end street, it has a quiet, relaxed feel as well as peaceful views. The 1,000-square-foot glass-enclosed veranda at the front of the house has a fireplace and overlooks the property's many pine, birch, and maple trees.

Address: *2211 E. 3rd St., Duluth, MN 55812, tel. 218/724–5434 or 800/879–5437.*
Accommodations: *4 double rooms with baths, 1 double with private non-adjoining bath.*
Amenities: *Clock radio, gas fireplace in 2 rooms; off-street parking.*
Rates: *$105–$125; full breakfast. MC, V.*
Restrictions: *No smoking, no pets.*

Bearskin Lodge

Dave Tuttle worked at Bearskin Lodge Resort when it was just an old lodge and several cabins 25 miles down the Gunflint Trail from Grand Marais and Lake Superior. Then, in 1973, while he was still a senior in college, he bought it.

Today it remains low-key and woodsy, but a bit more ambitious. Since it's adjacent to the Boundary Waters Canoe area, you'll find hiking and cross-country ski trails; boat, ski, and mountain-bike rentals; and a naturalist program. There's even a masseuse. The new lodge, built in 1980, has four large town houses; there are also 10 new or spruced-up log or log-frame cabins. The multilevel town houses, though within a wing of the lodge, feel secluded and each has a private deck. Some of the seven older cabins, built in the '20s, '30s, and '50s, have been remodeled to include room-brightening skylights above the beds. All are pleasant and have two or three bedrooms, woodstoves, and large, well-stocked kitchens. In addition, several have screened porches—critical during the buggy northwoods summers.

The rooms in both the town houses and cabins are simple and comfortable, with chenille bedspreads and pine furniture. Each of the five two- or three-bedroom log cabins is charming, though cabins 9 and 10, built in 1990 of Engelmann spruce, are especially lovely. These cabins have birch hardwood floors, braided rugs, brand-new kitchens as well-outfitted as any home's, and big screened porches, although they're a bit far from the lake.

One of the resort's most popular spots is the Hot Tub Hus, which guests sign up for ahead of time to use privately. Its walls, benches, and ceiling are pine, and it has a large deck and separate men's and women's changing rooms and showers.

Originally a summer-only resort, Bearskin now draws kudos from winter-sports lovers for its ice rink and 40 miles of cross-country ski trails (1 mile of which is lighted). Lodge-to-lodge skiing packages are available.

Address: *275 Gunflint Trail, Grand Marais, MN 55604, tel. 218/388–2292 or 800/338–4170, fax 218/388–4410.*
Accommodations: *10 2- to 3-bedroom cabins and 4 1- to 3-bedroom lodge town houses.*
Amenities: *Woodstoves, grills outside cabins; full meal service available in lodge dining room, wine and beer for sale; sauna, masseuse, spa house; sand beach, boat and mountain-bike rental, 40 miles of hiking/cross-country ski trails, ski school, ski rental, ice-skating rink; baby-sitting, children's program, naturalist program.*
Rates: *$110–$231; breakfast extra. D, MC, V.*
Restrictions: *No smoking in public areas of lodge, no pets.*

The Ellery House

If it's a comfortable family place you're looking for, Jim and Joan Halquist's beautiful 1890 Queen Anne is the place to stay. The house is on a fairly busy street, yet feels rather removed because of its ¾-acre lot, hilltop location, and backyard ravine with creek.

The large, sunny rooms, lit by large picture windows that face in three directions, are decorated in a trim, moderate Victorian style. The large bay window in the living room has a lake view that's best in the winter (shade trees partially obscure the view in summer). In the adjoining dining room, a collection of turn-of-the-century tables and cabinets surround the dark oak dining table.

Breakfast is served in the dining room or in three of the four guest rooms. All of these are delightful. The Ellery Suite, at the front of the house, has a small private balcony and 1920s-style bathroom. The Sunporch, a three-room suite, is made up of a cozy floral-wallpapered bedroom with a brass bed, a large bath with oversized claw-foot tub, and a sunny, plant-filled porch with a wood-burning stove and treetop views. The Thomas Wahl Room is particularly nice, with a tiny table for two tucked into a large lakeview bay window, the 1890s gas fireplace in the corner, the double marble shower, maple floors, and the cabbage rose hooked rug.

Joan, a violinist with the Duluth-Superior Symphony orchestra, encourages

duets on the parlor's baby grand piano. Jim, whose background is in hotels, makes a point of offering comfort and relaxation to tired and stressed-out guests. The popular Lake walk is just 2½ blocks from the inn, and the Halquists, both active, outdoorsy folks, can also recommend their favorite bike and cross-country ski trails; they even have a storage shed for any equipment you may bring. In addition, with two small children themselves, the Halquists don't mind accommodating the families of others. Their congeniality make the Ellery House very homey indeed.

Address: *28 S. 21st Ave. E, Duluth, MN 55812, tel. 218/724–7639 or 800/355–3794.*
Accommodations: *2 double rooms with baths, 2 suites.*
Amenities: *Fireplace in 2 rooms, 1 room with balcony, ceiling fans, fresh flowers; off-street parking.*
Rates: *$65–$98 winter, $78–$128 summer; full breakfast. AE, MC, V.*
Restrictions: *Smoking on porches only, no pets.*

The Mansion Bed & Breakfast Inn

Though imposing from the front, this 1928 rubblestone and half-timbered Tudor mansion is really oriented toward its backyard. And what a backyard: Five hundred feet of Lake Superior shore provides the house with incredible views from almost every room.

Built for mining executive Harry C. Dudley and his wife, Marjorie Congdon Dudley, daughter of Duluth lumber baron Chester Congdon, The Mansion is an inviting combination of grandeur and comfort. The main floor has a sunny dining room with a terrazzo floor, a wood-paneled library with a large fireplace and antique books, a large gallery with four window seats and three sets of French doors leading to a lakefront stone terrace, and a huge living room that opens onto a screened porch, a favorite of guests.

Sunny, lined with bear- and wolfskins and mooseheads, guarded by a suit of armor, and fitted with a huge lakeview window seat, the third-floor Trophy Room is the inn's designated quiet room. Guests use it for reading and dreaming, and "fall asleep here all the time," says proprietor Sue Monson, who, along with her husband, Warren, bought the building in 1983. Warren is a busy physician, so Sue, who likes to cater to the guests, runs The Mansion herself with some help from her three grown children and a small part-time staff.

The bedrooms that belonged to members of the Dudley family, such as the Anniversary Suite and the Master Suite, are the largest, but the coziest are the former maids' quarters, now called the Peach and Beige rooms. Some of the bedrooms, all of which are carpeted and contain some reproduction furniture, do pale in comparison to the absolute splendor of the Mansion itself, but as one of the guests said, "I can't imagine anyone coming here and not being completely impressed and comfortable."

The 7-acre grounds are given over to lawns, gardens, and a forest of northern hardwoods, pine, and cedar; there's also a private beach, where guests often build bonfires in summer.

Address: *3600 London Rd., Duluth, MN 55804, tel. 218/724–0739.*
Accommodations: *6 double rooms with baths, 4 doubles share 2 baths, 1-bedroom carriage house suite.*
Amenities: *Large screen TV and VCR in living room, kitchenette in carriage house; private beach, off-street parking.*
Rates: *$95–$195, $155 for carriage house; full breakfast. MC, V.*
Restrictions: *Smoking in library and on screened porch only, no pets.*

Pincushion Mountain Bed & Breakfast

After four winters with no snow in Flagstaff, Arizona, Scott Beattie, a longtime cross-country skier and instructor, moved to a place where snow was guaranteed. He and his wife, Mary, checked out locations around the country and came to a spot 3 miles up the Gunflint Trail from Grand Marais. They built the Pincushion Mountain Bed & Breakfast in 1986. The almost unreal quiet here is broken only by the occasional birdcall.

The modern pine building sits on the Sawtooth Mountain ridgeline, 1,000 feet above Lake Superior. The woodsy inn has fir beams, pine and aspen paneled walls, and country-style furnishings and knickknacks.

Downstairs is a living room equipped with a woodstove and a dining room where a hearty breakfast is served. There are spectacular views of Lake Superior and the surrounding pine, aspen, and birch forest. This is the true northwoods; don't be surprised if you see a deer, a moose, or even a bear passing by.

The four guest rooms upstairs are somewhat small but comfortable. The largest and probably the most desirable is the corner Pine Room, which has a fold-out love seat, a comfortably sized bath, and a majestic view of Lake Superior in the distance. The Birch and Aspen rooms have tiny but adequate built-in baths with showers only; the latter has no lake view. The Maple Room has a private bath across the hall.

Scott gives skiing lessons, rents and repairs skis, and grooms Pincushion's own 15½ miles of trails. Although Pincushion accommodates skiers in particular, its 44 acres are equally attractive in summer and fall when its ski trails are used for hiking. Because the inn's trails adjoin the 200-mile Superior Hiking Trail, Pincushion takes part in the north shore lodge-to-lodge hiking program and ski programs. There's also a 15½-mile, seven-loop mountain-bike trail system here, and an additional 200 miles in the woods nearby.

Address: *220 Gunflint Trail, Grand Marais, MN 55604–9701, tel. 218/387–1276 or 800/542–1226.*
Accommodations: *4 double rooms with baths.*
Amenities: *Fans, clock radios; sauna, mountain bikes and cross-country skis for rent, 15½ miles of cross-country skiing and hiking trails, 1 mile of lighted trails on winter Saturday nights, cross-country ski instruction, trail bag lunches available.*
Rates: *$70–$95; full breakfast, afternoon refreshments. D, MC, V.*
Restrictions: *No smoking, no pets; 2-night minimum stay on winter, late summer, and fall weekends; closed Apr.*

The Stone Hearth Inn Bed & Breakfast

In 1989, when Charlie Michels came to Little Marais, he wanted to buy some land on Lake Superior. Two years later he had a five-bedroom, 70-year-old inn, and a wife, Susan, who'd been one of his first guests.

The Stone Hearth Inn was the original homestead of the Benjamin Fenstad family. Benjamin built a log cabin on the site in 1893 and, in 1924, built the home that Charlie owns today. An accomplished Twin Cities carpenter and contractor, Charlie did most of the renovation work himself. He made 10 rooms into six, stripped the narrow-plank maple floors, added beams and molding downstairs, and collected stones from the shores of Lake Superior to build the large living-room fireplace.

Just 80 feet from the lake, the house has a wonderful, long porch furnished with Adirondack chairs, perfect for relaxing in these serene surroundings. French doors open from the simple dining room with a large handmade pine table in the center, and from the living room, where soft chairs and sofas flank the giant hearth and guests take turns playing the piano.

In all five guest rooms, you can fall asleep to the comforting sounds of the lake, but you'll get the best views from Rooms 2, 3, and 4. Room 2, a corner room in blue and white with a four-poster canopy bed, has a lake view even from its pink and white ceramic-tiled bathroom.

An old boathouse just 30 feet from the lake was renovated in 1992 and rebuilt as a two-unit cottage. One unit is a suite with a bedroom, bathroom, living room with sofa sleeper, and kitchenette. Both are upstairs and have fireplaces, whirlpool baths, and especially dramatic views from their picture windows.

Blueberry wild-rice pancakes, Austrian apple pancakes, lake trout sausage, and vanilla poached pears are perfect examples of Susan and Charlie's innovative cooking. On most clear nights, there is a bonfire down by the lake, with marshmallow s'mores provided by the Michels and, if you're lucky, northern lights provided by Mother Nature.

Address: *1118 Hwy. 61 E, Little Marais, MN 55614, tel. 218/226–3020, fax 218/226–3466.*
Accommodations: *6 double rooms with baths, 1 suite with kitchenette.*
Amenities: *Fireplace, coffeemaker, and whirlpool bath in 1 room and suite, kitchenette in suite, special dinners and trail lunches available; canoe and mountain bikes rentals, bonfire, lodge-to-lodge hiking program.*
Rates: *$79–$130; full breakfast in inn, Continental breakfast in boat-house double room, fully stocked kitchen in boat-house suite. MC, V.*
Restrictions: *No smoking, no pets.*

Caribou Lake B&B

I t's hard to find a bed-and-breakfast with a more spectacular setting than this one overlooking the clear water and surrounding forest of Caribou Lake. In 1989, when Jeanne and Carter Wells purchased this red cedar log house and guest cabin, built just over 10 years ago, they got all they wanted and more: They're right on a lake with lots of hiking and cross-country ski trails, swimming, boating, fishing, and wildlife-watching.

The lower-level suite doesn't have the same great views of the lake as the main-floor dining and living rooms. In addition, the low ceilings make it feel rather claustrophobic, despite the relatively spacious room with two double beds and large sliding-glass door. But it has a private sitting room with TV, a bathroom, and a fairly large sauna. The two-bedroom cabin has a kitchen and offers more privacy, but feels cramped. Nevermind, since most guests visit this area for the outdoors, few will find a better place to enjoy it than this hilltop retreat.

Address: *Box 156, Lutsen, MN 55612, tel. 218/663–7489.*
Accommodations: *1 suite, 1 cabin.*
Amenities: *TV, VCR, and sauna in suite; kitchenette, wood-burning stove and gas grill in cabin; tape players in both; 2 docks, boat and canoe rentals.*
Rates: *$85–$120; full breakfast, dinners and trail lunches available. MC, V.*
Restrictions: *No smoking, no pets.*

Fitger's Inn

O nly the stone walls in a few of the guest rooms and the lovely leaded-glass skylight and 19th-century iron registration cage in the high-ceilinged lobby reveal the origins of this inn on Lake Superior, near downtown Duluth: In the 1850s, it was a brewery. Now extensively renovated, it is on the National Register of Historic Places.

Although the guest rooms are furnished with reproduction antiques, they seem more like upscale hotel rooms than those of a historic inn. But all are spacious and have big beds, desks, wing chairs, and modern baths. Thirty-one rooms have lake views.

Fitger's is centrally located, convenient for exploring the town. It's also on Duluth's new Lake Walk, which goes past the Aerial Lift Bridge and ends in Canal Park. In summer, outdoor concerts are held nearby.

Address: *600 E. Superior St., Duluth, MN 55802, tel. 218/722–8826 or 800/726–2982.*
Accommodations: *42 double rooms with baths, 6 suites.*
Amenities: *Air-conditioning, phone, cable TV, clock radio in bedrooms, room service; conference facilities, including 160-seat theater; off-street parking, adjoining shopping and restaurant complex.*
Rates: *$85–$110, suites $135–$260; breakfast extra. D, DC, MC, V.*
Restrictions: *No pets.*

The Inn at Palisade Bed & Breakfast

This little five-unit motel, built in 1955 and now a unique B&B, lies in one of the prettiest coves on Lake Superior's north shore. Owners Mary and Bob Barnett were driving in the area in 1986 when the property caught their eye; it was in good shape, and the location was a winner.

The four main-level units have private entrances onto the parking lot and 1950's-pink ceramic-tile showers. They are all comfortably and neatly furnished, with small bay windows overlooking Lake Superior and the Inn's crescent-shaped beach. The common room has a fireplace, a large picture window also facing the lake, and an adjoining dining room where breakfast is served. On the building's lower level is one large room that contains a queen-size bed, a sitting area with a fold-out sofa, a table and chairs, a kitchenette, a fireplace, and two large picture windows. Also on this floor are a flagstone patio with a campfire circle, and stairs leading down to the beach. Adjoining the inn's property on the northeast side is Tettegouche State Park, with hiking paths and waterfalls.

Address: *384 U.S. 61, Silver Bay, MN 55614, tel. 218/226–3505, fax 218/226–4648.*
Accommodations: *4 double rooms with baths, 1 suite with kitchen.*
Amenities: *TV, clock radio, kitchen and fireplace in 1 room; campfire.*
Rates: *$80–$95; full breakfast, afternoon snack, coffee available all day. D, MC, V.*
Restrictions: *No smoking, no pets; closed mid-Oct.–May.*

Lindgren's Bed & Breakfast

This log house is now a B&B run by Shirley Lindgren, who is a real go-getter and then some. "My home is your home," she says, and a rather unique home it is, where the refined and the frontier mix below 18-foot beamed ceilings of knotty cedar. Just about every known denizen of the vast forests of the North Shore—from black bear, moose, and wolf to deer, owl, and beaver—reside in stuffed form in the living-dining area, which also has a fireplace, tall windows overlooking Lake Superior, and plenty of comfortable chairs and sofas. A large, handmade cabinet of cherry holds delicate crystal and fine china; across the room, a baby grand piano awaits a tune.

But for a double whirlpool bath in Bobby's Room, the two front bedrooms are identical, down to the king-size bed placed under huge windows overlooking the lake. The large rec-room–style basement has a fireplace, glass doors with lake access, a small bathroom, and beds for a dozen people.

Address: *County Road 35, Box 56, Lutsen, MN 55612, tel. 218/663–7450.*
Accommodations: *3 double rooms with baths, basement room with bunk and sofabeds.*
Amenities: *Cable TV in bedrooms, phones in 2 rooms, whirlpool in 1 room, fireplace in 1 room; bonfire pit, Finnish sauna, horseshoe pit, volleyball area, lodge-to-lodge hiking program.*
Rates: *$80–$110; full breakfast, lunch and dinner available. MC, V.*
Restrictions: *No smoking in public areas, no pets.*

Mathew S. Burrows 1890 Inn

Tired of the 9-to-5 life in Washington, D.C., David and Pam Wolff came back to Duluth, Pam's hometown, to open a bed-and-breakfast. They chose an imaginative red and green Queen Anne with an unusual gazebo-style front porch.

The public rooms—a music room with an upright piano and a parlor with a carved mahogany fireplace—are Victorian without the traditional Victorian clutter. But the house's standout feature is its white oak-paneled dining room, which has a carved built-in white oak mirrored buffet; a maple, walnut, oak, mahogany, and birch parquet floor; and the most magnificent blue and gold stained-glass window ever seen outside a church.

The best guest room is probably the Lakeview Suite, with its lace-draped four-poster canopy bed and twin French doors joining the bedroom to a private sitting room with corner windows and beautiful views.

Address: *1632 E. 1st St., Duluth, MN 55812, tel. 218/724–4991 or 800/789–1890.*
Accommodations: *2 double rooms with baths, 2 suites.*
Amenities: *Alarm clock, radio/tape player, fireplace and unique full-body marble shower in 1 suite; off-street parking.*
Rates: *$95–$125; full breakfast. AE, D, MC, V.*
Restrictions: *No smoking, no pets; 2-night minimum on summer weekends, closed Thanksgiving, Dec. 24–25.*

Naniboujou Lodge

Conceived in the 1920s as the cornerstone of an exclusive sportsmen's club, the Naniboujou Lodge, 15 miles northeast of Grand Marais, never grew beyond the hotel and its restaurant—but what a hotel and restaurant they are.

The lodge's focal point is the Great Hall, which has a huge 200-ton native rock fireplace. This room, now used for dining, is emblazoned with Cree motifs. The guest rooms are small but pleasant, remodeled and furnished with pine furniture and modern baths. Owners Tim and Nancy Ramey have kept the prices reasonable.

There is an abundance of recreational opportunities, but the lodge is definitely a place to lounge in the Adiron-

dack chairs and enjoy the views of Lake Superior.

Address: *U.S. 61 (HC 1, Box 505), Grand Marais, MN 55604, tel. and fax 218/387–2688.*
Accommodations: *24 double rooms with baths, 2 doubles share bath.*
Amenities: *Fireplace in 5 rooms, lake view from 12 rooms, restaurant; basketball and volleyball courts.*
Rates: *$45–$90; breakfast extra, afternoon tea. D, MC, V.*
Restrictions: *No smoking, no alcohol in restaurant, no pets; closed mid-Oct.–Mother's Day and weekdays Dec. 26–mid-Mar.*

The Superior Overlook B&B

Perched on a hill overlooking Lake Superior, 2 miles north of Grand Marais, this bed-and-breakfast truly lives up to its name.

Jack and Viola Kerber built their house in 1985 when they retired here from California. A few years later they converted the first floor to a three-bedroom B&B. It's a good spot for those who prefer to minimize their interaction with innkeepers, since there's a separate entrance, deck, living room with woodstove, and kitchenette with toaster oven, microwave, coffeemaker, and fridge.

It's quite a modern house—the living-room walls are light-blue cinder block and the ceiling is acoustic tile—but then the real view is outside, anyway.

The living room and the two guest rooms have wonderful views. The Deck Room can be made up with two twin beds or with one king-size; the Lake Suite has a queen-size bed, pink walls, a floral spread, a double whirlpool bath, and a separate entrance leading down a lake path.

Address: *U.S. 61, Milepost 112 (Box 963) Grand Marais, MN 55604–0963, tel. 218/387–1571 or 800/858–7622.*
Accommodations: *1 double with non-adjoining bath, 1 suite.*
Amenities: *TV, VCR, phone, and wood-burning stove in living room, kitchenette, sauna.*
Rates: *$90–$125; full breakfast. AE, D, MC, V.*
Restrictions: *No smoking, no pets.*

The Northwest and the Cuyana Iron Range
Including Brainerd and Detroit Lakes

When Twin Cities residents talk about "going up north," they usually mean up to Arrowhead, along the Lake Superior shore from Duluth to the Gunflint Trail. But to people in the more rural western parts of the state, "up north" means the Northwest and the Cuyana Iron Range, around Alexandria, Detroit Lakes, Brainerd, and Walker.

Studded with wooded lakes and state forests, threaded through with hiking trails and streams teeming with fish, the region is ideal for outdoorsy vacations. Here you'll find crystal-clear Lake Itasca, source of the Mississippi River, surrounded by the virgin pine forest of Itasca State Park. Leech Lake, much lovelier than its name implies, sits within the Chippewa National Forest; the town of Walker, on Leech Lake's southwestern corner, is a fishing favorite. Mille Lacs Lake, just east of Brainerd, is another popular body of water, and the towns of Detroit Lakes and Alexandria, to the west, have long attracted tourists for their proximity to a number of small, beautiful lakes. Farther north, in a much more rugged and thinly settled part of Minnesota, Lake of the Woods stretches its many fingers up into neighboring Ontario and Manitoba.

Besides such watery diversions as swimming, sailing, and fishing, there are plenty of other opportunities to enjoy the outdoors in these parts. The Heartland Trail, a blacktop bicycle path created from an old rail bed, runs 27 miles from Walker to Park Rapids. The North Country National Scenic Trail, 68 miles long, winds through the Chippewa National Forest between Walker and Romer. Among the many rivers designated as canoe trails are the Crow Wing River, Red Lake River, Pine River, and the Mississippi River, from Lake Itasca down to Anoka, just north of Minneapolis.

Tying into the region's logging past, several towns (notably Brainerd and Bemidji) are touted as "Paul Bunyan's Hometown." An even more exotic bit of history is represented in Alexandria: A rune stone there is said to be evidence that Viking explorers visited here in the 14th century.

Although Alexandria and Detroit lakes have long been tourist-oriented, traditionally the region was supported by logging and taconite mining. (The Cuyana is one of three iron ranges in the United States; the Mesabi and Vermilion ranges to the east are more familiar to Minnesotans.) Once the old-growth trees were felled and the mines were worked out, the region fell upon hard economic times, but it's making a modest comeback now, thanks in large part to tourism. Accommodations tend to be smaller and less fancy than those in Arrowhead or the St. Croix Valley, but consequently, prices are still refreshingly low.

Places to Go, Sights to See

Bunyan House Information Center (300 Bemidji Ave. (Rte. 197), Bemidji, tel. 218/751–3540). A so-called collection of the mythical lumberjack's tools and memorabilia is the main attraction here; there's also the requisite giant statues of Paul and his blue ox, Babe. Open Memorial Day–Labor Day, daily; weekdays the rest of the year.

Deer Town (U.S. 71, 1 mi north of Park Rapids, tel. 218/732–5135). Deer, goats, geese, and sheep roam around this re-created pioneer village, which also has a small museum, playground, and observation tower. Open Memorial Day–Labor Day, daily.

Itasca State Park (Rte. 200 and U.S. 71, about 35 mi southwest of Bemidji, tel. 218/266–2114). Minnesota's oldest state park is still one of its best—a 32,000-acre sanctuary of pine forest known for its excellent birding (at least one pair of loons stays on the lake each summer), hiking, biking, and cross-country ski trails. Lake Itasca contains the headwaters of the Mississippi River. Up here, you can cross the river by walking on a few smooth stepping-stones; farther down, it is a gentle, honey-colored stream, nothing like the muddy colossus it becomes. Also highly recommended: **Zippel Bay State Park** (Lake of the Woods, Williams, tel. 218/783–6252), which gives you a taste of wild northern Minnesota.

Lumbertown USA (U.S. 77, 15 mi northwest of Brainerd, tel. 218/829–8872). More than 25 replicas and restorations of 19th-century buildings re-create a logging town of the 1870s, complete with a maple-sugar plant, a general store, an ice-cream parlor, a pioneer home, a wax museum, an old-fashioned train, and a riverboat. Open daily,, Memorial Day–Labor Day.

Oliver H. Kelley Historic Farm (U.S. 10, 2½ mi southeast of Elk River, tel. 612/441–6896). A living museum of 19th-century agricultural practices, this farm on the banks of the Mississippi River has guides, dressed in period costume, out with their horses and oxen, demonstrating farm chores of the day. The original owner, Oliver Kelley, founded the Patrons of Husbandry, also known as the Grange, a farmers' fraternal organization that grew to have significant political influence in the 1870s. Open daily.

Paul Bunyan Amusement Center (junction of Rtes. 210 and 371, 2 mi west of Brainerd, tel. 218/829–6342). Offering the standard assortment of children's rides, minigolf, go-carts, and performing animals, this small park has one outstanding feature: a 26-foot animated statue of Paul Bunyan (with a 15-foot Babe, the blue ox, behind him) that spins tall tales to youngsters. Open daily, Memorial Day–Labor Day.

Sinclair Lewis Interpretive Center and Museum (junction of I–94 and U.S. 71, Sauk Centre, tel. 612/352–5201). There was no love lost between Sinclair Lewis and his hometown, Sauk Centre, when the Nobel-laureate-to-be depicted the town as "Gopher Prairie" in his novel *Main Street*. More than 70 years later, Sauk Centre folks have embraced their most famous native son, renaming a street after him. This museum is full of interesting artifacts related to Lewis and his hometown, which is a fairly typical Minnesota small town—neither gorgeous nor plain, but pleasant and practical. Here the **Sinclair Lewis Boyhood Home** (612 Sinclair Lewis Ave.) displays family memorabilia and 1900s furnishings.

Summerhill Farm (U.S. 71, 7 mi north of Park Rapids, tel. 218/732–3865). Several buildings of an old farmstead have been converted into this collection of gift shops selling country collectibles, art work, and handcrafted gifts. There's also a restaurant on the premises.

Restaurants

The area's restaurants, such as Bemidji's **Union Station** (Union Sq., 1st St. and Beltrami Ave., tel. 218/751–9261), serve a lot of walleye pike and prime rib. If you're looking for something different, head for the **Brauhaus** (U.S. 34, Nevis, tel. 218/652–2478), a little German place in the middle of the country, or **Companeros** (U.S. 226, Dorset, tel. 218/732–7624), a big, colorful Mexican spot in a very small town.

Tourist Information

Bemidji Chamber of Commerce (300 Bemidji Ave., Bemidji, MN 56601, tel. 218/751–3541); **Brainerd Lakes Area Chamber of Commerce** (110 N. 6th St., Brainerd, MN 56401, tel. 218/829–2838); **Detroit Lakes Regional Chamber of Commerce** (700 Washington Ave., Detroit Lakes, MN 56501, tel. 218/847–9202 or 800/542–3992); **Fergus Falls Chamber of Commerce** (202 S. Court St., Fergus Falls, MN 56537, tel. 218/736–6951); **Minnesota Office of Tourism, Northcentral/West regional office** (1901 S. 6th St., Box 443, Brainerd, MN 56401, tel. 218/828–2334); **Sauk Centre Area Chamber of Commerce** (1220 S. Main St., Sauk Centre, MN 56378, tel. 612/352–5201).

Hallett House

s you drive out of Crosby and approach the grand front lawn of Hallett House, you may feel like you've stepped back in time. A driveway that curves beneath oaks and jack pines brings you to the front door of a pale Georgian Revival house with green trim and a small arched portico. Inside, painted Georgian paneling suggests grandeur, but the lush green wool carpeting somehow shrinks the large rooms to livable size. Sun streams through the windows of a porch that's been made into a wicker-furnished guest room. The library, with a fireplace and built-in bookshelves, has the air of an old-fashioned men's club room.

Upstairs, past yellow-and-blue 1950s-era wallpaper with Early American scenes, the guest rooms give off that same feeling of luxury. The big, carpeted rooms, which have solid, often antique furniture and bay windows with venetian blinds, encourage the fantasy that you're staying in the home of some long-lost rich uncle. Here is the room of "the lady of the house," with its mirror-lined dressing area and vanity—you can almost smell the Chanel No. 5 and hear the faint tinkling of silver bracelets. Here is the master bedroom, with a baronial bed facing the bay window, or the maid's quarters, with her rather small bed and her own sitting room (and an up-to-date TV set). Down the hall, the eldest son's room seems to have been kept as it must have been before he

left for college, all hardwood floors and a big oak bedstead.

In truth, the house was built in the early '20s by E. W. Hallett, a construction and real-estate magnate who was once one of the richest men in the country. Hallett was a conservative man—he didn't lose his shirt in the Depression—and his house, though large, is not ostentatious, wearing its wealth lightly. He died in 1983 (at the age of 101!), and six years later a local couple, Kathy and Wes Pernula, bought the well-preserved home and turned it into a bed-and-breakfast. They've had the sense to leave well enough alone, adding only a few frills and figurines, most of them downstairs, so the delicious feeling of quiet privilege still prevails.

Address: *Hwy. 210 (Box 247), Crosby, MN 56441, tel. 218/546-5433.*
Accommodations: *5 double rooms with baths.*
Amenities: *Air-conditioning in 1 bedroom, cable TV in 2 bedrooms and in library.*
Rates: *$50–$70; full breakfast. AE, MC, V.*
Restrictions: *No smoking, no pets.*

Oakhurst Inn

t was perhaps the most prestigious house in the prosperous town of Princeton at one time, but when David and Suzie Spain bought Oakhurst in 1989, it was a cluttered near-ruin. It took two years of hard work to return the house to something close to its days of glory. Unlike the original owner, banker John Skahen, the Spains aren't made of money, so Oakhurst today feels more like a family home than a ostentatious mansion. Still, much of the grandeur remains.

Built in 1906, the three-story house is one of those Victorians that borrowed from many styles, hence the Queen Anne wraparound porch and the magnificent Romanesque fireplace in the front parlor. The front door opens onto a grand vestibule, with ceilings nearly 10 feet high, oak floors and woodwork, and a long bench built into one wall. To the right are the front and back parlors (the Spains have added oak wainscoting to the back parlor and turned it into a library); to the left is the dining room, complete with plate rail. The Spains hope to make the decor more consistent with one period: At present, an Eastlake chair, a Mission rocker, and a reupholstered camelback couch sit incongruously near one another. An air of homey middle-class nostalgia is perpetuated by Norman Rockwell plates, small stuffed bears, and braided area rugs.

Upstairs, the tasteful, comfortable guest rooms do better at creating a period look. The John J. Skahen Room,

for instance, features a velvet fainting couch and a pencil-post four-poster queen-size bed, covered with reproduction quilted lace. The smaller Sterling Room has a bathroom with such 1906-ish features as a pedestal sink, claw-foot tub, and wainscoting. The sunny Lucy Room has a white iron bed with lace coverlet, and lace curtains at the windows, making for a pleasant mixture of frill and simplicity.

The Spains and their children live on the third floor of this big house, and perhaps their presence has something to do with the down-to-earth family atmosphere of the place. Guests are welcome to visit Suzie in the kitchen, where they may be offered a chocolate-chip cookie or two while she talks of the horrors of renovation. While the remodelling was no doubt hard to live through, the result is a cozy success.

Address: *212 S. 8th Ave., Princeton, MN 55371, tel. 612/389–3553 or 800/443–2258.*
Accommodations: *3 double rooms with baths.*
Amenities: *Air-conditioning, TV/VCR in library.*
Rates: *$60–$75; full breakfast, evening refreshments. MC, V.*
Restrictions: *No smoking, no pets.*

Park Street Inn

This little jewel box sits on a little street in a little town you'd miss if you drove too fast. Nevis, once a prosperous logging town, now makes a bid for tourism with the nearby Heartland Bike Trail and Lake Belle Taine. The Park Street Inn represents this newer Nevis, although it is also rooted in the town's history.

Built in 1912 by Justin Halvorsen, a well-to-do banker and local land developer, the house is more of a bungalow than a mansion, but it was done up in style—all kinds of styles, in fact, for Halvorsen apparently was no purist. The compact oak stairway and banister were constructed out of state and brought to town by train. Other Midwestern craftsmen contributed a beveled-glass fan window and exquisite entry arches of carved oak in a French Empire style, with acanthus-topped fluted columns and flower-basket bas-reliefs. In contrast, an oak mantel sports the clean, simple lines of Mission-style design.

Halvorsen lost his money in the Depression and moved to California. Given that Nevis, too, was declining, it's surprising that so many of the original treasures in the house were still there by the time Kathy and Jerry Carney bought it in 1989. In converting it into a bed-and-breakfast, the Carneys have shown the utmost respect for the builder's idiosyncrasies, while bringing their own good taste to bear.

In the living room and dining area, subdued wallpaper and matching valances drape over lace-curtained windows. The Carneys' Eastlake chairs and rockers work surprisingly well, as do the folk-art engravings on the wall. Jerry tactfully introduced a modern stereo system (there's no downstairs TV) by installing the components inside a mahogany Victrola cabinet.

The upstairs is a bit less restrained, but still interesting. The largest guest room, which has a wicker-furnished sleeping porch facing Lake Belle Taine, also features a built-in cupboard bed whose oak arch came from a Lutheran church altar. Each room has its own wallpaper pattern and quilt—a handmade double wedding-ring quilt in one bedroom, a bright star pattern in another. The stuffed dolls and antique relics upstairs are tasteful, and in no way prevent the jewels here from sparkling.

Address: *Rte. 1 (Box 254), Nevis, MN 56467, tel. 218/652–4500 or 800/797–1778.*
Accommodations: *3 double rooms with baths, 1 suite.*
Amenities: *TV in sitting room.*
Rates: *$60–$75; full breakfast, evening refreshments. D, MC, V.*
Restrictions: *No smoking, no pets.*

Peters' Sunset Beach

One look inside the main lodge's dining room gives you the flavor of this classic lakeside resort: knotty-pine paneling, fish trophies, paintings of scenes from a Hiawatha-like Native American legend, light fixtures done up like painted drums, and a broad porch overlooking Lake Minnewaska.

The lodge, a gorgeous example of Craftsman-style design, is one of the resort's three buildings on the National Register of Historic Places. The place has changed a bit since train conductor Henry Peters jumped off the Soo Line in Glenwood and opened his summer hotel in 1915. It has grown from a small hostelry to a resort, complete with its own 18-hole golf course, accommodating up to 175 guests in a variety of up-to-date rooms, cottages, and luxury town houses. But it's still run by the Peters family, and they have restored the historic 1923 Annex to its old-fashioned appearance—making it, in the words of Henry's grandson Bill Peters, "our country inn."

From the outside, the Annex looks a lot like the main lodge, almost like a wing that detached itself and settled several steps away. Inside, the

Peterses have installed antique bedsteads, tables, and dressers, many of them wooden pieces from the turn of the century, to fit in with the refinished original woodwork. Quilts, made by a local artisan, grace each bed; the wallpaper is quietly floral. The whole

building has an agreeable, unpretentious air about it, although there are some discordant touches left over from the Annex's prerestoration interim years. Built-in couches, covered in tweedy fabrics, don't quite fit in, nor do the wall-to-wall carpeting and fluorescent lighting in the bathrooms.

Still, the Annex has a certain charm, and there are other compensations: The restaurant serves some of the best food in the area. The nearby town of Glenwood is pretty, the resort's grounds are gracious, and Lake Minnewaska itself is lovely. You can certainly see why Henry Peters made this the end of his line.

Address: *2500 S. Lakeshore Dr., Glenwood, MN 56334, tel. 612/634–4501 or 800/356–8654 in MN.*
Accommodations: *23 double rooms (12 in Court Bldg., 3 in Main Lodge, 8 in the Annex) with baths; 9 town houses sleep 4–6 people; 2 1-bedroom cottages, 5 2-bedroom cottages, 3 3-bedroom cottages, 1 4-bedroom cottage; 1 7-bedroom housekeeping cottage.*
Amenities: *Air-conditioning, cable TV in bedrooms, restaurant, snack bar, meeting room; beach, golf, tennis, racquetball, boat rentals.*
Rates: *$72–$96, $110–$222 for town houses and cottages; full breakfast and dinner. MC, V.*
Restrictions: *No pets; 2-night minimum, closed Oct.–Apr.*

The Robards House

Driving through Alexandria, with its wide, treeless Broadway, fast-food row, and numerous commercial tourist attractions, you might not believe a place like the Robards House could exist here. But go several blocks from the main drag and there it is, on a shady street, its graceful grounds stretching down to meet Lake Winona. With its shingled front gable, this quietly handsome brown-brick house looks something like a small-town creamery that sprouted a sloped roof, chocolate-colored shutters, and several extra rooms off the back. Built in 1889 by local hardware magnate Oscar Robards, it's listed on the National Register of Historic Places.

The spacious interior boasts high ceilings and Greek Revival oak moldings and door frames—some painted, some, thankfully, untouched—exuding a sense of late-Victorian elegance, with some Federal touches. Throughout the living room, parlor, and dining room, rich reds and greens are echoed in the wallpaper, carpeting, and drapery. It is all quite attractive, but the real beauty lies in the details, such as the Egypto-Celtic designs wrought into the window pulls and door hinges. The living-room decor includes velvet-upholstered oak sofas and chairs, a working Victrola with original records, and mementos of old Germany, heirlooms of owner Bernice Hillgruber (who now lives in California, leaving the daily operation to manager Rebecca Mulkern).

Upstairs, each room has been individually styled, though all have maple floors and antique furniture (or good reproductions). The Pederson Room, a likely honeymoon suite, features a broad bay window, a lake view, and a custom-built oak bedstead and armoire that don't look new at all. The Leroy Room, which also has a lake view, has Eastlake furnishings and its own little porch (marred somewhat by painted built-in cabinets that look like relics of a 1940s kitchen). The smaller rooms, the Kinkead Room (with twin beds) and the Cowling Room, are pleasant as well.

The spacious Penthouse Suite, which fills the whole third floor, has a smattering of antiques and a vintage stained-glass Palladian window. Its other amenities (a deck, a minilibrary, and a dining area off the sunken living room) make it more expensive, but its decor appears to be somewhat plain—something you certainly can't say about the rest of the house.

Address: *518 6th Ave. W, Alexandria, MN 56308, tel. 612/763–4073.*
Accommodations: *4 double rooms with baths, 1 suite.*
Amenities: *Air-conditioning, TV/VCR in living room.*
Rates: *$60–$165; Continental breakfast. MC, V.*
Restrictions: *No smoking, no pets.*

Spicer Castle

If you somehow missed the opportunity to live in an old country mansion circa 1913, here's your chance. This imposing house was built in 1895 by farm developer John Spicer, one of the founders of Minnesota's branch of the Democratic Party. According to current owner Allen Latham, Spicer's grandson, the last renovations on the house were done in 1913, shortly after it was wired for electricity, and the building hasn't been changed since. Set on the wooded shores of Green Lake, the Tudor-style half-timbered house was originally called Medayto Cottage, but in the 1930s, fishermen on the lake started referring to it as "The Castle," perhaps because of its crenelated tower. Though it's otherwise not particularly castlelike, the name stuck.

However beautiful its exterior, it's the interior that makes the Castle distinctive. The furnishings, rugs, china, and Craftsman-style lamps and clocks are all antiques and have been in place since the 1913 redecoration. Walking across the gleaming maple floors, through the living and dining rooms, the well-stocked library, and the grand porch overlooking the lake, you get the sense that you are not just viewing the past, but actually participating in it.

The first floor, with dark furniture and burlap wall coverings (a typical period Craftsman touch), might seem dark, but it's not oppressive—rather, it encourages quiet reflection and talk. In winter, it becomes downright cozy, as the fireplaces throw their flickering light on the ceiling beams.

Upstairs, it's almost like a different house. White beaded paneling and large windows give the place the bright air of a Nantucket summer cottage. Some renovation has been done up here, primarily in the bathrooms, but Allen and his wife, Marti, have kept to the period, with pedestal sinks and claw-foot tubs (some in the rooms themselves). The bedsteads and dressers are in various styles, but all belonged to the Lathams' forebears. Two equally well-preserved cottages offer more privacy.

Breakfast is served in the dining room in cool months, out on the lakeside porch in summer. There are no TVs, telephones, or air-conditioning. This is pure 1913—they won't be missed.

Address: *11600 Indian Beach Rd. (Box 307), Spicer, MN 56288, tel. 612/796–5870 or 800/821–6675.*
Accommodations: *8 double rooms with baths, 2 cottages.*
Amenities: *Ceiling fans, whirlpool bath in 1 bedroom and 1 cottage.*
Rates: *$60–$130; full breakfast, afternoon tea. AE, D, MC, V.*
Restrictions: *No smoking, no pets; closed weekdays Sept.–Apr.*

Carrington House

Save for its antebellum roof railing, the simple facade of Carrington House gives the deceptive impression that the rest of the house is similarly plain. It's the back that's really inviting—a long, enclosed porch with tall windows faces Lake Carlos, awnings shade the windows, and stairs lead down to a waterside deck.

Built in 1911, this is a typical lakeshore "cottage" of its era. Throughout the house, hardwood floors, high ceilings, and textured-plaster walls contribute to a calm, light-filled setting. The enormous living room, with its big fireplace and wicker furniture, mingles antiques and modern items.

Recently redecorated by owners Janet and Bruce Berg, the guest rooms each have a unique flavor, ranging from simple country to ornate. One unifying motif comes from the different stenciled patterns found on the walls of each room. In back is a cottage with pink furnishings and a whirlpool tub. Though some rooms are a little too frilly, the overall feeling is of a comfortable summer house made for easy relaxation.

Address: *4974 Interlochen Dr., Alexandria, MN 56308, tel. 612/846–7400.*
Accommodations: *4 double rooms with baths, 1 cottage.*
Amenities: *Air-conditioning, ceiling fans, cable TV on porch, whirlpool bath in cottage and 1 bedroom.*
Rates: *$80–$120; full breakfast. No credit cards.*
Restrictions: *No smoking, pets by prior consent.*

Heartland Trail Inn

The village of Dorset—population 38—was once the smallest town in the world to have its own bank. The bank has since closed, and in 1970, so did its three-room, two-story schoolhouse. Still, the town comes alive at night, thanks to four popular restaurants, and it also attracts cyclists on the Heartland Trail that runs between Walker and Park Rapids. Kris and Jim LaFleur became part of the local scene in 1993, when they bought this unusual building—the former schoolhouse, which had already been converted into a B&B.

Surrounded on three sides by fields and woods, the plain clapboard structure with its neat red roof still has a spare, wind-whipped look. The original three schoolrooms have been cleaned up and broken into six bright guest rooms, while the old cloak room was enlarged and turned into a common room for the guests. The refinished maple floors are cool and spotless, the walls freshly painted, and the sliding-glass doors factory-fresh. (Each room opens out onto a deck.) The hallways are furnished with old-fashioned school desks, maps, and chalkboards, and the stairways still show the wear-and-tear of generations of young feet.

Address: *Rte. 3 (Box 39), Park Rapids, MN 56470, tel. 218/732–5305.*
Accommodations: *6 double rooms share 3 baths.*
Amenities: *Air-conditioning, ceiling fans.*
Rates: *$45–$60; full breakfast. MC, V.*
Restrictions: *No smoking, no pets.*

Log House on Spirit Lake and Homestead

Bad weather put Lyle and Yvonne Tweten into the B&B business. After retiring to northern Minnesota, they bought 115 acres on Spirit Lake, built a house, and settled in. Then in 1984 a tornado in McIntosh, Minnesota, hit Lyle's boyhood home, a by-then decrepit white clapboard farmhouse that had been in the family since 1889. Several boards were ripped off, revealing a surprise underneath: The house was made of square-hewn poplar logs. The Twetens moved the structure to their land, setting it on a hill a few steps from the lake, and restored it as a B&B.

Inside the three-story house are the original whitewashed walls, reproduction fir floorboards, and period furnishings. The upstairs bedroom has a dark ceiling beam and old-fashioned rag rugs on the wide-plank floors. The lower-level bedroom is more modern and a bit frilly, but its private deck and porch are built from old silo wood. In 1993, the Twetens opened up the neighboring, turn-of-the-century Homestead, which they redecorated with canopy beds and antique wardrobes. Both homes are perfect for a lake-side retreat.

Address: *Ottertail Rte. 4 (Box 130), Vergas, MN 56587, tel. 218/342–2318 or 800/342–2318.*
Accommodations: *4 double rooms with baths.*
Amenities: *Air-conditioning, terry-cloth robes, fresh flowers, whirlpool bath in 1 bedroom.*
Rates: *$75–$110; full breakfast, welcome tray. D, MC, V.*
Restrictions: *No smoking, no pets.*

Nims' Bakketop Hus

Bakketop Hus means "Hilltop House" in Norwegian, and it's an appropriate name—the hillside views of rural Long Lake are perhaps the strongest asset of this large house, which Dennis and Judy Nims turned into a bed-and-breakfast when their kids grew up. (Judy is of Norwegian ancestry, hence the inn's name.) While there are some antique items here, most notably the huge buffet that dominates the living room, the overall decor befits a house built in 1975. It's essentially a suburban split-level writ larger than usual, with some rustic touches.

The mauve-and-blue Master Suite, popular with newlyweds, offers a skylight, an oversized whirlpool hot tub, and a view of the front garden. Another guest room, which opens onto a lakeview patio, has peach country French decor, with a draped canopy bed and a love seat.

Downstairs, a game room with pool table and player piano is available for guests, as is a large outdoor deck facing the lake.

Address: *R.R. 2 (Box 187A), Fergus Falls, MN 56537, tel. 218/739–2915.*
Accommodations: *3 double rooms with baths.*
Amenities: *Air-conditioning, cable TV and phones in rooms, oversized whirlpool in 1 bedroom.*
Rates: *$60–$95; full breakfast, evening refreshments. D, MC, V.*
Restrictions: *No smoking, pets by prior consent.*

Peace Cliff

Although this bed-and-breakfast isn't a historic old house—David and Kathy Laursen finished building the half-timbered, Tudor-style structure in 1989—it takes advantage of its lovely Leech Lake location with sunset views from every room.

The living room features an antique French tapestry; the dining room has Eastlake furniture. Upstairs in the tower, a Ralph Lauren–style library has tartan-covered rockers, leather wing chairs, and built-in bookcases. Two guest rooms are up here: the Belgian, with an immense 300-year-old walnut bedstead, and the Victorian, with an iron bedstead and floral wallpaper. In the bottom story are three other guest rooms, including the French Room, with its ornate furnishings.

Perhaps the house is still too new for all these weighty antiques, but Peace Cliff's most important assets—nature and the sunsets and serenading loons—make for not a bad retreat.

Address: *HCR 73 (Box 998D), Walker, MN 56484, tel. 218/547–2832.*
Accommodations: *3 double rooms with baths, 1 single with bath, 1 suite.*
Amenities: *Cable TV/VCR in common room.*
Rates: *$37–$100; full breakfast, evening refreshments. AE, D, MC, V.*
Restrictions: *No smoking, no pets; 2-night minimum summer weekends.*

Prairie View Estate

Thank goodness for Norwegian bachelor farmers who throw nothing away. When sisters Phyllis Haugrud, Carol Moses, and Janet Malakowsky inherited the 800-acre family farm from their unmarried uncle in 1990, his will forbade them to sell it. Inside this Craftsmanesque beige stucco house, they found loads of old family furniture, and decided to turn the home into a B&B.

Exposed rafters and dark wood furnishings—some more than 100 years old—create a portrait not only of old Minnesota farm life, but also of Old Norway. The three guest rooms have solid, well-made antiques—not fancy pieces, but often beautiful.

Some restoration has yet to be completed, but it's easy to ignore the remaining details when you sit enjoying breakfast on the lovely long, enclosed porch with hardwood floors. At Prairie View Estate, the past is alive and well.

Address: *Rte. 2 (Box 443), Pelican Rapids, MN 56572, tel. 218/863–4321.*
Accommodations: *1 double room with bath, 2 doubles share bath.*
Amenities: *Air-conditioning.*
Rates: *$35–$50; full breakfast, evening refreshments. D, MC, V.*
Restrictions: *No smoking, no pets.*

Stonehouse Bed and Breakfast

Stonemason Craig Nagel and his wife, Claire, built Stonehouse in 1988 on wooded acreage that's just a short walk from Lund Lake, a marsh with nesting birds. The low-angled house is somewhat stark and ordinary from the outside, but the Nagels have emphasized a sense of nature. The exterior walls are made of cedar and stone that Craig prepared; the pine interior walls and floors came from trees right on the property. Craig also split the stones for the fireplace. Claire added decorations and crafted the stained glass that appears here and there throughout the house.

There's a double bed in the bedroom and a queen-size bed in the living area, so up to four people can stay here at a time. Though comfortable, furnishings may remind some visitors of a good-quality motel—track lighting, nubby wall-to-wall carpeting, modern TV and kitchen appliances. One may wish that the Stonehouse were more eccentric and charming, like the Nagel's own house nearby, where breakfast is served. Still, this homemade (and well-made) cottage has the right location, nestled in a grove of pine trees, and its screened porch and stone-walled terrace are pleasant.

Address: *HCR 2 (Box 9), Pequot Lakes, MN 56472, tel. 218/568–4255.*
Accommodations: *1 cottage with double bed and queen-size bed.*
Amenities: *TV/VCR, kitchen.*
Rates: *$85–$115; full breakfast. MC, V.*
Restrictions: *No pets.*

Tianna Farms

Once a large, working dairy farm, this wooded 55-acre estate was opened as a bed-and-breakfast in 1991 by Peter Hawkins and Liza Vogt, grandchildren of the original dairy farmer. Though its outlines resemble a New England beach cottage, the 1920s-era house has an unadorned modernism that's part Prairie style, part Bauhaus.

Several details of the decor date from the mid-1970s, where the house underwent its last major redecoration, and they don't always work—the living room's handsome stone fireplace, for example, doesn't quite look right with the floral-upholstered sofas—but Frank Lloyd Wright himself would probably have approved of the library. The guest rooms are also a mixed bag. On the first floor, the twin-bedded Garden Room is country frilly. Upstairs, the Hunting Room looks heartily masculine, with maple floor, rifle collection, and woody-brown area rug.

The grounds include a tennis court, a greenhouse, and an elaborate wild-flower garden with an artificial waterfall.

Address: *Box 629, Walker, MN 56484, tel. 218/547–1306.*
Accommodations: *4 double rooms with baths, 1 suite.*
Amenities: *Air-conditioning, cable TV in living room and library; swimming dock, tennis.*
Rates: *$55–$110; full breakfast. D, MC, V.*
Restrictions: *No smoking indoors, pets by prior consent.*

Walden Woods

It's not nearly as austere as Thoreau's famous cabin in Massachusetts, but Walden Woods has the same back-to-basics spirit. Fourteen years ago, Richard Manly, a Minnesota-trained forester who had worked many years for the Audubon Society in New York City, built his own log cabin near Mud Lake, a wooded pond about 17 miles east of Brainerd.

Though recently constructed, Walden Woods doesn't look raw or artificially rustic. The Manlys' quietly tasteful antique furnishings, in an eclectic mix of styles, work well inside these Norwegian pine walls. A porch faces the pond and the surrounding woods. Up the split-log staircase is a well-stocked library. The guest rooms all have hardwood floors, antique bedsteads, and subdued floral curtains, and Anne Manly, a straw-weaver and basketmaker, has accented them with her work.

The worthier elements of civilization are provided—bathrooms are up-to-date, though with older-style fixtures. There are many beautiful clocks here, but the Manlys don't bother to wind them. As for TV and air-conditioning, who needs them when you can listen to the loons serenade at dusk on "Walden Pond"?

Address: *16070 Rte. 18 SE, Deerwood, MN 56444, tel. 612/692–4379.*
Accommodations: *4 double rooms share 2 baths.*
Rates: *$55–$75; full breakfast. AE, MC, V.*
Restrictions: *No smoking, no pets.*

Whistle Stop Inn

Named for its proximity to a set of railroad tracks, this 1903 Queen Anne Victorian opened as a B&B in 1992. Owners Jann and Roger Lee had always dreamed of opening a bed-and-breakfast, and while vacationing in Roger's hometown of New York Mills, they spotted the perfect house. They bought it and opened for business six months later. Originally owned by August Nylan, a Finnish newspaperman, the house's exterior is standard Victorian, but the Lees have added a whimsical touch inside while maintaining the original elegance.

Filled with railroad memorabilia and nostalgia—miniature trains, a red 1947 Coca-Cola machine, and even a mannequin dressed in authentic railroad gear—the parlor is almost a museum.

The rest of the house is more classically decorated with period antiques and photos of the Nylan family. Upstairs, the blue-and-rose Northern Pacific Room has a delicate but sizable antique armoire and a claw-foot tub. The sunny Great Northern Suite has the original pine woodwork and built-in glass shelves. A remarkably appointed house in every way, the Whistle Stop even has a working sauna.

Address: *Rte. 1 (Box 85), New York Mills, MN 56567, tel. 218/385–2223.*
Accommodations: *2 double rooms with baths, 1 suite.*
Amenities: *Ceiling fans; cable TV in suite and 1 bedroom; sauna.*
Rates: *$39–$59; full breakfast, evening refreshments upon request. MC, V.*
Restrictions: *Smoking on porch only, no pets.*

The Southwestern Prairie

Southwestern Minnesota, along with St. Louis and Texas, once
served as a gateway to the American West. The West that
begins here is the northern prairie, a vast sea of grass that
sustained herds of buffalo. This expanse was also the home of
one of the greatest of all Native American nations, the
Dakota—otherwise known as the Sioux, although that's
actually an insulting term that roughly means "snake." The
Dakota considered the region near the South Dakota border
sacred, and they quarried its soft red stone to make peace
pipes (hence the town named Pipestone). They believed that
their tribe originated here, and that the color of the stone came
from the blood of their ancestors.

The white people who settled here were predominantly German
and Scandinavian immigrants who brought with them
cherished relics of their homelands—the German influence in
New Ulm, for example, is still very strong. For all the prairie's
beauty, what the newer settlers valued even more was its rich
soil. Families like the Ingallses, whose daughter Laura grew
up to immortalize her Walnut Grove home in such books as
The Little House on the Prairie, were called sodbusters
because they had to plow up dense mats of roots to plant their
corn. It took a lot of pioneer grit, but once the land was plowed,
it yielded good crops.

On the prairie, the pleasures of life are generally on a small-
town scale. Many towns proudly celebrate their heritage with
summer events such as Pipestone's annual Civil War Festival
and Walnut Grove's yearly Little House pageant. Their small
county historical museums provide fodder for an hour's low-
key browsing, nothing more. St. Peter, a trim college town in
the bucolic Minnesota River Valley, was originally planned as
Minnesota's capital (until St. Paul's wheeler-dealers stole that
plum for themselves), and it still has the original wide streets,
along which parade many gracious homes. Other county seats,
such as Blue Earth and Pipestone, are equally prosperous and
charming, with typically handsome country courthouses

(often constructed from the same local quartzite that you can occasionally see cropping out even in the farm fields). The southwestern prairie's lesser communities, although pleasant, are practical rather than beautiful; many communities lost a good deal of their historic charm during the 1960s, when the main streets were modernized.

When it comes to outdoor activities, the offerings are quietly unspectacular. There's fishing and swimming in many fine small lakes here, especially around New Ulm and Mankato, but don't expect the pine-ringed, sky-blue waters of the North. The prairie terrain makes for pleasant, if unchallenging, cycling; a 68-mile loop has been mapped around the Pipestone countryside.

The mid-19th-century white settlers called the land "plains" because it is relatively flat and treeless. The prairie, however, is in fact anything but plain: It is one of the richest and most subtly beautiful ecosystems on earth. These days, farming has made untouched prairie as hard to find as the great herds of buffalo that once grazed here, but there are untilled patches to be found. Good places to start are in several of the state parks: Blue Mound State Park (near Luverne) has some attractive grasslands as well as a small buffalo herd; you'll also find grasslands in the Kilen Woods, near Worthington. Make your base camp in a town, then go out and explore the world of the Dakota. Like many things of subtle beauty, the prairie is better appreciated the more you learn about it.

Places to Go, Sights to See

August Schell Brewery (Schell Park, 18th St. S., off Rte. 15, Box 128, New Ulm, tel. 507/354–5528). One of the prettiest little breweries in the United States, Schell's is set on the founder's estate, where there is also a mansion and a deer park. It's not only the source of some fine beer (its Pils and Weiss beers have won national awards), it's also rich in regional history, for beer has been brewed here for more than 125 years. Schell's survived the Dakota conflict of 1862, local historians claim, because the Schell family maintained good relations with the local Dakota. Tours (including beer tastings) are available.

Katherine Ordway Prairie (near Sunburg, 7 mi southwest of Brooten, tel. 612/331–0750). Managed by the Minnesota Chapter of the Nature Conservancy, the Ordway Prairie comprises 582 acres of sharply rolling hills with numerous moist lowlands. It was once cultivated, and has not yet been completely taken over again by prairie plants, but it is still one of the best places in the state to see what Minnesota looked like before the coming of the *wasicu* (the Dakota term for "white man").

Laura Ingalls Wilder Museum (330 8th St., Walnut Grove, tel. 507/859–2358). Exhibits depict the life of the *Little House on the Prairie* author and her family, as well as the early history of the tiny town of Walnut Grove. Memorabilia include Laura's hand-stitched quilt, family photos, and a bench from the Congregational Church attended by the Ingalls family. The museum is generally open daily from May through October, with visits by appointment during the rest of the year, but it's best to call ahead.

Lower Sioux Agency (Box 125, Morton, tel. 507/697–6321). The Interpretive Center at this Mdewakanton Dakota community, set in the Minnesota River Valley south of Willmar, is key to understanding Dakota life and culture. Also on the grounds are Tipi Maka Duta, the Lower Sioux pottery shop, and St. Cornelia's Episcopal Church (listed on the National Register of Historic Sites). A powwow, open to the public, is held the second weekend in June.

New Ulm Glockenspiel (Schonlau Park Plaza, 4th and Minnesota Sts., New Ulm). New Ulm, settled by German immigrants in 1854, was nearly destroyed in the Dakota Conflict of 1862. Animated figures in this 45-foot-high musical clock tower depict the town's history daily at noon, 3 PM, and 5 PM, while the 37 bells in the carillon ring on the hour.

Pipestone Historic District (stop by Pipestone County Museum, 113 Hiawatha Ave. S, tel. 507/825–2563). Guided tours (on request) or self-guided tours (outlined in a free brochure) explore the historic center of the town of Pipestone, where 20 buildings are listed on the National Register of Historic Places. Nearly all were built before the turn of the century; local quartzite was used to render the then-fashionable heavy Romanesque style, which is full of quirky details.

Pipestone National Monument (1 mi north of Pipestone, then ½ mi west, tel. 507/825–5464). These quarries were legendary throughout Native America for their soft red stone, prized for making the sacred calumets (peace pipes) used by the Dakota and other tribes as well. Native craftspeople still quarry and make pipes here. The 283-acre monument also features an Indian Culture Center and walking trail.

Sod House on the Prairie (Rte. 2, Sanborn, tel. 507/723–5138). This authentic reconstruction of two pioneer sod houses—a poor man's dugout and a richer man's "soddy"—is open as a small museum of early settlers' life; it is also available for overnight guests as a bed-and-breakfast (*see below*).

Restaurants

Minnesota's special restaurants are nearly all in the eastern part of the state, but the **Calumet Inn** (104 W. Main St., Pipestone, tel. 507/825–5871) has a restaurant that's highly regarded for its creative touch with beef and pork. In New Ulm, the **Glockenspiel Haus** (400 N. Minnesota St., tel. 507/354–5593) serves good German food and the locally brewed Schell's beer. Though it's not the colorful joint it once was, the **Magnolia Steak House** (U.S. 75 exit off I–90, Luverne, tel. 507/283–9161) still has custom-aged beef, and its onion rings are legendary.

Tourist Information

Mankato Chamber and Convention Bureau (112 Riverfront Dr., Mankato, MN 56001, tel. 507/345–4519); **Minnesota Office of Tourism, Southern Regional Office** (Box 286, Mankato, MN 56001, tel. 507/389–2683); **New Ulm Chamber of Commerce** (1 N. Minnesota St., New Ulm, MN 56073, tel. 507/354–4217); **Pipestone Chamber of Commerce** (Box 8, Pipestone, MN 56164, tel. 507/825–3316).

Park Row Bed and Breakfast

L ike many of the older large houses in rural Minnesota, Ann Burck-hardt's bed-and-breakfast, a few blocks from St. Peter's Main Street, is two houses fused together. The larger of the two, a Carpenter Gothic, was built in 1874 with wooden gingerbread trim on its porch railings and eaves. In 1903, the house was purchased by a probate-court judge, who added what was tantamount to another building, a Queen Anne–style wing with an apron porch and a turreted circular staircase. After the judge's death in the 1930s, his home suffered the fate of many such big houses: It was turned into a duplex. A local professor bought it in 1971, bringing it back to its eclectic late-Victorian grace.

It's this combination of styles that Ann, who bought the house in 1989, has maintained in her decor. The interior is as eclectic as the exterior, but it has a homey Victorian look, as opposed to the dark, heavy version of Victorian. The downstairs is light and spacious. In the dining room, where a huge bay window draws in daylight from three directions, late-Victorian antiques blend with modern reproductions. Small-scale furnishings, bright stained-glass windows, and lace curtains reinforce the sense of sunshine and fresh air.

Each of the four guest rooms is furnished with period antiques and has its own ethnic theme. But Ann is not heavy-handed about it, and is simply out to create a *feeling* of Englishness (or Frenchness, or Germanness).

There's a Norwegian-style painted floor in the Scandinavian Room. In other rooms, bright colors and fabrics project the same decorative frilliness as the exterior gingerbread. It never gets cutesy, however.

"I want my guests to feel as if they're stepping back into 1910," Burckhardt says. Granted, it's a somewhat modernized 1910—there's wall-to-wall carpeting, done in a Victorian pattern—but the shower you take will be in a claw-foot tub with its original oak rim, and there will be no TV in your bedroom.

Expect an exceptional breakfast. The indefatigable Burckhardt commutes 66 miles to Minneapolis three days a week to work as a food journalist, so food is a passion with her. And, since she is a writer, reading is another passion: Books and magazines, mostly of local and regional interest, are displayed throughout the house. Pleasures here are quiet ones, but never unrewarding.

Address: *525 W. Park Row, St. Peter, MN 56082, tel. 507/931–2495.*
Accommodations: *4 double rooms share 2 baths.*
Amenities: *Air-conditioning, cable TV in living room.*
Rates: *$44–$69; full breakfast. D, MC, V.*
Restrictions: *No smoking, no pets.*

Sod House on the Prairie

When Stan McCone was growing up, older relatives told him tales of his forebears—sod-busting white settlers of the Great Plains, just like those that Willa Cather and Laura Ingalls Wilder wrote about. Since few trees sprouted on the grasslands, pioneers literally built their houses out of the earth. These sod houses, made of blocks of cut turf, were held together by the dense root systems of the prairie grass.

McCone dreamed of re-creating this lost type of architecture. After working for several years as a cattle buyer, he got a chance to make his dream come true when he learned that one of his neighbors in rural Sanborn had a patch of virgin prairie on his land. Soon Stan set to work, with the same kind of grit and sweat as his pioneer ancestors, cutting massive blocks of sod (he describes the sound as "the ripping of a giant canvas"). The result is two buildings set amid acres of (reseeded) prairie grass: a rudimentary "poor man's dugout" and a larger "rich man's soddy," both open to the public as a museum. For those who want a full dose of pioneer experience, the larger is a snug, rustic bed-and-breakfast.

The house's furnishings—antique bedsteads and buffets, kitchen and farm implements hanging on the walls and beams—are practical and sturdily beautiful. The only piece that could be considered at all fancy is the leather fainting couch that doubles as a bed,

across which is spread a heavy, shaggy buffalo-hide blanket.

Authenticity is the key word here. There are no wires or pipes running through the soddy's turf walls—heating comes from a potbellied stove, air-conditioning from open windows, light from oil lamps. The bathroom is a two-seat outhouse steps away; to wash, guests must pour water from a jug into the 100-year-old pitcher and bowl.

The McCones provide a simple, hearty country breakfast, incorporating high-quality meats, which is Stan's other line of business. If you want to cook your other meals, throw some logs into the mighty Monarch stove. One family spent a prairie Christmas here, cooking up a feast on the Monarch, with the soddy so snug that the kids padded about in shorts. Though few of us today would want to live day to day with the rigors of pioneer life, we can still savor a sample of it, thanks to Stan McCone.

Address: *Rte. 2 (Box 75), Sanborn, MN 56083, tel. 507/723–5138.*
Accommodations: *1 house with 2 double beds and outhouse.*
Amenities: *Wood-burning stoves.*
Rates: *$60—125; full breakfast. No credit cards.*
Restrictions: *No smoking, pets by prior consent.*

Fering's Guest House

Charles and Phyllis Fering freely admit that Blue Earth, while attractive, isn't a tourist hot spot, despite its attractive courthouse, many antiques shops, and lovely woods. The same can be said of this large frame Victorian house, built in 1889, where the Ferings have lived for more than 20 years. Rather than being a renovated showplace, it looks like the ideal small-town home, all porch and tall windows with a lush, shady yard. Original oak woodwork exists alongside more recent birch paneling and country-style wallpaper; family knickknacks are scattered about. When the Ferings opened their bed-and-breakfast in 1990, after most of their kids had grown and gone, they expected to attract folks who were just looking for a good night's lodging.

Still, the Ferings' guests often send them Christmas cards, bottles of wine, invitations to visit. Why? "We're like family," says Charles. They're affable, open-minded, and flexible—for example, although they usually serve only Continental breakfasts, once when guests were stranded by a sudden snowstorm, they whipped up three square meals a day until the snow cleared. That's small-town America for you.

Address: *708 N. Main St., Blue Earth, MN 56013, tel. 507/526–5054.*
Accommodations: *1 double room with bath, 2 doubles share bath.*
Amenities: *Air-conditioning, cable TV and phones in bedrooms.*
Rates: *$40—45; Continental breakfast. No credit cards.*
Restrictions: *No smoking, no pets.*

Prairie House on Round Lake

In 1879, Chicago commodity trader Owen Roche built this grand American Bracket-style house, nicknamed "Roche's Roost" and surrounded by a 2,500-acre estate on Round Lake. It's smaller than it used to be, having been truncated to save money during the Depression (in an odd twist, the bottom floor rather than the top was removed); the estate has shrunk to 44 acres, but it still remains a good place to escape urban stress.

Now owned by horse-breeders Ralph and Virginia Schenck, the house is set amid horse barns and wildlife preserves. Inside, there are some antiques (claw-foot tubs, some fine old tables) and beamed ceilings, but the wall-to-wall carpets, modern bathroom fixtures, and other furnishings suggest the interior of a suburban home more

than a country inn. Fresh flowers from the Schencks' greenhouse and the whinnying of their American paint horses help to remind you of your rural surroundings. Canada geese, white pelicans, and other waterfowl thrive in peace here. Outside of outdoor recreation, there isn't much to do here—but that's enough.

Address: *R.R. 1 (Box 97), Round Lake, MN 56167, tel. 507/945–8934.*
Accommodations: *1 double room with bath, 1 double with half-bath, 2 doubles share bath.*
Amenities: *Air-conditioning, lakeside beach, tennis court.*
Rates: *$45–$55; full breakfast. No credit cards.*
Restrictions: *No smoking, pets by prior consent.*

Wisconsin

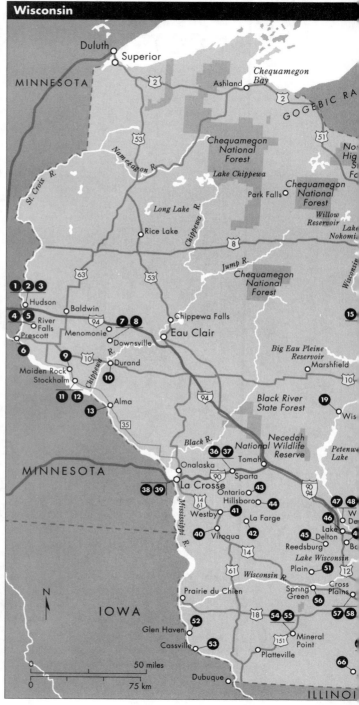

Wisconsin

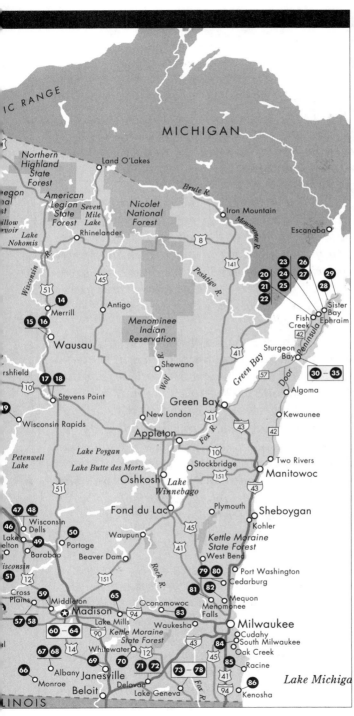

Milwaukee and Southeast Wisconsin

With a population of about 640,000, Milwaukee is Wisconsin's largest city and the nation's 24th largest; it covers nearly 96 square miles and has more than 15 suburbs. Metropolitan Greater Milwaukee includes a four-county area with a population of nearly 1.4 million.

Nonetheless, a genial atmosphere prevails in Milwaukee, which seems like not so much a big city as a large collection of neighborhoods with respect for small-town values. Streets are clean, homes are tidy, parks and green spaces abound. Modern steel and glass high rises occupy much of the downtown area, but the city's early heritage persists in the restored and well-kept 19th-century buildings that share the city skyline.

That heritage is diverse. Most Native Americans were gone by the mid-1840s, but a few Potawatomi huts could still be found as late as 1854 in what is now downtown Milwaukee. The city's population in 1845 was about 10,000, more than half of German descent. Many Germans arrived in the 1850s, along with Italians, Poles, Scandinavians, Serbs, and Irish. By the last half of the 19th century, Milwaukee's German population was so large that the city was often called the German Athens. Only the Polish and Irish populations came close in numbers, and English was rarely heard in some neighborhoods. The German influence is still found throughout the city in architecture, in language, and especially in food, with a legacy of Old World restaurants.

Today the city claims more than 50 ethnic groups and celebrates its "melting pot" origins with all kinds of ethnic and cultural festivals, along with the annual State Fair. Milwaukee has become known as the "city of festivals," stemming from the nationally known Summerfest, which kicks off each summer's activities on a Lake Michigan lakefront park. Another annual highlight is the Great Circus Parade, a July spectacle that features scores of antique circus

*wagons from the famed Circus World Museum in Baraboo.
More than a million people line the streets to watch it.*

*Besides the spectacular festivals, Milwaukeeans are proud of
their 137 parks, the Brewers baseball team, the lakefront, the
zoo, and the horticultural domes in Mitchell Park. The art and
natural history museums are quite good. The Milwaukee
Symphony plays at the Performing Arts Center, and there are
top-notch opera, ballet, and repertory companies.*

*Since Milwaukee is one of a handful of Midwest cities that has
a skywalk system, visitors staying in large downtown hotels
can walk to restaurants, shops, theaters, and sporting events
without having to step outdoors. The Riverspan part of the
system is the only skywalk in the nation built over a navigable
waterway, the Milwaukee River.*

*Milwaukeeans will readily admit their city doesn't dazzle like
Houston, or charm like San Francisco. But they don't mind.
At the same time, the city lacks the hard edge of a Detroit or a
Chicago, and they don't mind that, either.*

Places to Go, Sights to See

Cedarburg. Restored to achieve the look of the 1840s, when German immigrants first harnessed the nearby creek to power their new mills, the entire downtown area of Cedarburg has been listed on the National Register of Historic Places. One of those mills now houses the Stone Mill Winery (tel. 414/377–8020), which offers tours, and the adjoining Cedar Creek Settlement, a restored village jammed with restaurants, art galleries, and shops. The Ozaukee Art Center (tel. 414/377–8230), in a former brewery, displays the works of regional artists. Wisconsin's oldest covered bridge spans Cedar Creek just 3 miles from town.

Lake Geneva. Ringing the lakeshore are the country houses of the 19th-century wealthy, who could afford country quiet. Today's activities center around the water. There are seven public beaches, and boating is quite popular. A 26-mile footpath circles the lake, and there are 10 public golf courses and 10 hiking trails nearby, some of which are used for skiing in winter. Old World Wisconsin (north on Rte. 67, tel. 414/594–2116), a 50-building settlement comprising historic farmsteads and a village, is a short drive away.

Milwaukee. Beer made this city famous, but there's more to it than breweries, bratwurst, and ballparks. Its true life and backbone are found in its pockets of German, Polish, Serbian, African-American, Irish, and other ethnic communities.

Numerous festivals, parades, and restaurants celebrate the city's diversity. It has always had a lively arts scene; its reputation as a center of publishing and graphics design is growing. The Performing Arts Center (929 N. Water St., tel. 414/273–7206) boasts a symphony orchestra, as well as ballet, opera, and theater companies. The Broadway Theater Center (158 N. Broadway, tel. 414/291–7800) houses theater and light opera companies. The Milwaukee Repertory Theater, (108 E. Wells St., tel. 414/224–1761) a major regional company, is housed in a new theater complex. In an Eero Saarinen–designed lakefront building, the Milwaukee Art Museum (750 N. Lincoln Memorial Dr., tel. 414/224–3220) exhibits an impressive array of 19th- and 20th-century American and European artwork. The Milwaukee Public Museum (800 W. Wells St., tel. 414/278–2700) contains the fourth-largest collection of natural-history exhibits in the United States.

Racine. This city's best-known attraction, the S.C. Johnson Wax Building (1525 Howe St., tel. 414/631–2154), was designed by Frank Lloyd Wright and built in the 1930s, but it still looks like an office structure of the future. Free tours are given Tuesday to Friday; reservations are required.

Restaurants

One of the brightest stars in Wisconsin's culinary flag is **Sanford's** (1547 N. Jackson, Milwaukee, tel. 414/276–9608), an upscale storefront restaurant serving Franco-Californian creations. But ethnic fare is Milwaukee's specialty, and the proof is there for the eating at longtime favorites like **Karl Ratsch's Old World** (320 E. Mason St., tel. 414/276–2720), which serves German food, and **Old Town** (522 W. Lincoln, tel. 414/672–0206), where Serbian dishes are offered. In Kenosha, the place to eat is **Mangia** (5717 Sheridan Rd., tel. 414/652–4285), where inventive contemporary Italian dishes are served in an equally contemporary setting alongside the town square. **St. Moritz** (327 Wrigley Dr., tel. 414/248–6680), a Queen Anne summer cottage (read: mansion) on the shores of Lake Geneva, is proud of its *mesclún* salad, its garlicky rack of lamb, and other dishes featuring Wisconsin veal and salmon. For wood-smoked ribs and prime rib in a casual setting in Lake Geneva, head for **Celebration** (422 Wells St., tel. 414/248–2555).

Tourist Information

Cedarburg Visitor Information Center (City Hall, W63N645 Washington Ave., Cedarburg, WI 53012, tel. 414/377–9620); **Greater Milwaukee Convention & Visitors Bureau** (510 W. Kilbourne Ave., Milwaukee, WI 53203, tel. 800/231–0903, fax 414/273–5596); **Lake Geneva Area Chamber of Commerce** (201 Wrigley Dr., Lake Geneva, WI 53147, tel. 414/248–4416).

Allyn Mansion Inn

When Alexander Allyn built this palatial mansion in 1885 with Milwaukee architect E. Townsend Mix, his motto might well have been "If you've got it, flaunt it—and do it in good taste." Current owners Joe Johnson and Ron Markwell followed that dictum when renovating Allyn's home, which for decades had served as a furniture store and nursing home. The house, listed on the National Register of Historic Places, is considered Wisconsin's best-preserved example of the Queen Anne Eastlake style.

The duo filled the mansion's 23 rooms with American antiques that, along with six original gasoliers, French walnut woodwork, parquet floors, and 10 Italian marble fireplaces—four topped with grand Eastlake mirrors—create the very picture of late 19th-century elegance. The high coved ceilings in each of the three parlors have been repainted with floral scrollwork, as in Allyn's day, following the designs that were uncovered during restoration. The front room glitters with gold French wallpaper, and green velvet portières dangle from walnut rings over the doorway. Shutters on the tall windows shield the room's stately grandfather clock, Victorian tufted-silk sofa, and matching chairs from sunlight, and a cribbage board made from a walrus tusk stands ready on the marble coffee table. In another parlor is an 1890 Steinway grand piano originally from a convent (and now the focus of the inn's musicales). The dining room displays English china from Chicago's 1893 Columbian Exposition. In the library, floor-to-ceiling bookshelves accommodate a collection of books about the Windy City. The bathroom beyond has a galvanized tin tub dating from the 1880s, and the kitchen, anchored by a regal cream enamel stove manufactured in 1930, displays a calendar clock and a complete set of Flow Blue china.

The Empire Room is furnished completely in that period's antiques and dazzles guests with an 1830 tester bed and the slipper sofa at its foot, a mirror, fireplace clock, game table, curvy settee, and marble-topped table. In the Mary Elizabeth Room, guests can relax on the chaise longue before bedding down on the 10-foot-tall half-tester with velvet drapery.

Enormous trees and colorful flower beds surround the house, and the grand porte cochere, a replica, will have you looking for carriages to drive up and complete the picture.

Address: *511 E. Walworth Ave., Delavan, WI 53115, tel. 414/728–9090.*
Accommodations: *8 double rooms share 7 baths.*
Amenities: *Air-conditioning.*
Rates: *$80–$90, $50 single weekdays; full breakfast, evening refreshments. MC, V.*
Restrictions: *No smoking, no pets.*

The Hitching Post

There really is a stone hitching post next to this inn. The original was used to tether the horse belonging to Dr. William Hoyt, a distinguished doctor who began the home for his family in 1869. Dr. Post died in 1870 and the house was completed by his wife, Nancy, who, with no formal medical training, also took over her husband's practice and kept the household together until her son George completed medical school and took over both the practice and the home. The Colonial Revival home, now owned by Holly Smith, sits on a large, shaded, one-acre suburban lot at the edge of Menomonee Falls, a half-hour from downtown Milwaukee. Holly has landscaped the yard with lilac bushes, a wildflower garden, and 2,000 daylilies. Every spring, she adds to the garden color with hundreds of annuals.

The bright and airy living room, painted white and accented with floral stenciling, contains a number of Smith family antiques, including a mirror over the fireplace that belonged to Holly's great-grandfather and a large table clock. There are more antiques in the family room, where a comfortable sofa and easy chairs surround the fireplace. "In the winter, guests always find their way in here because it's so warm and embracing when we light a fire," Holly says.

Upstairs are two guest rooms. Dr. William's Room is furnished with an antique cedar chest, an antique rocker, and a king-size canopy bed with a cab-bage-rose pattern in pinks and greens on both the canopy and comforter. Dr. George's Room is decorated with blue-and-yellow sponge-painted designs, and is furnished with a maple double bed that belonged to Holly's grandfather; the quilt covering the bed was sewn by Holly's grandmother. Just down the hall from the guest rooms, Holly keeps a guest library of hundreds of best sellers, mysteries, and classics. Both guest rooms share the 1930s bathroom, which still contains a six-foot tub that's ideal for a long, relaxing soak, as well as the original sink, now topped by an antique mirror.

Holly serves her breakfast of home-made pastries and muffins, eggs, fresh fruit, juice, and gourmet coffee in the dining room, with its cabinet displaying Smith family china and silver, outdoors on the deck overlooking the wildflower garden, or in the guest rooms.

Address: *N88 W16954 Main St., Menomonee Falls, WI 53051, tel. 414/255–1496, fax 414/255–4552.*
Accommodations: *2 double rooms share bath.*
Amenities: *Air-conditioning, free newspaper, robes in rooms; nearby bike trail, pool, tennis courts.*
Rates: *$60–$75; full breakfast, evening refreshments. MC, V.*
Restrictions: *No smoking indoors, no pets.*

The Manor House

When auto executive James Wilson became vice president of the Nash Motor Company, headquartered in Kenosha, he had this grand estate constructed. Wilson's stately 1924 French Renaissance revival mansion, its brick and stone walls covered with ivy and topped by a slate roof, is designed in the style of the great English manor houses. Located in the city's Lakeshore Historic District, surrounded by other opulent homes and just across the road from Lake Michigan, the Manor is listed in the National Register of Historic Places. Encircled by landscaped grounds with towering trees and a wonderful formal English garden that includes some 40 species of carefully tended ornamental trees and shrubs, a sunken pool with a fountain, and a gazebo and arbor, the house could easily be the setting for a *Masterpiece Theater* presentation.

Guests enter the grand hall, with its heavy woodwork, slate floor, and thick rugs. A wide central stairway leads to the upstairs rooms. To the left down a wide hallway is the living room, which occupies one end of the first floor. A fireplace and a grand piano are the center of attention here. The library is paneled in mahogany, and contains a fireplace with marble and mahogany facing. The more informally decorated sunroom provides a view of the formal gardens. The grand dining room, with oak panelling, also has a fireplace. Guests eat at a massive table under the room's elaborate crystal chandelier.

Upstairs, the mansion's third-floor ballroom has been converted to a luxury suite that retains the original dark oak beams and coffered ceiling. A private balcony affords a view of Lake Michigan. Five large rooms on the second floor—three of which have lake views, and all of which have private baths and were recently redecorated—are furnished in Queen Anne antiques and reproductions. The mansion's carriage house was recently divided into two luxury suites.

Lest guests feel that The Manor really is a stuffy English country house, owner Laurie Novak-Simmons puts everyone at ease with snacks in the kitchen, piano-playing in the living room, and friendly conversation everywhere. She serves breakfast in the guest rooms, the garden, or in the dining room.

Address: *6536 3rd Ave., Kenosha, WI 53143, tel. 414/658–0014.*
Accommodations: *5 rooms with baths, 3 suites.*
Amenities: *Air-conditioning, phone, cable TV in rooms; whirlpool in 3 suites, honor bar in library, snacks and ice in kitchen; access to tennis courts, bike trails, fishing wharf, marina.*
Rates: *$99–$199; full breakfast. AE, MC, V.*
Restrictions: *No smoking in rooms. Inquire about pets.*

The Mansards on-the-Lake

This Second Empire–style house, built in 1867, sports a green mansard roof and neat rows of dormers. The structure has been occupied by a string of fascinating people: Its first owners were an inventor and his wife, a suffragette who worked as an editor; they were followed by a family of musicians and a circus acrobat whose wife, also a circus performer, did trick horseback riding. Today's owner is a retired Russian-language teacher who inherited the house and many of its furnishings from her mother.

The second and third floors are now self-contained suites, each with a living room, a bedroom, a bathroom, and a kitchen. The high-ceilinged Polonaise Suite, on the second floor, is decorated with theatrical posters from Eastern Europe that the innkeeper collected during study tours. Its kitchen has a full-size refrigerator, stove, and microwave oven, and is stocked with the makings for breakfast, including cheeses and the locally famous pretzel-shaped pastry known as Danish Kringle. The dining area, though small, has a view of Lake Michigan and contains a lively display of Polish circus posters, cut paper, and framed embroidery. Still other theatrical posters, these for European productions of *Romeo and Juliet* and *The Student Prince*, hang in the bedroom. An old-fashioned, metal, ice-cream parlor table and chairs sit beside the room's sunny bay windows. The crocheted bedspread was made by the innkeeper's mother who sat in the very

same wooden rocker you can relax in today. French doors open to a balcony with a lake view. The bathroom is "bigger than an airplane's," says the host—though not by much; it contains a tub and shower.

The third-floor Garret Suite has a Bohemian artist-in-residence ambience. Low dormer windows punctuate the sloped walls, and the living room is full of books and magazines. The white reproduction French provincial–style furnishings do little to enhance the room's charm—the living room's sectional sofa does even less. But a 1950s-style chrome dinette gives the kitchen lots of character, and its terrific view of the lake doesn't hurt, either. Here, too, the refrigerator is stocked with breakfast fixings.

This inn is a good bet for families or for guests who will be in town for longish stays. The back yard leads straight to Lake Michigan, and Racine's historic district is a stroll away.

Address: *827 Lake Ave., Racine, WI 53403, tel. 414/632–1135.*
Accommodations: *2 suites.*
Amenities: *Air-conditioning on 3rd floor, ceiling fans on 2nd floor.*
Rates: *$50–$65; breakfast fixings stocked in kitchens; MC, V.*
Restrictions: *No smoking, no pets.*

Riley House Bed and Breakfast

Built in 1903 as a wedding present for the future city attorney and his new bride, the Riley House is cute, tidy, and rather unassuming—every inch the embodiment of turn-of-the-century small-town America charm. You may have to remind yourself that this quiet South Milwaukee residential neighborhood, near the shore of Lake Michigan, is only a 15-minute drive from downtown Milwaukee.

Roberta—call her Bert—is the live wire of this innkeeping duo; her husband, Mark, is the resident chef and the hand behind the homemade chocolate truffles in every guest room. The couple uncovered the house's quarter-sawn oak woodwork and embossed wallcoverings. They also restored the double-decker oak mantels over the fireplace in the Gentlemen's Parlor, whose centerpiece is now a leather-upholstered Mission chair. The Greek Revival sofa nearby plays a comfy second. The upright piano in the Ladies' Parlor is the same age as the house—"which is why we *had* to have it." Bert can now look back with relief at the hours she spent stripping it of layer upon layer of blue paint. All their hard work paid off; the interior looks and feels authentically turn-of-the-century.

Upstairs, a newly furnished suite is papered in a light floral print that complements the carved, queen-size, cherry-wood bed, the Duncan Phyfe drop-leaf table, and an antebellum cherry-wood armoire retrieved from

Mark's family's attic. The bathroom has the inn's only whirlpool tub. In another of the guest rooms is a full-size, quarter-canopy bed made of walnut, and an Eastlake-style dresser. In the Mary Riley Room, both the white iron daybed and an ornately carved, Victorian double bed are covered with floral comforters and heaped with pillows.

You can expect a delicious breakfast here: an omelet or quiche, along with muffins and baked goods. Mark will deliver breakfast to your room if you like, or you can eat in the dining room, or on the shaded patio that looks out onto Oak Creek Parkway. Beyond, it extends to woodsy Grant Park and the Lake Michigan shoreline, where it hooks up with a 90-mile bike and hiking trail.

Address: *727 Hawthorne Ave., South Milwaukee, WI 53172, tel. 414/764-3130.*
Accommodations: *2 doubles share bath; 1 suite.*
Amenities: *Ceiling fans, turndown service, whirlpool in suite, TV and VCR in parlor; off-street parking.*
Rates: *$70–$95; full breakfast. MC, V.*
Restrictions: *No smoking. Inquire about pets.*

Stagecoach Inn

After careful restoration by historian Brook Brown and his wife, Liz, this compact Greek Revival limestone inn once again welcomes travelers as it did when stagecoaches stopped in Cedarburg on their journey between Milwaukee and Green Bay in 1853, when the house was built. Restoring the corner pub was the Browns' first project. They uncovered the tin ceiling, set up a long, well-used wooden bar where the original had stood, refinished the rough plank floors, brought in some handsome tavern tables, and—in a place of honor behind the bar, next to the vintage silver cash register and grandmother clock—installed the original pub's wooden signpost depicting a fleet of white steeds. This is where the inn's guests gather for breakfast every morning and where, in the evenings, they congregate for draughts of Sprecher, a local root beer, and for cards, games, conversation, or a peek into the scrapbooks that Liz kept of the restoration.

A prize wallflower bench from an old-time dance hall sits in the front-hall corridor, at the bottom of the steep, narrow cherry-wood staircase that leads to the guest rooms on the second and third floors. The rooms' sunny nooks and low dormers host a mishmash of rustic furniture, much of it 100-year-old pine purchased by the Browns during their previous careers as antiques dealers. Braided rugs and Oriental carpets warm the rough pine floors.

One suite has an exposed limestone wall, an antique oak dresser, and a whirlpool. Another, one of three that overlook Cedarburg's beautifully preserved old main street, has a hand-stenciled frieze on the walls and a cherry-wood country Victorian bed, wardrobe, and dresser. The walls of the third-floor rooms are also stenciled, and the furniture is antique pine; two rooms have whirlpool baths, and another has two sleigh beds and is brightened by a skylight. The only guest room on the ground floor is a suite. In it are an 1860 four-poster bed, a sturdy immigrant chest that still looks capable of transporting all your worldly possessions, and a well-worn Oriental carpet.

Across the hall from the pub is a branch of the Manitowoc-based Beernstsen Candy Store, which sells chocolate candies shaped like computers, fish, and even costumed pigs named Green Bay Porker and Swine Lake.

Address: *W61 N. 520 Washington Ave., Cedarburg, WI 53012, tel. 414/375–0208.*
Accommodations: *6 double rooms with baths, 6 suites.*
Amenities: *Air-conditioning, TV and whirlpool bath in suites, pub, gift shop.*
Rates: *$65–$95; Continental breakfast. AE, DC, MC, V.*
Restrictions: *No smoking, no pets.*

Washington House Inn

This cream-colored brick Victorian building, built on Cedarburg's main street in 1886, is actually the second hostelry to stand on this site; the first was established in 1846. Jim Pape, who restored Cedarburg's Stone Hill Winery (and spearheaded the town's historic-preservation movement), took on the task of returning the Washington House to its former glory. The building had been used as offices and apartments since the 1920s, and nearly the only thing that hadn't been modernized or covered up was the lobby's parquet floor. After removing decades' worth of "improvements," Jim and his wife, Sandy, decided to leave many of the building's broad supporting beams and rough limestone walls exposed, and set about filling guest rooms with regional period antiques.

Guest rooms are named after the pillars of 19th-century Cedarburg society. The Frederich Hilgen Room, dressed in Bradbury & Bradbury wallpaper popular in the late 1800s, has a half-canopy bed draped in burgundy paisley print, a vintage marble-topped walnut table, and two reproduction wing chairs flanking the tall, narrow, shuttered windows. The bathroom is done in 1-inch white tile, and contains a marble sink and an antique dresser.

Dr. Friedrich Luening's Room is genteelly rustic with its tall South Carolina pencil-post bed and its plank floor strewn with rag rugs. Patchwork quilts decorate the walls, and a fire

engine–red circular iron stairway from the old Pabst Brewery leads to the loft sitting area under the exposed-beam ceiling. Plants adorn the spa-like adjoining room, and there's a modern fireplace and a decidedly 20th-century double whirlpool bath.

Windows in the dining room, on the ground floor, overlook Washington Avenue, the town's main thoroughfare. But even when the comings and goings abate, there's plenty to look at inside, what with the pressed-tin ceiling, the farm tables, and the rustic Victorian chairs. On your way in or out, glance at the original hotel register on display in the spacious lobby.

The Washington House recently expanded with the addition of five rooms in nearby Schroeder House, an 1880s stone home now converted to an inn annex.

Address: *W62 N573 Washington Ave., Cedarburg, WI 53012, tel. 414/375–3550 or 800/554–4717.*
Accommodations: *34 double rooms with baths.*
Amenities: *Air-conditioning, phone, cable TV, and HBO in rooms; whirlpool bath in 31 rooms, gas fireplace in 14 rooms, social hour with local wine and cheese, elevator, sauna.*
Rates: *$59–$159; Continental breakfast. AE, D, MC, V.*
Restrictions: *No pets.*

American Country Farm

Hams once hung from the ceiling beams of this snug fieldstone cottage, built in 1844 as a smokehouse for a country estate. Today, guests can toast their feet in front of the building's original broad fireplace. The cottage, its original stone walls whitewashed on the interior, consists of a single room—with a tiny kitchen and bathroom—and is comfortably furnished with a king-size bed with white coverlet, a plump wing chair, and a sofa. Murky oil paintings of farm scenes adorn the two-foot-thick walls, and a large wreath hangs over the fireplace.

Outside the cottage's two Dutch doors is a private patio facing a wooded wildflower preserve. Also on the two-acre property are a grape arbor, a kitchen garden, and the original white stone barn and farmhouse sheltered by tall pines. Every morning, innkeeper and antiques dealer Donna Steffen arrives laden with hot baked goods for breakfast.

Address: *12112 N. Wauwatosa Rd., Mequon, WI 53092, tel. 414/242–0194.*
Accommodations: *1 double room with bath.*
Amenities: *Air-conditioning, TV, kitchen, fireplace.*
Rates: *$75 midweek, $95 weekends; Continental breakfast. MC, V.*
Restrictions: *No pets.*

Eleven Gables Inn on the Lake

Until 1965 this sprawling Carpenter's Gothic house and its grounds on Lake Geneva served as a private retreat for the rich and famous. Built in the 1850s, the white clapboard Victorian villa and adjacent coach house are only steps from the lake.

The rooms are individually decorated with a rainbow of fabrics and a mix of contemporary furnishings and antiques, such as the Wicker Suite's fainting couch and the Mildred Fasel Peach Room's 110-year-old brass-and-iron bedstead. In the Cornelius Vanderbilt, Jr., Room, the pair of barrel-backed velvet wing chairs are said to have been favorites of that frequent guest. Most of the rooms have a private balcony, veranda, or enclosed courtyard. There is a shortage of TLC here, however, especially in the breakfast room, which is clean but blandly furnished.

Address: *493 Wrigley Dr., Lake Geneva, WI 53147, tel. 414/248–8393.*
Accommodations: *6 double rooms with baths, 2 suites in coach house can be 2 or 3 rooms each.*
Amenities: *Cable TV, fireplace, wet bar, kitchenette in 3 rooms; private pier, bike and watercraft rentals.*
Rates: *$89–$125 midweek, $125–$149 weekends and holidays, packages available for cottage; Continental breakfast weekdays, full breakfast weekends. AE, DC, MC, V.*
Restrictions: *No pets; 2-night minimum weekends.*

Elizabethian Inn

As they say in real estate: location, location, location. Set on a long shady lot on the shore of Lake Geneva, two blocks from downtown, an hour's drive from Chicago, and 45 minutes from Milwaukee, this inn has it in spades. A gabled, 1903 Queen Anne clapboard with a square turret, a sunporch, and a deck, the inn looks—inside and out—like an archetypal "Grandma's house." The ivory-toned living room holds just a few of the inn's collection of English antiques and reproductions.

The largest of the guest rooms in the main house faces the lake and takes up the entire front upstairs. It's popular because of its spaciousness and lake view, its four-poster bed, and its tufted floral settee. Half of the inn's rooms are in the Kimberly House—originally a barn and converted to a residence at the turn of the century. The decor here is Laura Ashley/country style. A breakfast of omelets, quiche, corned beef hash, or waffles is served at a long trestle table in front of a fireplace in the Kimberly House or on the sunporch in the main house.

Address: *463 Wrigley Dr., Lake Geneva, WI 53147, tel. 414/248–9131.*
Accommodations: *10 double rooms with baths.*
Amenities: *Air-conditioning, turndown service, TV in living room; private pier.*
Rates: *$95 weekdays, $115 weekends and holidays; full breakfast. MC, V.*
Restrictions: *No smoking, no pets, 2-night minimum weekends.*

Lawrence House

Although this house, built in 1885, is one of the oldest in town, its owner and innkeeper, Larry Joseph, has opted for creature comforts over strict historical re-creation. Enjoy the luxurious double whirlpool baths in each room's sun-filled, oversize bathroom, loaded with towels and toiletries. Reached through French doors, these are a bit of heaven for those who love to soak and dawdle in the tub. Room decor ranges from the deep hunter green and burgundy tones of the walls, fabrics, and canopy bed of one first-floor room, to the softer peach and blue scheme and floral print wallpaper and fabrics in another. All the rooms have big-screen TVs and VCRs concealed in reproduction Victorian armoires.

Guests can gather in the upstairs sitting room or around the living room's fireplace. Joseph's seven-course breakfast often features such dishes as eggs Benedict, soufflés, or waffles, and is served in the dining room, the enclosed wraparound sunporch overlooking the lake, or the screened-in porch.

Address: *403 S. Lake Shore Dr., Lake Geneva, WI 53147, tel. 414/248–4684 or 800/530–2262.*
Accommodations: *5 double rooms with baths.*
Amenities: *Air-conditioning, whirlpool baths, cable TV, video library.*
Rates: *$120–$150; full breakfast, afternoon refreshments. AE, D, DC, MC, V.*
Restrictions: *No pets; 2-night minimum weekends in summer.*

Pederson Victorian Bed & Breakfast

When Kristi Cowles bought this picture-perfect 113-year-old Victorian house in 1990, she wanted to create an environmentally friendly B&B, so guests may see sheets and towels drying in the breeze in the backyard. The house, in the tiny hamlet of Springfield, only 3 miles north of bustling Lake Geneva, is surrounded by a white picket fence and shaded by stately maple and walnut trees. Guests are invited to enjoy the porch swing and a pair of wicker rockers, or a hammock strung between two trees. Inside, the parlor and sunroom have old-fashioned floral-print carpets and are furnished with Victorian antiques and overstuffed chairs and sofas. The downstairs room, the Jennie Williams, has its own bath and turn-of-the-century furniture accented with wicker pieces. The three rooms upstairs are furnished with antique beds and dressers; they share a spacious bathroom with an antique clawfoot tub.

Kristi's prizewinning feta veggie quiche is a favorite on the extensive vegetarian breakfast menu; traditionalists can still choose from such dishes as apple-cinnamon pancakes with Wisconsin maple syrup or homemade fruit muffins.

Address: *1782 Hwy. 120 North, Lake Geneva, WI 53147, tel. 414/248–9110.* **Accommodations:** *1 double room with bath, 3 doubles share bath.* **Amenities:** *Air-conditioning, ceiling fans; hammocks and porch swing.* **Rates:** *$55–$85, $45 single weekdays Nov.–Apr.; full breakfast. MC, V.* **Restrictions:** *No smoking, no pets.*

T.C. Smith Inn

T.C. Smith came to Lake Geneva in 1844 and soon became a successful hardware dealer. In 1845 he built this mansion, blending elements of Greek Revival and Italianate styles. The home, an inn since 1987, is on the National Register of Historic Places and retains much of its grandeur. The large corner lot is surrounded by the original wrought-iron fence and is landscaped with stone walkways, flower beds, shrubs, shade trees, and a pool and fountain. Inside, the parlor boasts a Tiffany chandelier and a marble fireplace, and the entry hall and parlor have their original parquet and hardwood floors and woodwork. Unfortunately, these are the only public areas, other downstairs rooms having been converted to guest quarters.

All of the rooms are furnished with antiques, including some 19th-century paintings. The Renoir Garden Room has a huge bed with large brass medallions depicting cherubs and a matching wardrobe. The Autumn Room has unique wallpaper, made by drying real leaves and pressing them onto a paper backing; a marble fireplace and whirlpool make this one of the inn's most luxurious rooms.

Address: *865 Main St., Lake Geneva, WI 53147, tel. 414/248–1097 or 800/423–0233.* **Accommodations:** *6 double rooms with baths, 2 suites.* **Amenities:** *Air-conditioning, fireplace in 4 rooms, 3 whirlpools; lake views, bikes, nearby beach, tennis, shopping.* **Rates:** *$125–$175 weekdays, $175–$245 weekends; full breakfast. AE, D, DC, MC, V.* **Restrictions:** *Inquire about pets.*

The Victorian Belle

The oak trees that shade this stately Victorian are almost as old as the house itself, which was completed in 1891. Although the exterior is restrained by the standards of the day, the rooms inside are faithful re-creations of the period's over-the-top decor. Furnishings are Victorian and the stained-glass windows, oak floors, pocket doors, and the fireplace, rimmed by vibrant blue-green glazed tiles and a mantelpiece full of floral carvings, are all original. The dining room, in which host Barb Jaeger serves such breakfasts as her signature deep-fried French toast or whole-wheat pancakes with peaches and cream, is illuminated by a century-old brass chandelier; its corner china cabinet is filled with antique dishes.

Susanna's Room is the favorite of most guests, with its hand-stenciled walls draped with antique clothing, heirloom brass bed, rolltop desk, and private deck that faces a sprawling yard filled with shade trees and perennials. Although the house is on the town's main street, it's in a residential neighborhood a few blocks from the business district.

Address: *520 W. Wisconsin Ave., Oconomowoc, WI 53066, tel. 414/567–2520.*
Accommodations: *2 double rooms with baths.*
Amenities: *Air-conditioning, TV in living room; picnic table.*
Rates: *$70; full breakfast. MC, V.*
Restrictions: *No smoking, no pets.*

William's

This small, 85-year-old, two-toned blue cottage fills most of its corner lot in a quiet residential neighborhood 10 minutes from the lake and downtown. The smallish yard is big enough for two well-tended rock gardens and a bed of daylilies, with benches for contemplation.

Inside, the furnishings are unassuming, with a few standout family antiques, such as the treadle sewing machine and the wedding china on display in the dainty dining room. The small Victorian-style guest rooms have floral prints and light colors. One room has a curvaceous walnut bed, another a brass bed. The sunny octagonal room in the corner turret, with its low post bed and refinished hardwood floors, suggests an attic hideaway.

Innkeeper William Loftus is a former chef, and his made-from-scratch gourmet breakfasts might include strawberry crepes or quiches, along with raisin bran muffins and cinnamon bananas.

Address: *830 Williams St., Lake Geneva, WI 53147, tel. 414/248–1169.*
Accommodations: *4 double rooms share bath.*
Amenities: *Air-conditioning, TV and VCR in living room.*
Rates: *$65–$80; full breakfast. MC, V.*
Restrictions: *No smoking, no pets.*

Madison and Environs

*Scenic Madison, with a population of 195,000, is a thriving
center for business, government, education, and recreation.
The ethnic and cultural diversity of the University of
Wisconsin–Madison campus and the charged political
atmosphere created by Madison's role as state capital add to
the city's appeal.*

*Madison lies on the edge of Wisconsin's "driftless area"—a
region bypassed by Ice Age glaciers some 10,000 years ago.
Marked by deep, narrow valleys and steep, wooded hills, the
region covers most of southwestern Wisconsin and was the
scene of a major lead-mining boom in the 1830s. The city has
been known since settlement times as Four Lakes, with Lakes
Mendota, Monona, Wingra, and Waubesa lying within or just
outside the city limits.*

*The city center is on an eight-block-wide isthmus between
Lakes Mendota and Monona, with a skyline dominated (by
ordinance) by the 285-foot dome of the state capitol. The city,
filled with green spaces and conservation areas, includes more
than 30 city parks. In addition, three state parks are within a
20-minute drive of downtown Madison. The university
campus, stretching for more than a mile along the Lake
Mendota shore, is considered to be one of the nation's most
beautiful, and it has been a backdrop for a number of feature
films. Interesting nooks and crannies make the campus a
perfect spot for a stroll. At the western edge of the campus sits
the First Unitarian Society Meeting House, one of Frank
Lloyd Wright's finest designs. Madison's wide variety of
architectural styles, dating from the mid-19th century to the
present, include a handful of private homes designed by
Wisconsin's native son.*

*Madison is not a stranger to culture. There are several major
cultural venues, including the University of Wisconsin's
Elvehjem Museum of Art, the Madison Art Center, and the
State Historical Society Museum. The Madison Civic Center*

offers an extensive program of music, theater, and entertainment, including touring concerts and Broadway shows, and is home to the Madison Symphony and the Madison Repertory Theater. Downtown Madison hosts more than 100 annual events, including the Wisconsin Chamber Orchestra's outdoor summer concerts on Capitol Square and the annual Art Fair on the Square, which attracts thousands of browsers for art, entertainment, and food. In addition, the university's theatrical, musical, and film offerings add spice and variety to the cultural scene.

Madisonians are a sports-minded lot. University of Wisconsin's football, basketball, and hockey events draw large crowds. Badger football games are, in essence, an afternoon-long party where the Rose Bowl–winning team attracts more than 70,000 red-clad fans to Camp Randall Stadium. Softball is a summer passion; city leagues have some 400 organized teams. Boating, sailing, canoeing, and bicycling are also tremendously popular. In addition, over 100 miles of cross-country ski trails in the city and county offer a wide variety of terrain for winter athletes.

For the most part, Madison is free of suburban sprawl, with green spaces and farms between the city and outlying communities such as Cross Plains. Middleton and Monona are separate entities, but only city-limits signs insulate them from Madison. East and south of Madison, the land smooths out into rolling hills and farm fields where herds of black and white cattle graze. To the east, Lake Mills is convenient to either Madison or Milwaukee. Aztalan, near Lake Mills, was a Native American village where the Middle Mississippian culture existed from 1075 to 1175. It is now a state park.

Places to Go, Sights to See

Blue Mound. West of Madison, Blue Mound State Park (tel. 608/437–5711) has hiking trails, picnic areas, a swimming pool, a large campground, and viewing towers offering glorious vistas.

Elvehjem Museum of Art (800 University Ave., tel. 608/263–2246). The university's museum is one of the state's best, with a permanent collection of paintings, sculpture, and decorative arts dating from 2300 BC to the present.

Farmers' Market. Held on Capitol Square each Saturday from May through October, this extensive farmers' market has several hundred vendors offering baked goods, flowers, and fresh produce.

Henry Villas Park Zoo (702 S. Randall Ave., tel. 608/266–4732). The zoo exhibits nearly 200 species of animals and has a children's zoo (open Memorial Day through Labor Day) where youngsters can pet and feed animals. The zoo is located in Vilas Park, which has a swimming beach, tennis courts, and shady picnic areas.

State Street. A lively pedestrian mall runs between the capitol and the college where coffeehouses, ethnic cafés, and shops vie for the attention of passersby.

University Arboretum (1207 Seminole Hwy., tel. 608/263–7888). Away from downtown, the arboretum has more than 1,200 acres of natural plant and animal communities, such as prairie and forest landscapes, and horticultural collections of Upper Midwest specimens. The large lilacs and apple-tree gardens are spectacular in spring.

University of Wisconsin. The college opened in 1849 with 20 students. Today, with an enrollment of 42,000, it occupies a 1,000-acre campus on the shores of Lake Mendota. Guided walking tours of the campus may be arranged at the visitor information center in the *Memorial Union* (800 Langdon St., tel. 608/262–2511).

Wisconsin State Capitol (tel. 608/266–0382). The city center, on an eight-block-wide isthmus, is anchored at one end by the state capitol. Free tours of this magnificent Roman Renaissance structure take you through the Rotunda, the Supreme Court Room, the Senate and Assembly chambers, and the Governor's Conference Room.

Bicycling

The 23-mile **Sugar River State Trail** (tel. 608/527–2334 for information and fees) runs from New Glarus to Brodhead, crossing the Sugar River and its tributaries 14 times. The **Military Ridge State Trail** (tel. 608/935–2315 for information and fees) traces the path of the Old Military Ridge Trail of the mid-1800s for 39.6 miles between Verona and Dodgeville.

Canoeing

Canoeists can explore all four Madison lakes. **Lake Wingra,** where no motorboats are allowed, is a favorite. The **Yahara River** runs from Lake Mendota into Lake Monona, then south to Lake Waubesa and Lake Kegonsa. From there, it continues south through farmland and the town of Stoughton, joining the **Rock River** at a point just below Fulton, some 25 miles from Madison. The Rock River meanders through more countryside, and the towns of Janesville and Beloit before entering Illinois, and eventually running into the Mississippi. The current of both rivers is slow; some dams will require portaging, and in low water additional portages may be necessary. Access is available at the lakes and towns that the rivers run through, as well as spots where roads cross over them.

Fishing

Northern pike, walleye, smallmouth and largemouth bass, bullheads, catfish, and a variety of panfish are found in southern Wisconsin's plentiful waters. Rainbow, brown, and brook trout are stocked in specially designated streams. Local bait and tackle shops or resorts can tell you where to look for fish, or recommend a professional guide.

Restaurants

Madison's Farmers' Market provides many of the ingredients for the dishes at **L'Etoile** (25 N. Pinckney St., tel. 608/251–0500), where regional food with a French flair is served in the shadow of the capitol building. **Ovens of Brittany** (305 State St., tel. 608/273–4900) is where to find hearty French-country fare, as well as the University of Wisconsin's intelligentsia, who've made this a hangout for the smart set. **Quivey's Grove** (6261 Nesbitt Rd., tel. 608/273–4900) dishes out sturdy Midwest cuisine in an 1855 farmhouse.

Tourist Information

Greater Madison Convention & Visitors Bureau (615 E. Washington Ave., Madison, WI 53703–2952, tel. 608/255-2537 or 800/373–6376).

Arbor House

T his handsome Greek Revival building began life in the 1830s as a one-room pioneer home. That original structure, the oldest residence in Madison, is preserved as the living room of the Arbor House. In 1854, an inn was attached to the front of the small house. Called the Plow, the inn was a stagecoach stop on the route from Madison to the west. Travelers could eat and drink downstairs or visit the upstairs dance hall to work off excess energy. The building began to deteriorate after the stagecoach gave way to the railroad, but was saved in the 1940s when an art professor at the nearby University of Wisconsin purchased the historic structure and restored it, adding a rear wing that contained his studio.

The home as been a B&B since 1986, and today, thanks to careful restoration, the entire building retains its pioneer feel, with original pine and oak floors, stone fireplaces, and narrow hallways. But innkeepers Cathie and John Imes are not only preserving a venerable building. They're also developing an environmentally friendly B&B, with organic cotton sheets and towels, wool carpets and rugs, organic soaps and bath products, and water- and energy-saving plumbing and lighting—all while providing a quiet, luxurious retreat in the city.

The front rooms of the building, which served as the tavern in the 1850s, are now luxurious quarters called the Tap Room. Brass fixtures, a fish tank, and an old porthole window create a nautical theme, while a wet bar reminds guests of the room's original purpose. The antique brass bed in the Cozy Rose Room is made up with floral-patterned linens; one of the original stone fireplaces and a double whirlpool bath add to the relaxing, romantic mood. A view of the wooded yard and two skylights in the vaulted ceiling betray the origins of the top-floor suite called the Studio. Once the professor's atelier, it's now dominated by a brass bed with a lively Southwestern-design quilt; there's a separate dressing room, and another skylight crowns the cedar-paneled whirlpool room.

Breakfast is served on an enclosed pine-paneled porch that overlooks the flower garden, or outdoors on the shaded stone patio.

Address: *3402 Monroe St., Madison, WI 53711, tel. 608/238–2981, fax 608/238–1175.*
Accommodations: *4 double rooms with baths, 1 suite.*
Amenities: *Air-conditioning, radio in rooms; TV in 3 rooms, refrigerator in 2 rooms, whirlpool bath in 2 rooms; phone, TV, fax, and computer available in common room; croquet, badminton, bird-watching; bike path across street.*
Rates: *$85—$115; Continental breakfast weekdays, full breakfast weekends, evening refreshments. AE, MC, V.*
Restrictions: *No smoking, no pets.*

Collins House

This sturdy brick Prairie-style house, built for a lumber magnate in 1911, was divided into apartments, then used as an office building, and then abandoned. But it was on a prime corner lot in Madison's historic district, next to a small city park and overlooking Lake Mendota. So in 1985, Barb and Mike Pratzel bought it and dismantled its "modernizations," to reveal ceilings with oak and mahogany beams, decorative leaded-glass windows, and the clean geometric lines of Prairie design. Then they polished the rare red-maple floors, filled the house with a collection of vintage Mission and Arts and Crafts furnishings that complement the exquisite woodwork, and opened it as a bed-and-breakfast.

In the living room, a hassock and armchairs are grouped around a fireplace bordered in large, unglazed, moss-green tiles, which are surrounded by a massive mahogany frame and mantel. The ceiling has beams, and an oak-leaf frieze is stenciled on the cream-colored walls; moldings are dark mahogany. Twin leaded-glass fronted bookcases mark the entry to the library, whose frieze is in the Arts and Crafts style; inside, a plump upholstered armchair and sturdy rockers ring a well-worn Persian rug. Outside the library are three lakefront sunporches. Breakfast is served on one of the porches, where guests can watch the sailboats and crew teams, and, in winter, ice skaters and ice fishermen. Barb and Mike, who also own a gourmet catering firm,

often serve Swedish oatmeal pancakes in the morning.

The light and airy guest rooms upstairs have handmade quilts, soothing color schemes, and striking Mission and Arts and Crafts furniture. The largest room affords views in three directions, over Lake Mendota and the capitol building's dome. A tea cart filled with begonias and an immense oak breakfront and matching secretary give the room, which stretches the entire width of the house, a turn-of-the-century feel. Another suite, created by removing a wall between two small bedrooms, has its own balcony facing Lake Mendota.

The Collins House is only a short walk from the capitol, the university, State Street shops, a park on Lake Mendota, and Lake Monona.

Address: *704 E. Gorham St., Madison, WI 53703, tel. 608/255-4230.*
Accommodations: *2 double rooms with baths, 3 suites.*
Amenities: *Phone in rooms, whirlpool tub in 2 suites, TV in 1 room, TV and VCR in common room, video film library.*
Rates: *$65–$125; full breakfast. MC, V.*
Restrictions: *No smoking. Inquire about pets.*

Fargo Mansion Inn

The Wells Fargo Company was doing rather well in 1890, so when E.J. Fargo bought himself this grand house, he set about making it even grander. To the already stately Queen Anne building, Fargo added a gabled third floor, the cupola atop the showpiece octagonal turret, and an elaborate, gabled porte cochere. Over the years, however, the house fell into disrepair, and sat empty and condemned until it caught the eye of a developer who drove past it after making a wrong turn: Barry Luce decided then and there to buy it. He completely renovated it, and the house became an inn, furnished with antiques from the town's Opera Mall Antiques Center, which the developer and his partner, Tom Bolks, also operate.

The sunny, spacious living room, a popular spot for weddings, is a Victorian confection full of sculpted moldings and other architectural furbelows. The focal point is the fireplace of laurel-wreath-patterned tiles framed by an ornately carved wood mantelpiece; the shelves above are crammed with figurines and antique clocks. The music room holds a huge Federal dining table, two matching side tables, and two movable cabinets. The everyday dining room, wainscoted in oak, is no less elaborate, from its mirrored Victorian buffet and sideboard to the Corinthian columns that frame the doorway into the adjoining solarium. The small library contains a Victorian pump organ, a sled filled with antique

dolls and teddy bears, and a vintage toy ironing board.

Of the guest rooms upstairs, the Master Suite is the most popular because of its private balcony and its size: large enough to dwarf a bed with an 8-foot-tall headboard and to accommodate a teardrop chandelier and the plump velvet sofa by the white marble fireplace. A "secret" doorway, disguised as a bookcase, opens to reveal one of the inn's signature modern marble bathrooms; this one also has a whirlpool tub. The other rooms, of varying sizes, are decorated in late-Victorian style and filled with antiques.

On the house's double lot, lovely gardens of shrubbery and banks of daffodils have replaced the bear pit in which Mr. Fargo staged battles between bruins for the entertainment of his guests.

Address: *406 Mulberry St., Lake Mills, WI 53551, tel. 414/648-3654.*
Accommodations: *8 double rooms with baths.*
Amenities: *Air-conditioning, Jacuzzi in 5 rooms, TV in living room, conference facilities.*
Rates: *$73–$160; full breakfast. MC, V.*
Restrictions: *No smoking, no pets.*

Mansion Hill Inn

Considered by Madisonites to be the height of opulence when it was built in 1858, this ornately carved sandstone Romanesque Revival mansion still upstages its neighbors in the historic district. Swagged with double tiers of delicate wrought-iron balconies, it would be more at home in New Orleans. Inside, a spiral staircase anchored by an immense, intricately carved newel post rises four stories from the jewel-box foyer to a turreted belvedere with sweeping views of the city. The tawny marble floor, flamboyant floral arrangements, elaborate gilt moldings, friezes, and rich detailing create the atmosphere of a small European hotel and set the tone for the entire inn.

The small front parlor is arranged with conversational groupings of Rococo Revival–style furniture: settees upholstered in rose damask, side chairs with velvet ottomans. Guests can warm up at the elegant marble fireplace, or sashay over to the Emerson square grand piano for a musical interlude. The carved walnut dining table, original to the mansion, holds plates and pitchers of refreshments and newspapers from near and far to which guests are welcome to help themselves.

Each of the guest rooms is individually and lavishly decorated, and most are embellished with ornate cornices and ceiling medallions and elegant, modern, marble baths. In nine of the rooms, French doors open onto pleasant terraces. The Lillie Langtry Room has a white-marble fireplace, a veranda, wallpaper hand-painted in neo-Grecian patterns, Renaissance Revival furniture, and a bed draped in lace. The room known as the Turkish Nook recalls the 1890s craze for Orientalia: The wallpaper depicts the opening of the Suez Canal, and the bed, whose spread is a Near East–style tapestry, sits under a lacy sultan's tent. Velvet pouf ottomans complete the look. Rooms on the lower levels are smaller and not as elaborately decorated, but have their own patios.

You can have breakfast delivered to your room, along with your choice of morning newspaper, or arrange to eat in the parlor.

Address: *424 N. Pinckney St., Madison, WI 53703, tel. 800/798–9070, fax 608/255–2217.*
Accommodations: *11 double rooms with baths, 6 with sitting areas.*
Amenities: *Air-conditioning, phone, TV, and stereo in all rooms; 9 rooms with terraces, whirlpool in 8 rooms; private wine cellar and catered dinners available, teleconference facilities; 24-hour valet service and valet parking, access to health club.*
Rates: *$100–$250 single, $20 additional person; Continental breakfast. AE, MC, V.*
Restrictions: *No pets.*

Middleton Beach Inn

In this country-contemporary house, floor-to-ceiling windows frame spectacular views of Lake Mendota. But there's plenty to look at inside as well. The place is a showcase for the antique treasures that the peripatetic Dueslers collected during years of living in New England.

Antique sleds and sleighs are their particular weakness, and in the living room there's a sleigh parked by the window, covered with dolls and toys, and a sled that doubles as a coffee table. The room also holds a tavern table from the original Pabst Brewery, a pear-shaped oak Scandinavian grandfather clock, and a cabinet retired from the Wisconsin State Capitol (and now filled with collector marbles and four generations' worth of Duesler family teddy bears). By day sunlight pours through a skylight and the huge lakeview windows. A modern marble fireplace that takes up an entire wall warms winter nights.

The Victorian Suite's window wall and veranda allow for sweeping lake views, and its red velvet Victorian settee is as curvaceous as the nude in the painting (posed for, says the owner, by none other than Marilyn Monroe). The huge, skylit bathroom has a whirlpool and a vanity mirror. The Carriage Room, also skylighted, has a 19th-century country feel, with its Shaker-style bed, Jenny Lind trunk, cane-seat rocker, and drum table fashioned from a vintage Baker's chocolate container. The blue and white Schoolhouse Room,

smaller than the others, is enlivened by memorabilia from Mr. Duesler's pre-innkeeping career at Oscar Meyer, such as a toy Wienermobile. The hefty oak headboard of the queen-size bed in the Country Suite is embellished by intricate carving.

Two generations of Dueslers—outgoing, involved hosts—run this family business. Each morning they cook up crêpes, quiches, French toast, omelets, or bananas Foster, and urge their guests not to worry about the calories they consume; the many sports and athletic activities nearby will help them work it off.

Address: *2303 Middleton Beach Rd., Middleton, WI 53562, tel. 608/831–6446.*
Accommodations: *4 double rooms with baths.*
Amenities: *Air-conditioning; whirlpool in 2 rooms; phone and TV in room optional, TV and sound system in common room; free health-club access, canoe and water sports.*
Rates: *$65–$145; full breakfast, afternoon refreshments. AE, MC, V.*
Restrictions: *No smoking, no pets.*

Canterbury Inn

When Trudy Barash bought a dilapidated 1924 brick building in downtown Madison, she planned to fulfill her dream of opening a bookstore and coffee house. In 1991, after an award-winning renovation, Canterbury Booksellers Coffeehouse opened, offering authors' readings and musical performances in the café. Trudy's successful new venture didn't take up all the space in the building, however, so she commissioned six unique rooms and a large parlor for a second-floor B&B.

As the name suggests, the Canterbury Inn derives its inspiration from Chaucer's stories. Guests are greeted by a mural of medieval Canterbury, and murals also enliven each bedroom, all of which are named after a pilgrim in the *Canterbury Tales*. (Don't

worry—there's a cheat-sheet for those who can't remember the Miller from the Wife of Bath.) Otherwise, the spacious rooms are far from medieval. Done in muted jewel tones, each offers a queen- or king-size bed, overstuffed wing chairs and sofas, a refrigerator, TV, and CD player.

Address: *315 W. Gorham Street, Madison, WI 53703, tel. 608/258–8899 or 800/838–3850.*
Accommodations: *2 double rooms with baths, 4 suites.*
Amenities: *Air-conditioning, phone, TV, CD player, robes, and refrigerator in rooms, whirlpool in suites, VCR available, gift certificate for bookstore.*
Rates: *$80–$250; Continental breakfast, evening refreshments. MC, V.*

Enchanted Valley Garden

Guests are lured to Ken and Marcia Helgerson's inn by its natural surroundings, which offer days full of outdoor pursuits. Located in a farming community 30 minutes west of Madison, the modest contemporary house sits on five acres of woods and fields, perfect for long walks and bird-watching. It's just 4 miles from Indian Lake Nature Preserve, a 442-acre park with hiking and natural cross-country ski trails.

Guests will enjoy the irises that bloom in May, as well as a succession of other blooms throughout the summer. Bounty from the Helgersons' herb and vegetable garden goes into the farmstyle breakfast, served in a sunny kitchenside nook with broad picture windows, or on a deck that commands panoramic views of the trees, wildflow-

ers, and hills. Any surplus from the garden makes its way to Madison's Farmers' Market each Saturday.

The two guest rooms, both with queensize beds, are anonymously modern, with small windows. Guests would do better to relax in the central den, which has an old-fashioned iron stove, a TV, and floor-to-ceiling windows that look out on bird and squirrel feeders.

Address: *5554 Enchanted Valley Rd., Cross Plains, WI 53528, tel. 608/798–4554.*
Accommodations: *2 double rooms share bath.*
Amenities: *Badminton, croquet, hiking in adjoining woods.*
Rates: *$50–$60; full breakfast, snacks. No credit cards.*
Restrictions: *No smoking, no pets.*

Jackson Street Inn

A retired Montana rancher built this foursquare clapboard house with oak and maple woodwork, a cross-beamed oak ceiling, patterned oak paneling, a sweeping oak stairway, beveled glass windows, a glass-paneled pocket door, and an Italian marble fireplace. That was in 1899. Now the house is an inn run by a retired couple who've lived here for more than 35 years. Its fine turn-of-the-century craftsmanship is diminished only by the downstairs carpeting and furniture, which, except for the pair of huge Eastlake buffets with beveled-glass windows in the spacious dining room and parlor, is undistinguished.

The guest rooms are done in antiques and have delicately patterned floral paper on the walls and quilts on the beds. The color scheme of the largest bedroom takes its cue from a blue and white handmade Amish quilt, and the cushioned seats in the bay windows overlook a quiet, residential street.

Address: *210 S. Jackson St., Janesville, WI 53545, tel. 608/754-7250.*
Accommodations: *2 double rooms with baths, 2 doubles share bath.*
Amenities: *Air-conditioning and ceiling fans in rooms, TV in downstairs living room, phone and refrigerator in upstairs hall sitting room; putting green, shuffleboard.*
Rates: *$55-$65; full breakfast. MC, V.*
Restrictions: *No smoking in guest rooms.*

Past and Present Inn

F irst came the gift shop, carrying quaint collectibles and dried floral wreaths made on the premises. Next, tired of watching shoppers go elsewhere for lunch, owner Joyce Niesen opened a dining room that soon became legendary for its bacon-lettuce-tomato soup and cheesecakes. Then, three guest suites were added to this contemporary, colonial-style house to accommodate people hiking the nearby Ice Age Trail and anglers who wanted to fish for trout in adjacent Black Earth Creek. The two-bedroom suite, reached by an outside staircase, has private decks at each end, a mix of old and new furnishings, and a kitchen. The other two suites, on the ground floor, face Black Earth Creek, and are done in a country Victorian style with rattan furnishings, antique tables and chairs, and floral patterned wallpaper.

Each has a refrigerator and a double whirlpool bath.

Guests may order breakfast from the restaurant menu, which features omelets and other egg dishes, Belgian waffles, and specialty pancakes.

Address: *2034 Main St., Cross Plains, WI 53528, tel. 608/798-4441.*
Accommodations: *1 2-bedroom suite, 2 1-bedroom suites with whirlpool.*
Amenities: *Air-conditioning, phones, TV in each suite; restaurant, gift shop.*
Rates: *$75-$150; full breakfast (in restaurant). MC, V.*
Restrictions: *No smoking, no pets.*

University Heights Bed and Breakfast

Local pharmacist Clement Bobb and his wife Bertha built this imposing brick foursquare-style home on Madison's up-and-coming west side in 1923 and proceeded to raise eight children in the house. Now this stately home, on a large lot shaded by century-old oaks, is in one of Madison's most historic and architecturally interesting neighborhoods, an easy walk from the University of Wisconsin campus.

Betty and Bill Smoler, the home's third owners, bought it to fulfill their dream of opening a B&B. Inside, the living room boasts a large brick fireplace and original woodwork. Oak cabinets with beveled-glass doors and an ornate oak arch separate the living and dining areas. Upstairs, the Regent Room is a suite furnished with an Arts and Crafts-style queen-size bed and 19th-century wardrobe. The Chancellor Room has an iron bedstead and an antique American wardrobe and table. The Provost Room boasts a 19th-century bed and matching desk.

Betty serves breakfast on the sunny, all-season porch or in the more formal dining room. Guests are welcome to enjoy the shaded brick patio at the rear of the house—and its large hot tub.

Address: *1812 Van Hise Ave., Madison, WI 53705, tel. 608/233–3340.*
Accommodations: *2 double rooms with baths, 1 suite.*
Amenities: *Air-conditioning, whirlpool bath in suite, TV in common area; hot tub.*
Rates: *$65–$125; full breakfast. AE, MC, V.*
Restrictions: *No smoking, no pets.*

Victoria-on-Main

This high-style Queen Anne house, on a corner adjacent to the university campus, was built by Whitewater's mayor in 1895, and the pediments, pillared porch, and octagonal, cone-topped turret signal the residence of a prominent citizen.

Inside, all the rooms are decorated in Laura Ashley wallpaper and fabrics, and filled with antiques and bric-a-brac. Each guest room features a different Wisconsin hardwood. The Bird's Eye Maple Room contrasts blue and white chintz against the golden-toned wood; leaded-glass windows add a touch of elegance. In the Cherry Room, a six-foot-tall cherry headboard stands out against the airy, floral-print wallpaper. The most striking feature of the Red Oak Room is a fireplace of blue fleur-de-lis-patterned tiles, with a metal grate emblazoned with cavorting Grecian nymphs.

Breakfast, served in the bright and sunny kitchen, may include caramel-baked French toast, quiche, baked eggs, or the inn's special puffed apple dish.

Address: *622 W. Main St., Whitewater, WI 53190, tel. 414/473–8400.*
Accommodations: *1 double room with bath, 2 doubles share bath.*
Amenities: *TV in sitting room, kitchen available for guests' use.*
Rates: *$48–$75; full breakfast. MC, V.*
Restrictions: *No smoking, no pets.*

Wisconsin River Valley
Including Wausau, Baraboo, and Spring Green

Running north to south, the Wisconsin River wiggles through the center of the state before suddenly veering west to join the Mississippi. At times there is a distinct herd mentality here, from the Holsteins munching on the grassy banks to the armada of out-of-state vans and mobile homes making their way down U.S. 51 (which parallels the river) to Wisconsin Dells and other tourist meccas.

There's a sharp contrast between the original Winnebagos—the Native American tribe that just three centuries ago silently canoed the river's course—and their 4-wheeled namesakes, especially during the summer crush. That's when small towns up and down the river host a stream of history pageants, arts festivals, crafts fairs, band concerts, fireworks displays, athletic competitions, and other weekend happenings.

The state's most-touristed town, Wisconsin Dells, is where the Wisconsin River twists through walls of castellated sandstone. Originally called Kilbourn, the town officially changed its name in 1931 in an unabashed attempt to draw more visitors to the picturesque region, which had garnered national renown through the stereoscopic photographs of H.H. Bennett. It may have succeeded too well. Outside of a museum dedicated to early photography in the H.H. Bennett Studio and an exciting 15-mile boat ride through the gorge, the overall experience for some has become homogenized. It doesn't help that the roads leading in and out of the dells are lined with hundreds of "family fun" venues and neon-laced motels that wink at passersby like so many painted ladies.

These pressures have not yet reached Baraboo, the original winter quarters of several circuses, including those owned by the five Ringling brothers, Baraboo natives. This pleasant community, which took its name from an early French trader,

Baribault, is home to the Circus World Museum and other Big Top–related attractions. When you're tired of circuses, take in the International Crane Foundation. This fascinating center for the study and preservation of endangered cranes is 5 miles north of town, off U.S. 12.

Spring Green is internationally renowned as the home of architect Frank Lloyd Wright. Thousands of visitors annually tour the buildings of Taliesin, his home and school on the Wisconsin River, just south of town. American Players Theater offers first-class professional productions of Shakespeare and other classics in repertory every summer in an open-air theater. There's also excellent canoeing on the Wisconsin River and bicycling on local backroads. Farther south on Route 23 from Spring Green is the House on the Rock, Wisconsin's single most popular tourist attraction. This surreal museum of kitsch is one of those places you have to see to believe—it houses everything from the world's largest carousel to a gigantic whale and sea monster diorama to replicas of the British Crown Jewels.

Wausau, the largest city in north central Wisconsin, is known for its annual June Log Jam Festival, with lumberjacks, Civil War re-enactors, arts-and-crafts booths, music, and world-class kayak racing on a special man-made course along the Wisconsin River. The city also has an excellent art museum, the Leigh Yawkey Woodson Art Museum, as well as fine restaurants, shopping, and nearby Rib Mountain State Park, with hiking in summer and cross-country and downhill skiing in winter.

Places to Go, Sights to See

Baraboo. Circus World Museum (426 Water St., tel. 608/356–0800), the original Ringling Bros. winter home, re-creates the razzle-dazzle era with an outstanding collection of circus wagons and big-top performances featuring today's circus stars. Both Devils Lake State Park (3½ mi south on U.S. 12, tel. 608/356–8301), featuring Devil's Lake and several prehistoric Native American mounds, and the International Crane Foundation (5 mi north on U.S. 12, ¼ mi east on Shady Lane Rd., tel. 608/356–9462), a preserve for endangered crane species, offer guided and self-guided tours.

Portage. This river town's historic district has a cache of elegant homes worth touring; one of them is the author Zona Gale's (804 MacFarlane Rd., tel. 608/742–4959), now the public library. The Old Indian Agency House (Rte. 33E, tel. 608/742–6362) of 1832, the Surgeon's Quarters (Rte. 33E, tel. 608/742–2949) from the 1820s, and the adjoining 1850s Garrison School recall the pioneering era with their period furnishings.

Spring Green. Frank Lloyd Wright chose this farming community on the Wisconsin River for his home, Taliesin, and for his architecture school, Hillside Home (3 mi south on Rte. 23, tel. 608/588–7900), both of which can be toured from May through October. The House on the Rock (9 mi south on Rte. 23, tel. 608/935–3639), eccentric builder Robert Jordan's tour de force perched atop a chimney-like rock 450 feet above the Wyoming Valley, is an architectural wonder of a different stripe. The complex, begun in 1940, includes waterfalls, massive fireplaces, and the millionaire's eclectic collections of dolls, paperweights, mechanical banks, armor, and much more. American Players Theater (Rte. C, Spring Green 53588, tel. 608/588-7401) offers four or five classic plays each summer season. The setting is a natural outdoor amphitheater, and patrons can picnic on the grounds before the show.

Stevens Point. A branch of the University of Wisconsin (tel. 715/346–4242) is situated here, and campus tours can be arranged. A planetarium and observatory in the Science Building are open year-round, as is the world's largest computer-assisted mosaic mural. The Museum of Natural History (Albertson Learning Resources Center, University of Wisconsin, tel. 715/346–2858) features one of the country's most comprehensive collections of preserved birds and bird eggs. The regionally famous Stevens Point Brewery (2617 Water St., Stevens Point 54481, tel. 715/344–9310) offers tours and samples.

Wausau. The Andrew Warren Historic District (3rd St. and surrounding area) encompasses 10 blocks of historic homes built between 1868 and 1934. You can pick up maps at the Visitors Council (300 3rd St., Suite 200, tel. 800/236–9728) in Washington Square, the center of Wausau's historic Third Street pedestrian mall. The Grand Theater (415 4th St., tel. 715/842–0988) was recently restored to its 1926 splendor at a cost of over $2 million; the Greek Revival structure is now home to the performing arts in the area. The Leigh Yawkey Woodson Art Museum (Franklin and 12th, tel. 715/845–7010) is best known for its annual Birds in Art exhibit. It also has a fine permanent collection.

Wisconsin Dells. The scenic dells of the Wisconsin River are one of the state's foremost natural attractions. Created over thousands of years by the river cutting through soft limestone to a depth of 150 feet, the Upper and Lower Wisconsin Dells are nearly 15 miles of fantastic soaring rock formations. While the sandstone cliffs, majestic pines, and gently flowing waters are still popular, man-made attractions nearly overshadow the region's natural wonders. Virtually everything in the dells is casual; shorts and T-shirts are allowed nearly everywhere, and swimsuits, tanning lotion, and comfortable shoes should be considered standard equipment. For more information on dells attractions, dining, and lodging, contact Wisconsin Dells Convention and Visitors Bureau (701 Superior St., Wisconsin Dells, WI 53965, tel. 800/223–3557).

Restaurants

The **Springs Resort Dining Room** and **Grill on the Green**, both at the Springs Resort (off Rte. C, 2 miles south of Spring Green, tel. 608/588–7000), offer continental fare in the Dining Room and more casual meals in the Grill; both overlook woods and a golf course. The town's **Round Barn** (¼ mi west of Rte. 23N and U.S. 14, Spring Green, tel. 608/588–2568), only a little more formal than when the cows ate here, segues from sandwiches to giant Wisconsin steaks. The **Silver Coach** (38 Park Ridge Dr., Stevens Point, tel. 715/341–6588), a railroad car that once streaked through Stevens Point, now turns out a "fish fry" as upscale as its art aeco quarters with salmon, garlic shrimp, and tuna. **The Cottage** (1502 Post Rd., Plover, tel. 715/341–1600), where dining is in the comfy rooms of an 1860s house, does a signature beef Wellington. **Wally's House of Embers** (935 Wisconsin Dells Pkwy., Wisconsin Dells, tel. 608/253–6411), is famous for barbecue ribs, veal dishes, prime rib, and salmon—not to mention the Sunday brunch. **Michael's Supper Club** (2901 Rib Mountain Dr., Wausau, tel. 715/842–9856), is a popular dinner spot that serves excellent fish and seafood, pasta, prime rib, and steaks, as well as wonderful desserts.

Tourist Information

Portage Chamber of Commerce (301 W. Wisconsin Ave., Portage, WI 53901, tel. 608/742–6242); **Spring Green Travellers Guide** (Box 3, Spring Green, WI 53588, tel. 608/588–2042); **Stevens Point Convention & Visitors Bureau** (660 Main St., Stevens Point, WI 55481, tel. 715/344-2556); **Wausau Convention & Visitors Council** (Box 6190, Wausau, WI 54402–6190, tel. 800/236–9728); **Wisconsin Dells Visitors & Convention Bureau** (701 Superior St., Wisconsin Dells, WI 53965, tel. 800/223–3557).

Dreams of Yesteryear

Designed in 1901 by architect J.H. Jeffers (who was also the architect for the Wisconsin Pavilion for the 1904 St. Louis World's Fair), Dreams of Yesteryear was singled out from among its Victorian peers by Bonnie and Bill Maher, a couple determined to save the attractive, grand old Queen Anne from destruction. Bonnie, an antiques collector, recognized the value and potential in the oak woodwork, hardwood floors, leaded-glass windows, and footed tubs that remained in the house. She replaced a rotting roof with wooden shingles and restored the Queen Anne lines of "a chimney you could watch the sunset through." Then, with the major overhaul completed, she began "gathering" Victoriana. The voluptuously carved parlor sofa became theirs when a stranger telephoned to say, "Aunt Minerva just died at 93—could you use it?"

Today that sofa, along with a revolving library table discovered at a church bazaar, faces the fancy fireplace with its Victorian cascade decorations and surrounding tools. Sheet music for "Lola" sits on the vintage upright piano, alongside a 1904 phonograph that still has its wooden needles. Bonnie's lavish breakfasts, which feature local cranberry juice and pecan-stuffed French toast, are served on the inn's original dining-room set.

Upstairs, it's hard to choose between Gerald's Room, done in French blue, with a pineapple-post bed and tiny balcony; Isabella's Room, with an elaborately carved headboard, an ivy-filled bay window, and a cozy reading nook; Florence Myrna's Room, with gardenia wall coverings and its own deep green ceramic-tiled bathroom lit by antique wall sconces; and the cozy Maid's Quarters, done in peach, with telephone access and a desk that appeals to business travelers.

Bonnie's newest additions are the two suites on the third floor. Each has a bedroom and sitting room. One is furnished with a white wrought-iron bed and has a whirlpool bath, while the other is done in brown wicker and has a black wrought-iron bed.

Address: *1100 Brawley St., Stevens Point, WI 54481, tel. 715/341–4525.*
Accommodations: *2 double rooms with baths, 2 doubles share bath, 2 suites.*
Amenities: *Air conditioning, fans in rooms, whirlpool in 1 room, fireplace in common room.*
Rates: *$55–$125; full breakfast. AE, MC, V.*
Restrictions: *No smoking, no pets.*

Historic Bennett House

Historic Bennett House is a pleasant alternative to the many hotels and resorts in the Wisconsin Dells. A handsome 1863 Greek Revival mansion, the inn takes guests back to a gentler era. It was here that Civil War veteran Henry Hamilton Bennett became a pioneer photographer; his stop-action pictures, the first ever done, are displayed today in the Smithsonian Museum. Gail and Richard Obermeyer, a former stage actress and a university communications professor, are running the inn in their retirement years. "We wanted the change of seasons. We'd visited relatives in the Dells and loved it." The couple knew exactly what they wanted: the intimate atmosphere of a European bed-and-breakfast and a "historic home with warmth and charm," Gail says.

First they found the perfect house, complete with a white picket fence and only a block from downtown and the Wisconsin River. Then they waited for it to come on the market—which it soon did.

Guests from as far away as Germany and South Korea have come to this casually elegant inn. Before dinner, visitors relax with a glass of wine on the floral-patterned sofa or in a pair of wing chairs drawn up to the white, wood-burning fireplace in the living room. Breakfast is served at the communal table in the other half of the long room, which has a walnut-toned china cabinet and buffet and, on cool days, an open fire. Here Gail brings out the house specialty, eggs Bennett. There's also a small, cozy parlor with a TV and comfortable chairs.

The ground-floor suite has a bedroom with Eastlake furniture, a parlor furnished with a loveseat, antique table and chairs, and a framed antique tapestry; there's also a VCR and film library. Upstairs, the English Room has the original black floors, a walnut canopy bed, and an antique armoire from Britain. It shares a bathroom with the snug Garden Room, fitted with a brass bed and wicker furniture. The bathroom, with its gold fixtures, hand-painted Italian sinks, and claw-foot tub, is so seductive that some guests call it therapy.

Address: *825 Oak St., Wisconsin Dells, WI 53965, tel. 608/254–2500.*
Accommodations: *2 double rooms share bath, 1 suite.*
Amenities: *Air-conditioning, TV in suite and common room, fireplaces in common rooms.*
Rates: *$70–$90; full breakfast, early morning coffee, evening refreshments. No credit cards.*
Restrictions: *No smoking, no pets.*

Rosenberry Inn

The Artzes' innkeeping career started one day when they went antiques-hunting and strayed too far from home. "We'll stay in a B&B," Pat informed her dubious husband. Next thing they knew, they were renovating a mansion of their own in a community "where people didn't have to lock their doors."

The good news about their choice, a 1908 Prairie schoolhouse built for Judge Rosenberry in Wausau's Andrew Warren Historic District, was that they could afford it if they did the renovation work themselves. The bad news was that there was plenty to do; back in the 1940s, the place had been turned into efficiency apartments.

Today, each guest room contains a tiny kitchen, eating nook, bath, and rustic Victorian furnishings—patchwork quilts, wooden rockers, and braided rugs. The four first-floor bedrooms still have tiled working fireplaces; rooms with western exposure are the sunniest and most spacious. In the romantic Hat Room, on the eastern side, antique headpieces adorn the walls, an old record cabinet now holds books, and there's an antique grapevine-canopy bed. On the second floor, where pressed-tin ceilings have been added, the bedrooms are filled with more attractive furniture—a calliope horse, a stencilled bed, and a wicker settee.

You won't find a dining room or parlor; instead, guests congregate in the third-floor common room for breakfast served on an old farmhouse trestle table. The imposing staircase that leads there is crammed with vintage teddy bears and lined with mannequins showcasing the couple's collection of antique clothing.

Across the street the Artzes converted the DeVoe House, the oldest home in Wausau, into two guest suites; both the downstairs and upstairs accommodations contain whirlpool tubs, fireplaces, and open-to-view kitchen appliances, all in one large room with partitions. Throughout the house are collections of antique hope chests, patchwork quilts, and, in the room under the rafters, a rope-suspended porch swing.

Both establishments on this quiet, almost aristocratic residential street have porches and gardens for relaxation. They are also only a quick walk from downtown.

Address: *511 Franklin St., Wausau, WI 54401, tel. 715/842–5733.*
Accommodations: *8 double rooms with baths, cottage has 2 double rooms with baths.*
Amenities: *Air-conditioning, fireplace in 4 rooms.*
Rates: *Rosenberry Inn $60, DeVoe House $90; Continental breakfast. MC, V.*
Restrictions: *No pets.*

Stewart Inn

Banker and lumberman Hiram Stewart made a fortune in booming Wausau at the end of the 19th century. In 1905, he commissioned well-known Chicago architect George Maher to design a mansion befitting his wealth and place in the community. Stewart became the lucky beneficiary of Maher's genius—the architect produced a masterpiece of the Prairie School style pioneered by his friend Frank Lloyd Wright.

When planning a project, Maher commonly chose a local plant and a geometric design to provide a unifying design theme throughout the structure. For Stewart's home, Maher used the tulip and a three-segmented arch. Tulips crown the tops of the columns on the front porch. The massive front door is arched at the top, as is the picture window in the living room.

The interior of the house is spectacular. From the mahogany-paneled entry hall, guests ascend three marble stairs to the spacious living room. The home's eighteen rooms range from the third-floor ballroom to a cozy parlor next to the living room. There are six fireplaces, including one in the living room that is framed by a dazzling glass-and-ceramic mosaic. A dozen kinds of wood were used for paneling, moldings, stair railings, floors, cabinets, and built-in benches, buffets, and bookshelves. One art glass tulip chandelier provides light in the living room, while another massive stained-glass chandelier hangs over the dining-room table. Original leaded-glass windows are still found throughout the house. Innkeepers Dennis and Chikako Massey have filled the house with both contemporary and antique furnishings, as well as collections of Japanese ceramics, pottery, furniture, dolls, wedding kimonos, and prints—many of them from Chikako's family.

A grand staircase leads upstairs past a large framed antique tapestry to the guest rooms. The most popular is Room 2 (the Masseys don't name their rooms), with its balcony and fireplace. It was Stewart's master bedroom. The smaller Room 3 has a fireplace, a TV, a white wrought-iron bed, a lovely collection of Japanese dolls, a private bath, and access to the balcony. The guest rooms without private baths all have sinks, the height of luxury in 1905.

The house, which is on the National Register of Historic Places, is in the center of Wausau's impressive Andrew Warren Historic District, and only a few blocks from downtown's shopping, entertainment, and restaurants.

Address: *521 Grant St., Wausau, WI 54401, tel. 715/848–1852.*
Accommodations: *1 double room with bath, 2 doubles and 1 single share bath.*
Amenities: *Air conditioning in 2 rooms, fireplaces; bicycles.*
Rates: *$60–$80; full breakfast, afternoon refreshments. No credit cards.*
Restrictions: *No smoking indoors; no pets.*

Bettinger House

Marie Neider's hilltop brick home, built in 1904, has been in her family since 1913, when her grandfather moved in. Today, it's a walk-in album of family history: Vintage photos line the walls of the house where her grandmother, a midwife, delivered more than 300 of Plain's babies.

Relatives' names are scrolled in brass on the doors of the four guest rooms. Uncle Edmund's Room has a handmade Star of Bethlehem quilt and matching wallhanging, white ruffled curtains, and floral stenciling. The front room, named for Grandma Elizabeth, looks like a schoolgirl's bower, complete with a dainty wicker dresser.

The common rooms are more modern and have less personality than the rest of the house. Breakfast is informal; guests gather around the oak kitchen table. Wicker chairs and a swing on the front porch catch the action in this small town, but don't let the relaxed atmosphere fool you: the Bettinger House fills up fast in the summer because it's only 7 miles from Spring Green and its many attractions.

Address: *855 Wachter Ave., Hwy. 23, Plain, WI 53577, tel. 608/546–2951.*
Accommodations: *2 double rooms with baths, 3 doubles share 2 baths.*
Amenities: *Air-conditioning.*
Rates: *$50–$60; full breakfast. MC, V.*
Restrictions: *No smoking indoors, no pets; 2-night minimum summer weekends.*

Breese Waye

Portage, Wisconsin's third-oldest city, sits where the Fox River, flowing north toward the waters of Green Bay, comes within a mile of the Wisconsin River. It was here, in 1880, that banker Llewellyn Breese built the Breese Waye—a brick Victorian mansion, later remodeled to give it a vaguely Greek Revival look.

In the front foyer, a fireplace with sculpted tiles of classic Grecian profiles catches your eye immediately. The rest of the family rooms are less distinctive, unless you're after velvet swivel chairs and reproduction Early American hutches.

Guest rooms, however, have a lot to offer. The Surgeon's Quarters has a collection of antique physicians' instruments, two rocking chairs, and an extra-large bathroom with bright white tiles. The young, or perhaps the young at heart, may prefer the Toy Room, full of owner Gretchen Sprecher's collection of dolls, stuffed animals, and other playthings. Don't let the toys keep you from noticing the room's gorgeous parquet floors and spoolback rocker.

Address: *816 MacFarlane Rd., Portage, WI 53901, tel. 608/742–5281.*
Accommodations: *4 double rooms with baths.*
Amenities: *Air-conditioning, TV and VCR in common room.*
Rates: *$55–$65; full breakfast. No credit cards.*
Restrictions: *No smoking indoors.*

Candlewick Inn

Built by lumber baron and civic leader Henry Wright in the 1880s, this classic Victorian has been carefully restored to its late-19th-century elegance. The original quarter-sawn oak woodwork includes intricately carved crown molding in the living and dining rooms and library. The living room, furnished with antique and reproduction wing chairs and sofas, has a green glazed-brick fireplace and a large bay window that looks out onto a comfy screened porch. Adjoining the living room is the more casually furnished library, which besides books, houses a TV and VCR. The dining room has a fireplace rimmed in blue glazed bricks and a built-in buffet with leaded-glass doors; a crystal chandelier hangs from the beamed ceiling. It's here innkeeper Dan Staniak serves his delicious homemade muffins.

Upstairs, the five guest rooms include the Lane Room, popular with honeymooners because it has a pink glazed-brick fireplace, a king-size brass bed, and a sitting area with wing chairs in the large bay window. The McCord Room features an antique sleigh bed, and the Wright Room has an antique oak bed, washstand, table, and chairs.

Address: *700 W. Main St., Merrill, WI 54452, tel. 715/536–7744 or 800/382–4376.*
Accommodations: *3 double rooms with baths, 2 double rooms share bath.*
Amenities: *Air conditioning, fireplace in 2 rooms and common rooms.*
Rates: *$55–$110; full breakfast, afternoon refreshments. MC, V.*
Restrictions: *Smoking on porch only; no pets.*

Hill Street

All the woodwork in this Queen Anne house is hand-carved, making Kelly and Jay Phelps' Hill Street one of the nicest bed-and-breakfasts in Spring Green. The grand central staircase has a striking design, and throughout the main floor you'll find contemporary furnishings mixed with Mission style chairs and tables.

Guest rooms, named after prominent settlers of the town, are each decorated differently. Most attractive is the Harry Gray Room, banded by four windows in a turret alcove, with a brass bed and a ceiling fan. The Marion Kanouse Room has a half-canopy bed with a floral-print quilt, wicker chairs, a love seat, and a Victorian dresser; a quilt made by Kelly's grandmother hangs on the wall. In the basement are two guest rooms furnished in a con-

temporary style, as well as the TV lounge.

Before setting out, guests can breakfast on Doris's giant pancakes with home-grown raspberries or the house specialty, French toast stuffed with pecans and cream cheese, or enjoy the morning on the wraparound porch with its wicker chairs and swing.

Address: *353 W. Hill St., Spring Green, WI 53588, tel. 608/588–7751.*
Accommodations: *5 double rooms with baths, 1 double and 1 triple share bath.*
Amenities: *Air-conditioning, ceiling fans.*
Rates: *$65–$75; full breakfast. MC, V.*
Restrictions: *No smoking indoors, no pets; 2-day minimum weekends June–Oct.*

Nash House

The Nash House, in Wisconsin Rapids, recalls some of the state's historic past. Built in the early 1900s, it was home to Guy Nash, father of Philleo Nash, special assistant to President Harry S. Truman and head of the Federal Bureau of Indian Affairs. When Phyllis and Jim Custer bought the house in 1987, their love of historical homes prompted them to draw the Nash family's past into the inn's future by naming the rooms after Philleo and his siblings.

The beds in the three guest rooms are covered with antique quilts; Philleo's Room, decorated in mauve and white, features one crafted by a local Amish woman. Jean's Room displays hand-stenciled furniture, while Tom's Room has an antique brass bed and walnut highboy. Each sunny bedroom has floor-to-ceiling windows and all rooms offer the comfort of a private bath (Jean's and Tom's have claw-foot tubs).

Breakfast is usually served on the screened back porch, giving guests a chance to appreciate the array of daylilies, phlox, and impatiens blooming in the inn's garden.

Address: *1020 Oak St., Wisconsin Rapids, WI 54494, tel. 715/424–2001.* **Accommodations:** *3 double rooms with baths.* **Amenities:** *Air-conditioning, ceiling fan in rooms, fireplace in common room; tandem bike.* **Rates:** *$45–$50; full breakfast, afternoon refreshments. AE, D, MC, V.* **Restrictions:** *No smoking, no pets.*

Parkview

Tom and Donna Hofmann used 43 rolls of wallpaper and 35 gallons of exterior paint to turn this Queen Anne Victorian into a bright, homey place. A few steps from downtown on a corner in Reedsburg's historic district, Parkview is surrounded by other Victorian homes and churches. But Parkview is different. Built in 1895 by a local hardware merchant, the house has an abundance of ornate hinges and doorknobs, not to mention original oak woodwork throughout the house. The yard behind the house is just as fanciful, crowded with a playhouse, goldfish ponds, stone flower pots, trellises, and a windmill built of pebbles.

The guest rooms upstairs are furnished with antiques bought at local auctions. One room has a high-top bed with carved head- and footboards; another, a deal dresser with a swinging mirror; another features a brass bed.

Address: *211 N. Park St., Reedsburg, WI 53959, tel. 608/524–4333.* **Accommodations:** *2 double rooms with baths, 2 doubles share bath.* **Amenities:** *Air-conditioning, ceiling fan in rooms, fireplace in common room.* **Rates:** *$55–$70; full breakfast, refreshments on arrival. AE, MC, V.* **Restrictions:** *No smoking, no pets.*

Pinehaven

Enjoy the ride between the twin columns of spruce trees lining the drive of the 80-acre Pinehaven retreat. Overlooking a private pond on the edge of Baraboo, the house is the dream of Lyle and Marge Getschman, who began its construction in 1971.

In the living room, sliding glass doors frame bucolic vistas, a wall of white luma stone surrounds a dramatic modern corner fireplace, and there's a baby grand piano that guests are free to play. There are two levels of guest rooms, all with private baths and three with queen-size beds. Of the four rooms, the Victorian, done in white wicker, has the most dramatic views.

You can sit in the screened porches or outside on shady decks, swim, row, or lounge on rafts. Other activities include strolling to the nearby Baraboo River, or petting one of Pinehaven's nine sturdy Belgian draft horses. The horses team up in the summer for wagon rides and in the winter for sleigh rides.

Address: *E13083 Rte. 33, Baraboo, WI 53913, tel. 608/356–3489.*
Accommodations: *4 double rooms with baths, 2-bedroom guest house with kitchen.*
Amenities: *Air-conditioning, candy in rooms, fireplace in common room; small private lake with paddleboat and rowboat.*
Rates: *$65–$95; full breakfast (no breakfast in guest house), apple cider on arrival. MC, V.*
Restrictions: *No smoking, no pets.*

Sherman House

In 1904, Chicago architect Robert Spencer, a close friend of Frank Lloyd Wright, was hired to design this 14-room house. The stucco-and-sandstone, Prairie-style home, which overlooks the Wisconsin River, was commissioned by wealthy Chicago attorney J.M. Sherman as a summer retreat.

The living and dining rooms, which retain their original woodwork, are divided only by back-to-back tan brick fireplaces, angled to form two sides of a triangle. The point of the triangle directs the eye out through wide doors to the large screened porch, which overlooks a shady yard, towering oaks, and the river below. Innkeeper Norma Marz serves breakfast on the porch when weather permits. With the exception of a couple of antique tables, the downstairs is furnished in comfortable, if slightly frayed, sofas and chairs.

Upstairs, the woodwork is painted white, and Norma has painted each room a solid color–deep green, peach, sage green, and mauve–to contrast with the woodwork, creating an uncluttered backdrop for her mixture of antique and contemporary furnishings. Ask for a room with a river view.

Address: *930 River Rd., Box 397, Wisconsin Dells, WI 53965, tel. 608/253–2721.*
Accommodations: *3 double rooms with baths, 1 suite.*
Amenities: *Air conditioning.*
Rates: *$50–$65; Continental breakfast. No credit cards.*
Restrictions: *No pets. Closed Nov.–Mar.*

The Swallow's Nest

Although the Swallow's Nest bed-and-breakfast, a modern cedar-shingled lake house, is nestled among tall timbers and wildflowers of the forest, you can catch a glimpse of the lake's sparkling water from the house's windows. This scenery is the inspiration for the photography and paintings of innkeeper Rod Stemo.

The house is built around a sunny, two-story atrium. An open staircase leads to a bridge that overlooks the plant-filled atrium and connects the four guest rooms. In the Tamarack Room, blue-gingham-covered walls and lace curtains offset an antique mirrored dressing table. Paintings and floral plates grace the soft pink walls of the Wild Rose Room, complementing the room's heirloom English walnut furniture. Twin knotty pine beds and deep green and rust accents make the Whispering Pine Room quite masculine. The suitably named Sunburst Room is done in pale yellows, with a queen-size brass bed.

After a breakfast served by Mary Ann Stemo, guests can take a woodland walk or rent a boat to explore the lake.

Address: *141 Sarrington St., Box 418, Lake Delton, WI 53940, tel. 608/254–6900.*
Accommodations: *4 double rooms with baths.*
Amenities: *Air-conditioning, fireplaces in common rooms, pool table, TV in common room.*
Rates: *$65–$70; full breakfast. MC, V.*
Restrictions: *No smoking, no pets.*

Victorian Swan on Water

Joan Ouelette's Victorian Swan on Water, appropriately named for its Water Street address, is easy to find—the town's water tower looms behind it. A row of pine trees screens the tower from the 100-year-old blue clapboard house, which is flanked by a beautiful garden of annuals and perennials.

Ivy trails through the home's sunny dining room where the daily three-course breakfast is served. Before retiring to one of the four bedrooms, guests can relax in the garden's double porch swing or in the Victorian drawing room, which has distinctive black-walnut inlaid floors and elaborate crown moldings.

In the peaches-and-cream Newport Chaney Room, Jean turned an alcove into a sitting area with a skirted table and two antique chairs. The Rothman Room features a hand-carved antique dressing table. Its bathroom has a claw-foot tub, a pedestal sink, and cabinets made to match the walnut and maple floor. The Balcony Room, romantically decorated in rose and lilac chintz, has a canopy-draped wrought-iron bed; a small balcony overlooks the front yard and Water Street.

Address: *1716 Water St., Stevens Point, WI 54481, tel. 715/345–0595.*
Accommodations: *4 double rooms with baths.*
Amenities: *Air-conditioning, fireplace in parlor.*
Rates: *$50–$70; full breakfast. AE, D, MC, V.*
Restrictions: *No smoking, no pets.*

Hidden Valleys
Including La Crosse and Prairie du Chien

The rumpled rural terrain known as Hidden Valleys hugs the eastern edge of the Mississippi River as it flows southward from La Crosse to the Iowa border, rolling inland in some spots for 60 or so picturesque miles. As viewed from the window of a plane, the land is a pincushion of church steeples and grain silos, towers of strength that neatly summarize what this somnolent slice of small-town America is all about.

Faith first arrived in these parts in the person of Jesuit priest Jacques Marquette, who busily converted Native Americans even as he and explorer Louis Jolliet searched for the Mississippi in the 17th century. Agriculture appeared not too long afterward, as successive waves of immigrants from several European nations literally set down roots in the rich topsoil.

Many of these communities proudly maintain their Old World character, a task made easier by their relative isolation. The region has the Midwest's largest concentration of hardwood forests and is unblemished by an interstate, allowing the Norwegian heritage to survive in Westby and helping Hillsboro to keep its distinctive Czech culture. In New Glarus, founded in 1845 by immigrants from Glarus, Switzerland, many of the residents are still bilingual—a pleasant discovery for visitors to such annual events as the Heidi Festival in June, the Volksfest in August, and the Wilhelm Tell Festival on Labor Day weekend. Like the other festivals in the area, these are genuine ethnic celebrations that have so far resisted being cloying.

Another ethnic enclave is Mineral Point, just south of Dodgeville along U.S. 151. Here Cornish miners in the 1830s sat out winters in underground dwellings called badger holes. The lead and zinc mines contributed to Wisconsin's admittance to the Union in 1848, and the prospectors' dugouts accounted for its nickname as the Badger State. Mineral Point today is a growing artists' colony featuring a wide variety of influences, but its English history is still very much in evidence, from the old stone houses to the formidable meat pies called pasties. Visitors to Mineral Point should not miss Pendarvis, a state historic site with a collection of restored limestone and log Cornish cottages from the 1840s.

The two largest towns in the region, La Crosse and Prairie du Chien, were both settled by French traders looking to exploit their locations on the Mississippi River. The distance between these ports can be leisurely traversed via riverboat or Route 35. The latter, part of the Great River Road, is a 55-mile drive that offers a succession of scenic vistas; it's particularly spectacular in October, when the statewide "Colorama" autumn festival is in full swing.

Places to Go, Sights to See

Cassville. Visit Stonefield Village (north on Rte. VV, tel. 608/725–5210), home to the State Agricultural Museum and a replica of an 1890s village, complete with costumed guides. Across the road, Nelson Dewey State Park (tel. 608/725–5374) is a perfect place to catch the drama of river-bluff vistas.

Bike Trails. The Elroy-Sparta State Trail (tel. 602/463–7109) was the first abandoned railroad grade to be converted to a recreation trail. It winds through 32 miles of wooded valleys, small towns, and railroad tunnels, with interpretative stops, parking, and picnic facilities along the way. The valley's other biking trails include the Great River State Trail (tel. 608/534–6409), 22½ miles along the Mississippi Valley, and the 23-mile Sugar River State Trail (tel. 608/527–2334) that runs south from New Glarus.

La Crosse. The Convention and Visitors Bureau in Riverside Park (tel. 608/782–2366) is also the home of Riverside USA, an animated exhibit describing life on the Mississippi. The bureau also provides maps for a Heritage Tour, which details 42 historic buildings throughout the town, beginning at the Hixon House (429 N. 7th St.), now the County Historical Museum, and including the G. Heileman Brewery and Christina Winery. Nearby, La Crosse Queen (tel. 608/784–2893 or 608/784–8523) and Island Girl (tel. 608/784–0556) offer paddleboat river excursions. Granddad's Bluff towers 530 feet above the city; the summit offers a panoramic view of three states and three rivers.

New Glarus. "Little Switzerland" honors the Alpine life of its founders in the pastoral Swiss Historical Village (612 7th Ave., tel. 608/527–2317), where 12 reconstructed buildings depict the homes, trades, and skills of the Swiss who first settled here, including a tour of a 19th-century cheese factory. Events such as the

Wilhelm Tell and Heidi festivals, and the Volkfest, Polkafest, and Winterfest take place throughout the year and include arts-and-crafts fairs, outdoor music, and historical plays.

Norskedalen (Rte. PI, west of Westby, tel. 608/452–3424). "The Norwegian Valley," as it translates, has grown from an arboretum to a 400-acre expanse that includes log farmsteads. Maps guide hikers past corn and tobacco fields, oak and spruce forests, prairies, ponds, and springs. Cross-country skiers use the trails in the winter.

Prairie du Chien. Remains of the American Fur Trading Company's stone warehouses and fort survive on St. Feriole Island. In 1870, fur fortunes built opulent Villa Louis Mansion (531 N. Villa Louis Rd., tel. 608/326–2721), home of Wisconsin's first millionaire. Today, tours are offered daily from May through October. Along the river behind the mansion, the St. Feriole Island Railroad's restored railroad cars are filled with shops. Nearby, Lawler Park has swimming beaches and marinas.

Restaurants

In Monroe, you have your choice between **Baumgartner's Cheese Store & Tavern** (1023 16th Ave., Monroe, tel. 608/325–6157), in the town's historic square, serving bulky cheese sandwiches and a local brew, or a fancier meal at the century-old **Idle Hour Mansion** (1421 Mansion Dr., Monroe, tel. 608/325–1200), where the Sunday champagne brunch is popular. You're back in history once more at the **Westby House** (200 W. State St., Westby, tel. 608/634–4112), where, in a Victorian tea-shop setting, you can order Wisconsin cheeses, sandwiches, salads, and rich homemade desserts. The **New Glarus Hotel** (100 6th Ave., New Glarus, tel. 608/527–5244) no longer accommodates guests overnight but does serve authentic Alpine dishes such as fondue and raclette. The **Chalet Landhaus** (801 Rte. 69, New Glarus, tel. 608/527–5234), housed in a town landmark, has a similar menu. In Mineral Point's Chesterfield Inn, another 19th-century site, **Ovens of Brittany** (20 Commerce St., Mineral Point, tel. 608/987–3682) serves its legendary baked goods, along with quiche and other light entrées.

Tourist Information

La Crosse Convention & Visitors Bureau (Box 1895, Riverside Park, La Crosse, WI 54901, tel. 608/782–2366); **Mineral Point Chamber of Commerce** (Box 78, Mineral Point, WI 53565, tel. 608/987–3201); **New Glarus Chamber of Commerce** (Box 713, New Glarus, WI 53574, tel. 608/527–2095); **Prairie du Chien Chamber of Commerce** (Box 326, Prairie du Chien, WI 53821, tel. 800/732–1673); **Sparta Chamber of Commerce** (101 S. Water St., Sparta, WI 54656, tel. 608/269–4123).

The Duke House

ven though it is in the Midwest, this 1870 Federal-style house—one of the oldest in Mineral Point—feels like a New England Victorian. Darlene Duke and her husband, Tom, packed up their antiques collection and drove out of the East Coast fast lane in search of a more pleasant way of life.

One of the reasons Darlene loves the light and airy house is that there are so many windows she can do her needlework even on a gloomy day. The focus of the creamy white living room is the working fireplace; a plush pastel Chinese rug warms the broad-planked floor. An old brass trunk serves as a coffee table, and there's a Colonial drum table under the newel post. These and a few reproduction pieces give the room a lived-in, homey atmosphere, perfect for the early evening social hour that the Dukes feel is the best time of the day.

The house is built on the area's highest point of land, so the views from the upstairs bedrooms capture most of the small city, which is almost untouched by time. The four-poster bed in the Canopy Room is covered with a crocheted string spread and a canopy, and the finials are shaped like pineapples, the symbol of hospitality. With its pierced-tin lamp, its low, wooden Colonial-era rocker, the steamer trunk in the huge walk-in closet, and the copper warming pan affixed to the wall, the room is comfortable but not precious.

Across the hall, in Grandma's Room, more pineapples appear on the four-poster bed, complemented by floral wallpaper, a white rug covering well-polished floorboards, a decorative kerosene lamp, and bookcases filled with tomes of area history and lore. Other pieces find their way here from Duke's Antiques, which is only a short stroll away, close to the artisans' shops that occupy the former miners' dwellings.

Address: *618 Maiden St., Mineral Point, WI 53565, tel. 608/987–2821.*
Accommodations: *2 double rooms share bath.*
Amenities: *Air-conditioning, fireplace in common room.*
Rates: *$48–$57; full breakfast, morning coffee and Cornish appetizers delivered to bedroom doors. MC, V.*
Restrictions: *No smoking, no pets; closed Mar.*

The Franklin Victorian

W.G. Williamson, a prominent Sparta banker, personally inspected every piece of wood that went into the interior of this raspberry-red clapboard Victorian. His high standards are evident the minute you cross the white-columned front porch. The floors are of glowing maple complemented by black ash and quarter-cut oak. Pocket doors of curly birch lead to a parlor with russet ceramic tiles, a beveled-glass window, and a double-manteled fireplace with fluted Corinthian columns—elegant reminders of the late 1800s, when Sparta, with its spas and mineral waters, was a hub of social activity.

Cordial innkeepers Jane and Lloyd Larson have integrated their family heirlooms into the house. In the dining room, which has an elaborate parquet floor with a "braided" border, is a buffet with floor-to-ceiling glass doors, showcasing china that's been in Jane's family for three generations. In the parlor, Jane's grandfather's Civil War–era miniature pump organ, an instrument he played at funerals, keeps company with a boxy Victorian velvet sofa trimmed in mahogany, and its honor guard of stuffed velvet chairs that belonged to her great-grandparents. The intricate "sunset" stained-glass window faces west, providing a vivid late-afternoon glow to the stairway landing.

Guests love the Wicker Room, with its white wrought-iron bed and wicker furnishings that contrast with the dark blue floral-design wallpaper. Most requested, however, is the Master Bedroom, which has a grand tiled and decorative columned fireplace, an immense oak headboard Lloyd Larson crafted with wood from the wall of a judge's chamber, and a tall highboy of bird's-eye maple that belonged to Jane's parents. Its bathroom, with tongue-and-groove wainscoting, still boasts the original marble-topped sink.

Guests can enjoy a private chat in the upstairs sitting room, or sit in rocking chairs and sip lemonade on the side and front porches. They overlook this corner lot in a quiet residential neighborhood, where trees loom taller than dormers and turrets.

Address: *220 E. Franklin Pl., Sparta, WI 54656, tel. 608/269–3894.*
Accommodations: *2 double rooms with baths, 2 doubles share bath.*
Amenities: *Air-conditioning, fireplace in common room; canoe rental, shuttle service for bikers and canoeists.*
Rates: *$60–$80; full breakfast, early morning coffee. MC, V.*
Restrictions: *No pets, no smoking.*

The Inn at Wildcat Mountain

All tall white pillars, with a classic Georgian air, this inn looks like the White House of woodland Wisconsin. A Greek Revival mansion on the edge of tiny Ontario, it was built in 1910 with high hopes: Its builder, who had made a fortune growing ginseng and shipping it to Asian buyers in Chicago, planned to rent rooms in the house to tourists. But the proposed railroad never made it this far, and the interior of the gorgeous house was carved up into apartments.

After undergoing a monumental restoration, the building is the dream come true of innkeepers Pat and Wendall Barnes. With their children grown and gone, turning their home into a bed-and-breakfast seemed natural: "How else could I justify buying a house like this?" Pat laughs. She says she enjoyed restoring the building and likes entertaining people who appreciate the cherry, oak, and bird's-eye maple woodwork she spent years of her life refinishing.

Pat describes her former life as "collecting things," an understatement once you see the period pieces and vintage clothing hung everywhere on walls, clothes trees, and mannequins. A fan revolves on the parlor's lofty ceiling, and lace-curtained windows rise even higher than the dignified grandfather clock. The focal point of the room is a 1905 oak secretary. The dining room, connected to the parlor by a columned entry, is set with a silver candelabra whose lights flicker on the Philippine mahogany sideboard.

Of the four upstairs rooms, the most asked for is the Balcony Room, which has a turn-of-the-century brass bed and its own curved balcony. The back room, called Shady Rest, boasts the house's only closet, as well as a four-poster bed and a bare wooden floor.

The 5-acre woodland setting, in the lap of the forested Wildcat Mountain State Park, makes the inn especially popular with outdoor-sports enthusiasts. Guests can rent horses or canoes at nearby outfitters. Or they can just loll on Pat's wide, inviting front porch or in the spacious backyard and watch the butterflies flit by.

Address: *U.S. 33 (Box 112), Ontario, WI 54651, tel. 608/337-4352.*
Accommodations: *4 double rooms (1 sleeps 3 people) share bath.*
Amenities: *Air-conditioning, ceiling fans.*
Rates: *$45–$85; full breakfast, early morning coffee and tea, afternoon refreshments. MC, V.*
Restrictions: *No smoking, pets in kennels outside only.*

The Jones House

This regional showcase looks as grand as it did on the day it was built; oddly enough, it was hardly lived in. William Jones, once commissioner of the Bureau of Indian Affairs for President McKinley, erected the 16-room redbrick mansion in 1906 as a homecoming present to himself after his stint in Washington. He died soon after and his will forbade its sale until the death of his wife and children. Boarded up intact, a housekeeper religiously dusted it twice a week until 1986, when June and Art Openshaw purchased it.

A grand, boxy staircase winds around one of the seven unusual fireplaces. The stairs rise from the foyer to a stained-glass skylight that casts patterns on the entrance carpet. The mahogany-beamed dining room is graced by forest-green woodland scenes painted above the wainscoting. A green-tile fireplace warms guests during breakfast. Twin sideboards topped by graceful arches glint with beveled glass, and padded velvet window seats on either side of the fireplace overlook the broad side lawn. To complete the *après la chasse* feel, the hardwood floor is covered with moss-green carpet.

The Persian and floral-print rugs, dark patterned wallpapers, and brass light fixtures, all of which came with the house, create a decidedly masculine atmosphere. The small Ladies' Parlor overlooking the front walk, however,

provides respite with its garlands of roses painted on its high, pale walls.

In the Master Suite, a white-tile fireplace, the original needlepoint chairs, and a floral covering on the daybed in the suite's sitting room also create a more feminine air. A screen door leads to a porch-top balcony that overlooks the town. The adjacent front bedroom, with a view of the spreading side yard as well as the avenue, boasts another white-tiled fireplace and a Colonial-reproduction four-poster bed with pineapple finials on the posts. The Ivy Suite, which overlooks the hills to the north of town, has a green-tiled fireplace and a Colonial-reproduction four-poster; the smaller back bedroom, in contrast, has a country-antique look.

There are traces of Mr. Jones still in the house: Outside the Master Suite stand the master's antique golf clubs; his leatherbound books still line the library's shelves; and his umbrella hangs on the door of the vestibule.

Address: *215 Ridge St. (Box 130), Mineral Point, WI 53565, tel. 608/987–2337.*
Accommodations: *1 double room with bath, 1 suite, 1 suite and 1 double share bath.*
Amenities: *Fans in rooms, 7 fireplaces.*
Rates: *$50–$80; full breakfast. No credit cards.*
Restrictions: *No smoking, no pets.*

Just-N-Trails

Ask Don and Donna Justin why they added a bed-and-breakfast to their 213-acre working farm and they just laugh, "We'd been doing it free for 15 years anyway for all the relatives." The accommodations are "all things to all people," claim the friendly, laid-back couple, who delight in welcoming guests. Their 50 head of Holstein often provide visitors with a late-night show (no cover charge)—the birth of a calf. An athlete's nirvana, their spread has 10 miles of groomed and mapped hiking and ski trails, six nearby cycling trails (the area calls itself "the bike capital of America"), and five rivers close at hand where guests can fish or go canoeing.

The farm is also a romantic getaway spot with three private cabins and Laura Ashley–decorated rooms upstairs in the farmhouse. The Granary cabin has a front porch from which you can watch the sun sinking past the fields and wooded hills. The cabin decor is on the kitschy side—plastic pine boughs with twinkling lights, lots of cows and teddy bears—but it has

Amish bentwood rockers made by local craftsmen and its own whirlpool bath. The beds are invitingly comfortable with an abundance of pillows that make reading a pleasure.

The second log cabin, Little House on the Prairie, has a log bed, country-style furnishings, and a whirlpool bath in the loft under skylights. The Paul Bunyan, the two-bedroom cottage, is made of aspen logs from the farm's woodlots, and is furnished with a log bed and other rustic pieces. It also boasts a double whirlpool, and a second floor porch from which to watch deer come out of the nearby woods. All three cottages have kitchenettes and the Paul Bunyan is accessible to wheelchair users.

Guests in the farmstead's bedrooms—such as the Maple Room with a green, pink, and white floral scheme and double sleigh bed of bird's-eye maple—get the same nine-pillow treatment as those in the cabins. The morning wake-up call is a wren's warble or perhaps a moo, followed by Donna's hearty, farm-style breakfast on the glassed-in sunporch. There's also a microwave guests can use when the hungries hit, as sometimes happens after a ramble on the hills up to the farm pond and down again via the Bambi trail—so named to reassure novice skiers.

Address: *Rte. 1 (Box 274), Sparta, WI 54656, tel. 608/269–4522 or 800/488–4521.*
Accommodations: *3 double rooms with baths, 2 doubles share bath, 2 1-bedroom cabins, 1 2-bedroom cabin.*
Amenities: *Air-conditioning, fireplace and whirlpool tub in cabins; hammock, picnic tables; cross-country ski rentals, snow tubes available free; "traditional agrarian fitness center with pitchfork and hay bales."*
Rates: *$65–$250; full breakfast. AE, D, MC, V.*
Restrictions: *No smoking, no pets.*

Martindale House

When Anita Philbrook opened the Martindale House in a quiet residential section of La Crosse, she was concerned that bed-and-breakfast establishments "were a fad, like the vitamin craze." But repeat guests—from as far away as England, Spain, and Scandinavia—have proved there's no cause for concern. "I offer not just a bed, but an experience," Martindale's polished hostess maintains. Luckily, it includes a hearty Swedish breakfast served on the fifth-generation family china patterned in wedding-ring gold, with antique silver coffee spoons, in the white, bright Scandinavian-style dining room lined with a traditional collection of family portraits.

The imposing green-shuttered house is a grand architectural mélange of Italianate cupola and Colonial clapboard, with an bungalow–style wraparound porch to boot. Combatting years of disrepair, Anita restored moldings and chandeliers discovered in the basement and returned them to their proper places; she also resurrected the iron fence, unearthed in the carriage house. Then she replanted the entire garden.

Inside, the parlor is a historian's delight. The room contains a stately grandfather clock, an antique chess table, antique Oriental rugs on the blond-oak floors, floor-to-ceiling windows flanked by their original shutters, and a piano that's been in her husband's family for five generations.

The white staircase in the foyer leads to four bedrooms. The Martindale Room features an 1800 cannonball bed, a warming pan, porcelain dolls in cradles, and quilts from the nearby Amish community. The French Room derives its name from the carved Louis XVI bed that came from a castle in Lyons; its other highlight is the carved-wood chest made by Anita's Swedish grandmother. The English Room offers a fireplace, a garden view, and a lace-canopied four-poster bed. This room has the advantage of a vast, soothing bathroom, dubbed by guests "the rub-a-dub." The antique beds in the sunny yellow Scandinavian Room were made in 1740 and came from a convent, and the Lappland dolls on display there belonged to Anita's grandmother. Anita recently renovated the 1860 carriage house into a three-room suite that's furnished with antiques, but has the modern convenience of a heart-shaped double whirlpool.

Address: *237 S. 10th St., La Crosse, WI 54601, tel. 608/782-4224.*
Accommodations: *4 double rooms with baths, 1 suite.*
Amenities: *Air-conditioning, use of portable phones; several languages spoken.*
Rates: *$80–$145; 4-course breakfast. MC, V.*
Restrictions: *No smoking, no pets.*

Mascione's Hidden Valley Villas

Phil and Mary Ann Mascione, as Italian as Chicagoans can get, do not come across at first as isolated rancher types. In fact, the fellow with the big grin and hearty handshake was the sports photographer for the *Chicago Tribune* for years. But when their kids grew up and moved away, the couple came here—to a hidden valley reached by a back road that weaves through stands of pine along the bluffs of the Kickapoo River.

All by themselves, the Masciones built an Alpine-style guest retreat. Phil scoured the countryside for weathered boards from fallen barns while Mary Ann collected American crafts. They created a minivillage of chalet-type guest villas that overlook pastures where young holsteins, relaxing before their milking careers begin, graze peacefully.

The Golden Antler villa follows a hunting-lodge motif and comes complete with mounted stags' heads, skis, snowshoes, and antlers used as racks for an antique gun collection. The Camelot villa's decor has a medieval theme. Both villas have two bedrooms in a loft space. The first floors have wagon-wheel chandeliers, fireplaces made of local fieldstone that Phil collected, complete kitchens including microwaves, dining areas, and a shared bathroom. They also have decks with umbrella tables and barbecue grills.

Three new two-person chalets have been added. The snug living room of each has a fireplace and, in the corner, a small minikitchen. Upstairs, under the slanting ceiling, Phil built impressive pine beds that Mary Ann carved and painted in keeping with the theme of each chalet: the Cheyenne, the Aztec, and the Eagle's Nest.

Mary Ann cooks a hearty breakfast of eggs Benedict or soufflé with local bratwurst and serves it in a separate dining cottage, whose entryway houses a gift-and-antiques shop.

Set back in the pines on a hill is an Olympic-size pool surrounded by a deck and umbrella tables. The 80-acre property has two trout ponds, a croquet court, and a baseball field, as well as miles of meticulously tended walking trails.

Address: *Rte. 2 (Box 74), Hillsboro, WI 54634, tel. 608/489–3443.*
Accommodations: *2 2-bedroom villas and 3 1-bedroom villas, all with baths.*
Amenities: *Air-conditioning, coffee maker, microwave, and fireplace in villas; hiking trails, pool.*
Rates: *$85–$185; full breakfast, snacks stocked in rooms. No credit cards.*
Restrictions: *Smoking limited, no pets; closed early Nov.–Apr.*

Westby House

Pat Smith is not a native of these parts—indeed, she claims she's here to "add a little variety to Westby's sturdy Norwegian mold," but she knows the territory. She grew up in St. Louis, and Westby was traditionally the halfway stop en route to Madeline Island, where her family spent summers.

In 1984, Pat purchased a country manor–style house built in the 1890s by a successful Norwegian immigrant. The mansion's signature Queen Anne witch's turret caught her eye, and as luck would have it, no paint marred the fine oak woodwork, and the light fixtures, stained glass, and imposing pillared fireplaces were still in place.

Upstairs in an otherwise undistinguished hallway, the original dining-room buffet stands guard over a pair of spacious front bedrooms. The Tower Room has a small bathroom and a down-quilt-covered brass bed set into an alcove of bay windows. The Fireplace Room has a brass bed, tiled fireplace, and a rocking chair; a TV helps to compensate for a lackluster view of storefronts just off the town's main street. The two rooms are connected by double doors and can be rented as a suite. The Anniversary Room is almost a suite, with reproduction wing chairs and a sofa forming a conversation group in its bay window. Its brass bed merits the handmade quilt and white eyelet comforter. The Greenbriar Room's caned chairs, rag rugs, marble-top washstand, and old-fashioned white iron bed, topped with another antique quilt, has the look of Grandma's house—comfortable but not fancy.

When Pat bought the house, she vowed never to cross the kitchen door. Ironically, she now runs a public restaurant in the three adjoining dining rooms. Polished wooden floors, bare wooden tables, and ice-cream-parlor chairs mingle with an antique upright piano and a fireplace replete with ceramic tiles and a mirror over the mantel.

This very Norwegian town is especially lively during the Syttendai Mai festival in May, when rooms are spoken for well in advance; the Old World Norskedalen Village, 6 miles away, attracts Pat's Scandophile guests year-round.

Address: *200 W. State St., Westby, WI 54667, tel. 608/634–4112.*
Accommodations: *2 double rooms with baths, 4 doubles share 2 baths.*
Amenities: *Air-conditioning, TV in rooms, fireplaces in common rooms, restaurant, gift and antiques shops.*
Rates: *$60–$80; Continental breakfast weekdays, full breakfast weekends, refreshments on arrival. MC, V.*
Restrictions: *No pets.*

The Country Manor

German pancakes have long been the specialty of Berlin-born, Milwaukee-bred Ursula Henke, but she never dreamed she'd be whipping up a fresh batch every Sunday. Nor did she and her husband, Eugene, picture themselves retiring to a small town in Wisconsin to run a bed-and-breakfast—until they stayed a night in one. Its owner knew of a deserving restoration project nearby—a solid 1860s brick farmhouse set in the wooded hills on the edge of town.

The Hinkes furnished their inn's living room with a comfortable sofa and wing chairs set on a braided rug, facing the fieldstone fireplace. The sunny, white parlor, more formally furnished, boasts an Victorian sofa, desk, chair and tables. French doors connect the parlor to the bright dining room, where

they've situated their pride and joy, a Civil War–era rocker.

Upstairs, each bedroom is sparkling and white from the walls to the German coverlets, china washing sets, and chamber pots. There are also Amish wicker rockers to sit in while taking in the view of shady elms and furrowed fields.

Address: *W5456 Boma Rd., La Crosse, WI 54601, tel. 608/787–1719.*
Accommodations: *1 double room with bath, 2 doubles share bath.*
Amenities: *Air-conditioning, fireplace in common room.*
Rates: *$60–$78; full breakfast. No credit cards.*
Restrictions: *No smoking, no pets.*

The Geiger House

Marcus and Penny Neal searched far and wide until they discovered a sleepy river town where time seemed to stand still. Then they combed it for a house that could hold their collection of antique furniture. The stately Greek Revival home they finally settled upon is on a spacious corner lot just two blocks from the Mississippi River. A trim white picket fence marks the spot.

Many of the inn's rooms do indeed showcase the Neals' vintage country-primitive furniture; the front bedroom boasts a rough-hewn table and an antique upright piano anchors the sitting room. Two bedrooms have views of the stunning Mississippi River bluffs behind the town. The front porch of the house provides box seats for Cassville's annual Twins Parade,

where Penny, a twin herself, is always front and center.

In the rear of the house, a grove of cherry, apple, and plum trees produce a cloud of blossoms in the spring. In winter, the dining room's fireplace makes a cozy gathering spot for breakfast.

Address: *401 Denniston St., Cassville, WI 53806, tel. 608/725–5419.*
Accommodations: *1 double room with bath, 4 doubles share 2 baths.*
Amenities: *Air-conditioning, fireplace in common room; bikes, shuttle to river ferry.*
Rates: *$45–$60; full breakfast, morning coffee, afternoon refreshments. MC, V.*
Restrictions: *No smoking, no pets.*

Oak Hill Manor

First a word about breakfast: *Gourmet* magazine has asked for the eggs Benedict recipe. Lee and Mary De Wolf used to own a restaurant, and it shows in the wonderful assortment of eggs, crêpes and sausages, and the fresh-baked bread. The couple's other passion is their terraced garden, complete with an English gazebo, which guests can enjoy from an old-fashioned swing on a porch that spans the 1908 foursquare house.

The proud farmwife for whom the house was built insisted on being able to survey the comings and goings from both directions, so the inn sits diagonally on its corner. The house showcases some of the lady's upscale tastes: Original ivory-embossed wallpaper hangs in the entry hall; the dining room is appointed with oak pocket doors and a built-in buffet; the living-room fireplace has tall wooden Ionic columns and a shiny brass grate; and rich oak woodwork is visible throughout. Upstairs, off a wide, sunny hall that leads to a cheery gathering room, are the two most popular bedrooms: Sylvia's, with a white-tiled, pillared fireplace, and Josephine's, with a private sunporch filled with wicker furniture.

Address: *401 E. Main St., Albany, WI 53502, tel. 608/862–1400.*
Accommodations: *4 double rooms with baths.*
Amenities: *Air-conditioning, fireplace in 1 room and common rooms; bikes.*
Rates: *$45–$55; full breakfast, evening refreshments. MC, V.*
Restrictions: *No smoking, no pets.*

The Parson's Inn

The cross on the rooftop is the clue that you've found the Parson's Inn—a 12-room, turn-of-the-century brick rectory that once served the church right across the street. Just off the wraparound porch, which overlooks the wooded river valley and the hills beyond town, is the original priest's office. "It's where I signed my marriage papers," says Mary Huser, mother of proprietor Julie Cull and a native of this secluded pocket of the state.

In decorating the inn, mother and daughter combined eclectic furnishings with family antiques such as the rolltop desk in the living room. Mary's grandmother's bird's-eye maple bed with ruffled half-canopy sits in Granny's Room, and the dining-room set was Mary's mother's wedding present—it's now where Julie serves her own mother's melt-away pecan rolls and homemade jellies for breakfast.

The Belle Suite's fireplace has been bricked over, but there's a rag rug on the floor, a handmade basket-pattern quilt on the bed, and a dresser and chest built into an alcove; from its awning-shaded deck, the nearby bluffs spread out before your eyes.

Address: *Rock School Rd., Glen Haven, WI 53810, tel. 608/794–2491.*
Accommodations: *2 double rooms share bath, 1 suite.*
Amenities: *Air-conditioning.*
Rates: *$45–$68 ($85 for 4 in suite); full breakfast, afternoon refreshments. No credit cards.*
Restrictions: *Closed Nov.–Mar.*

Sugar River Inn

The Sugar River is the source of many pleasures for the Albany community and its visitors. The inn's backyard is on the river shores, so guests can linger in the gazebo and watch canoes drift by or enjoy the view from the windows of the inn's country-style bedrooms—the Oak Room even has a small balcony.

Jack and Ruth Lindberg have furnished their 1920s brick home with Colonial-reproduction furniture, but their unique touches are what give the rooms charm. The quilt on the Country Room's four-poster Shaker-style bed depicts the same farm scene you see on the room's wallpaper border. The Rose Room's antique dolls and toys fit in perfectly with its pink walls and white lace. The Jenny Lind Room is home to a small library.

Ruth sends her guests off with a hearty breakfast featuring her "golden treat," a mélange of granola, golden raisins, bananas, vanilla yogurt, and honey, while a full cookie jar awaits guests at the end of every afternoon.

Address: *304 S. Mills St., Albany, WI 53502, tel. 608/862–1248.*
Accommodations: *1 double room with bath, 3 doubles share bath.*
Amenities: *Air-conditioning, fireplace in parlor, turndown service.*
Rates: *$45–$60; full breakfast, wake-up coffee, afternoon refreshments. MC, V.*
Restrictions: *No smoking, no pets.*

Trillium

These two cottages are nestled amid 85 acres of rolling hills in the heart of Amish farm country. The innkeepers, the Boyett family, live in the nearby frame house, and farmwife Rosanne Boyett arrives each morning with a freshly cooked breakfast for guests. Rosanne's husband laboriously hauled sandstone from the banks of the nearby Kickapoo River to build a huge fireplace in each cabin.

Grandma's Cottage, the smaller of the two, has a sitting room with a humble and well-used look that comes from overstuffed and antimacassared armchairs and treadle sewing machines; the sofabed allows the room to double as a bedroom. Beyond an arched doorway is a cozy inner bedroom with a neatly folded double wedding-ring quilt at the foot of the bed. An old woodstove dominates the kitchen (with a 1950s electric range as backup). The Hill Cottage has a open living-dining-kitchen area arranged around the stone fireplace. Upstairs are three bedrooms. Both cottages' spacious covered porches are set with rocking chairs. Paths lead to a brook and waterfall in the woods and circle fields of grain.

Address: *Rte. 2 (Box 121), La Farge, WI 54639, tel. 608/625–4492.*
Accommodations: *1 1-bedroom room cottage, 1 3-bedroom cottage, each with bath.*
Amenities: *Fireplaces, kitchen, hammocks, porch swings.*
Rates: *$65–$70 double; full breakfast. No credit cards.*
Restrictions: *No pets.*

Victorian Garden

Trees shade the arched front porches of this 110-year-old Victorian belle located on a quiet street in Monroe. But what makes you catch your breath is the double lot's gardens, crossed by meandering brick pathways.

The guest rooms are named after the garden's flowers, which can be seen from the rooms' windows. In the spacious Sweet Jasmine Room are a king-size bed, an antique loveseat, and a bay window that affords a particularly lovely view. The Rosebud Room has an antique double bed and a private bath. A small adjoining single room can be rented with either the Sweet Jasmine or the Rosebud room.

The large shared bath is spectacular: roses bloom on its black wallpaper and its folding screen. Live plants twine around the claw-foot tub and antique pedestal sink, and French doors overlook the garden.

Privacy is foremost in the Secret Garden dormer suite, with its own white staircase, skylights, television alcove, refrigerator, and microwave. The sunny bathroom even comes with a rubber duck in the whirlpool.

Address: *1720 16th St., Monroe, WI 53566, tel. 608/328–1720.*
Accommodations: *1 double room with bath, 2 doubles share bath, 1 suite.*
Amenities: *Air-conditioning; whirlpool tub, microwave, and refrigerator in suite; robes.*
Rates: *$45–$150; full breakfast. MC, V.*
Restrictions: *No smoking, no pets.*

Viroqua Heritage Inn

Restraint was the last thing the Boyle family had in mind when they built this Victorian extravaganza in 1890, and present owner Nancy Rhodes-Seevers has lovingly restored every last curlicue. This grand house rises in blue-shingled splendor, its porch embossed with a floral garland, and its corner tower topped with a conical cap.

More flowers bloom inside on the carved, ornately tiled fireplaces. Polished hardwood floors peep out from under the Oriental rugs in the parlor, and nearly outshine the brass and crystal chandelier. Lace curtains, a pair of fringed settees upholstered in tapestry print fabric, and a globe gas lamp complete the mood. In the music room is another intricately carved fireplace, as well as a baby grand piano

and a working Victrola.

Each guest room is furnished with antiques; the largest has a brass bed and a sitting area in the turret, and shares a balcony that overlooks the garden. Nancy is adding a third-floor suite complete with fireplace, whirlpool, and 1840s four-poster bed.

Address: *220 E. Jefferson St., Viroqua, WI 54665, tel. 608/637–3306.*
Accommodations: *2 double rooms with baths, 2 doubles share 1½ baths.*
Amenities: *Phones and TV available for rooms; robes, refrigerator, and microwave available to guests.*
Rates: *$50–$75; full breakfast. AE, D, MC, V.*
Restrictions: *No smoking indoors, no pets.*

Hiawatha Valley
Including Hudson, River Falls, and Stockholm

Wisconsinites owe their outdoorsy image to the year-round opportunities nature provides them. But you don't have to strap on snowshoes or float a kayak to appreciate what the residents of the rugged wedge of water, prairie, forest, and farmland take for granted. Instead, spend a couple of hours on the Great River Road (Route 35), which snakes along the east bank of the Mississippi River and continues along the St. Croix River.

Navigating the rising and falling terrain is like riding the chest of a gently snoring giant, but the eye-popping scenery guarantees that you won't fall asleep at the wheel. This primeval nature show hasn't changed since the days of Chief Red Wing and Princess Winona. Limestone bluffs fringed with fir trees rise dramatically around you, while hawks and eagles dip in and out of shadows. All along the way, old river towns such as Hudson, Prescott, Alma, Maiden Rock, and Stockholm cling to coves and bluffs, each imparting its own unique personality.

Many things in this area look as it they've just jumped off hand-tinted postcards: vintage bandstands centered in shady parks, elegant mansions recalling the glory days of the lumber barons, red-and-white farmsteads sprinkled on the surrounding hills. Given this heady dose of Americana, it should come as no surprise that the village of Pepin was inspiration for Laura Ingalls Wilder's first book, Little House in the Big Woods.

The fur trade and logging industry shaped the area, as newly rich lumber barons filled towns with mansions that seemed to spring up almost overnight. Today, the area is the playground of Minnesotans looking for an escape from the urban pressures of Minneapolis and St. Paul. And they find it. With state and local parks providing hiking, biking, and cross-country trails; with canoeing and motorboating on the Mississippi and on the St. Croix, which is a National Scenic River; and with plenty of shopping, historic sites, and winding back roads, it's easy to while away a weekend or a week.

The calendar is filled with antiques shows, arts-and-crafts fairs, and farmers' markets on warm-weather weekends, but autumn is the finest time of year in Hiawatha Valley. Be prepared. The trees start turning in early September, causing the valley's biggest tourist logjam and making film and accommodations premium items.

Places to Go, Sights to See

Hoffman Hills State Recreation Area (9 mi northeast of Menomonie, north of Rte. 29/12 and west of Rte. 40, tel. 715/673–4725). If you're entranced by western Wisconsin's theater of ecology, here's a chance to see it all. Marshes, ponds, streams, prairies, meadowlands, and hardwood forests mingle on the 655 acres, which incorporate 8½ miles of trails. A 2-mile loop to the observation tower includes a nature trail.

Nelson Cheese Factory (Rte. 35, Nelson, tel. 715/637–4725). The fifth-generation family-owned shop produces 50 varieties of what the state's cows are best at.

Mabel Tainter Memorial Auditorium (205 Main St., Menomonie, tel. 715/235–9726). This tribute to a lumber baron's daughter was built in 1980—an imposing Romanesque-style fortress harboring a jewel box of a theater done in Victorian Moorish style. Frequent performances range from jazz concerts to children's theater. Tours are also offered.

Red Cedar Trail (from Menomonie at Rte. 29 south to Dunnville on Rte. Y). This limestone-surfaced trail follows an abandoned railway right-of-way along the wooded banks of the Red Cedar River to its junction with the Chippewa River 15 miles south. Owls, eagles, deer, otter, and beaver share their habitat with hikers, bikers, and cross-country skiers.

Stockholm. This tiny Mississippi River hamlet shows many signs of its Swedish heritage, from the names in its romantic graveyard to the stores offering food and antiques, art from the old country in galleries, shops of traditional wares, and a charming old-time museum in the former post office.

Restaurants

The valley's specialty is its Friday fish fry, found in nearly every small town's bar and grill. **The Harbor View** (1st and Main Sts., tel. 715/442–3893) in Pepin is one of those corner cafés, but with a twist. While it retains its "just folks" atmosphere, the place has become a destination for Twin Citians, undaunted by a 90-mile drive and no-reservations policy when they're hungry for Swedish dumplings, coq au vin, or salmon with shiitake mushrooms. **The Creamery** (1 Creamery Rd., tel. 715/664–8354) in Downsville comes up with equally imaginative food, from lamb curry to fettuccine with morels, in a contemporary setting with a river valley view. Durand's **Cafe Mozart** (311 W. Main St., tel. 715/672–4103) ladles out *Gemutlichkeit* along with its Wiener schnitzel, while Prescott's **Steamboat Inn** (307 Lake St. N, tel. 800/262–8232) is a classic '50s supper club with the bonus of a riverside deck. **La Pommeraie** (417 2nd St., tel. 715/381–5353) in Hudson serves outstanding French country cooking, plus pasta, homemade bread, and pastries.

Tourist Information

Prescott Chamber of Commerce (Box 244, Prescott, WI 54021, tel. 715/262–3284); **River Falls Chamber of Commerce** (115 E. Elm St., River Falls, WI 54022, tel. 715/425–2533); **Hudson Chamber of Commerce** (421 2nd St., Hudson, WI 54016, tel. 715/386-8411 or 800/657-6775).

The Boyden House

P.Q. Boyden, mayor of Hudson, built this grand Victorian Gothic mansion in 1879 for $10,000, paid in cash. Nine owners later, Minnesota Orchestra violinists and innkeepers Julie Ayer and Carl Nashan treat guests to the kind of Sunday musical soirees in the music room that hearken back to the long-gone days of quieter pleasures. In one of the two adjoining parlors, separated by walnut-stained pine pocket doors, the innkeepers have awarded a place of honor to a 1926 Steinway grand piano. An antique pump organ, an Edison cylinder phonograph, and an old Victrola ensconced beside an ornately carved white marble fireplace are proudly displayed in the other. Performances are followed by sherry and pastries in the dining room, which guests share with a vintage Ayers teddy bear in a cane-seated high chair on wheels. All the rooms still have the woodwork, oak floors inlaid with walnut, and brass fittings that were picked out by Mayor Boyden.

Lace curtains filter sunlight onto the built-in butler's pantry resplendent with brass hardware. Carl's hobby, making Tiffany-style stained-glass lamps, is in evidence throughout the house. A particularly fine example of his work is the dragonfly-motif lampshade in the back parlor beside the antique backgammon table that awaits competitive guests. The dramatic black walnut staircase leads to the two-room Boyden Suite, which is furnished in Renaissance Revival style. Table lamps with Carl's stained-glass shades pro-

vide light for reading. Also in the sitting room are a marble-topped table and matching Victorian chairs, as well as a day bed. The highlight of the suite is the carved walnut queen-size bed and matching marble-top dresser, along with a Louis XV settee.

On some weekends, area innkeepers get together dressed in Victorian garb for a game of croquet on the double lawn that is still bound by an iron fence: Guests in modern attire are invited to join. The inn, amid the opulent residences of Hudson's former magnates, overlooks the St. Croix River just a short jaunt down the hill.

Address: *727 3rd St., Hudson, WI 54016, tel. 715/386-7435.*
Accommodations: *1 suite.*
Amenities: *Air-conditioning, ceiling fans, silk robes, fireplace in parlor.*
Rates: *$225 per weekend; full breakfast, early morning juice and coffee. No credit cards.*
Restrictions: *No smoking, no pets. Open weekends only, May–Oct.; 2-night minimum.*

The Knollwood House

The comfortable atmosphere of the two-story Knollwood House and the warm hospitality of owners Jim and Judy Tostrud quickly transform guests into friends. Built in 1886 with red bricks from a local factory, the house, set on 85 acres in the rolling Kinnickinnic River Valley, draws people into its rich history. Jim farms the land, as his father did before him, and Judy, a horticulturalist, fills the landscape with perennials and hydroponic plants. Inside, you'll appreciate the Tostruds' personal touches, displayed in the plants that grace the windowsills and the family heirlooms that furnish the rooms.

Christie Ann's Room is filled with Tostrud family memorabilia. The queen-size bed with carved head- and footboards and matching dresser and armoire belonged to Jim's parents. An Amish quilt covers the bed. The suite includes an unusually spacious bathroom with tub and shower.

The Sherlock Wales Room, a smaller room with wainscoting and an antique brass bed, overlooks a garden and small goldfish pond below the window. The aptly named Garden Room on the first floor allows guests access to the plant-filled solarium, which has a hot tub, and to the Day Room, which indeed has a daybed, and a small enclosed porch. The Garden and Day rooms are usually rented as a suite.

The kitchen contains an antique cast-iron stove, a glazed pottery water cooler, and a farmhouse pie cabinet with glass doors to tempt the hungry. Judy prepares a down-home breakfast featuring muffins made with the strawberries and raspberries she grows herself. The meal is served in the dining room, in the solarium, or in the flower garden beside the swimming pool.

There is no lack of activities at Knollwood: Just about everything you could want is right outside the door. Badminton, croquet, basketball, softball, shuffleboard, boccie, a swimming pool, an in-ground trampoline, and a 180-yard par-three golf hole are found within the 3½-acre yard. The more ambitious athlete can try the 2 miles of well-maintained hiking and cross-country ski trails nearby.

Address: *N. 8257 950th St., Knollwood Dr., River Falls, WI 54022, tel. 715/425–1040 or 800/435–0628.*
Accommodations: *2 double rooms with baths, 1 double and 1 suite share bath.*
Amenities: *Air-conditioning, ceiling fans, robes, fireplace in common room; hot tub, pool.*
Rates: *$80–$150; full breakfast. No credit cards.*
Restrictions: *No smoking, no pets.*

The Oak Street Inn

Prescott's city founders, William Copp and Orrin Maxson, built this graceful Italianate clapboard mansion back in 1854 to demonstrate how civilized the river settlement, where the St. Croix joins the Mississippi, had become. The house's many metamorphoses include service as a church and parsonage, a hospital annex, and a piano-melodeon factory before the Johnsons undertook its renovation as, they now recall with amusement, "a lark."

The small parlor, framed by severe Italianate arches and dressed in warm tones of yellow and green, with small-paned windows and gleaming hardwood floors, is home to a plush Italianate settee and a low, marble-top table that's been in young innkeeper Ann-Marie Johnson's family "forever." But the showpiece is a working old melodeon that she ably demonstrates for willing listeners. Corinthian pillars define the adjoining dining area, whose buffet is filled with her grandmother's china.

Downstairs, the feminine Elizabeth Room, done in delicate shades of rose, has a four-poster brass bed, Brentwood rocker, a dressing room, and a bathroom equipped with what Ann-Marie deems essential: a great reading light thoughtfully positioned over the claw-foot tub. Upstairs, the Jenna Room occupies the home's original master bedroom and is decorated in shades of rose and green. Original woodwork, oversize windows, and an antique rocker and bed give the room a traditional feel. Across the hall is Grandpa's Room, a small room that includes grandpa's 1920s steamer trunk. The room has a single bed, and is rented only in combination with the Jenna Room.

Guests are served bountiful Scandinavian breakfasts in the dining room, on the front porch, which is furnished with wicker furniture, or on the sprawling, shady lawn.

On a quiet street that's five blocks from Prescott's historic main street, the Oak Street Inn overlooks the river bluff a few blocks away. Ann-Marie supplies directions to nearby Carpenter Nature Center and Kinnickinnic State Park and, as president of the city's Chamber of Commerce, stories of early Prescott as well.

Address: *506 Oak St., Prescott, WI 54021, tel. 715/262-4110.*
Accommodations: *2 double rooms (1 with adjoining single) with baths.*
Amenities: *Air-conditioning, turn-down service.*
Rates: *$60–$85, Grandpa's room $25–$30; Continental breakfast weekdays, full breakfast weekends, refreshments on arrival. MC, V.*
Restrictions: *No smoking, no pets.*

The Phipps Inn

T his Queen Anne house has remained virtually untouched since its debut in 1884. From the octagonal tower under the witch's-cap roof to the wraparound veranda with scrolled friezes and pedimented gables, the house, which is on the National Register of Historic Places, is the showplace of the river town.

William Phipps, a prominent Hudson banker, politician, and philanthropist, moved to town to serve as land commissioner for the railroad, and certainly wasn't averse to living well. The interior of his former house is equipped with six fireplaces that are flamboyantly carved, guarded by Ionic columns, and set with Italian tiles. Ornate brass hardware, stained-glass windows, and parquet flooring in intricate geometric designs add to the "got it, flaunt it" look.

Innkeepers John and Cyndi Berglund bought the mansion intact but empty. This gave them the mandate of filling it with antiques from the St. Croix River Valley, including an 1890s pump organ and tufted Victorian sofas and chairs in the two parlors. In the music room, they've installed a snazzy 1920 baby grand piano that's set these days with afternoon snacks. Guests linger over breakfast in the dining room, warmed by sun streaming through the stained-glass windows and by one of the fireplaces.

The Bridal Suite boasts a wicker canopy bed, a fireplace with Italian ceramic tile, and a wicker table. The Master Suite has a canopied pine four-poster bed, another fireplace, and a large, climb-through window that leads to a private balcony. Victoria's Room, a more intimate hideaway done in a black-and-gold Victorian floral motif, is furnished with a brass bed and antique armoire; Queen Anne's Room features hand-stenciled walls, a wicker four-poster canopy bed, and windows that capture the afternoon sun.

Above all looms the third floor's grand ballroom. Once the sight of the Phipps's elegant gatherings, it has been converted into the Willow Chamber, and the Peacock Chamber. Guests will find Jacuzzis in all the bathrooms.

Address: *1005 3rd St., Hudson, WI 54016, tel. 715/386–0800.*
Accommodations: *6 double rooms with baths.*
Amenities: *Air-conditioning, fireplace in 5 rooms and in common rooms, whirlpool tub in 6 rooms; bikes, dinners, and picnics available with advance notice and at an extra charge.*
Rates: *$89–$159; full breakfast, champagne and cookies on arrival. MC, V.*
Restrictions: *No smoking, no pets.*

Cedar Trails Guesthouse

This was a working farm until 1984. These days, there's a new deck—big enough to hold a hoedown—surrounding the comfy, modernized 80-year-old farmhouse, where city folk can watch cattle amble to the barn and horses enter the paddock. Proprietor Barb Anderson also invites guests to mosey over to her second farm nearby, where she "raises sweaters." Her sheep provide wool for the handmade comforters and mattress pads that warm the guest beds in the six-level house.

The furnishings are an eclectic mix ranging from art deco squatting peacock chairs to framed needlework pillow shams. One guest room features an antique rooming-house washstand with drawers, while another has a modern sleeping loft complete with a futon set by a window. The overall effect is informal. "It's like visiting relatives, without the relatives," Barb claims, inviting guests to raid the cookie jar. The living room has a welcoming overstuffed couch and chair and turn-of-the-century rocker, and the picture window in the parlor offers lovely views of the pines beyond the long driveway.

Address: *Rte. C, Downsville (mailing address: Rte. 4, Box 175, Menomonie, WI 54751), tel. 715/664–8828.*
Accommodations: *2 double rooms with baths, 2 doubles share bath.*
Amenities: *Air-conditioning.*
Rates: *$45–$65; full breakfast. MC, V.*
Restrictions: *No smoking, pets outside only.*

The Creamery

Although this redbrick building began life in 1904 as a co-op creamery turning local cream into butter, today, thanks to a tasteful renovation by a family of hands-on proprietors, the building has a clean, contemporary look. The windows of its bright, white dining room frame a garden terrace sloping to a wooded lake. The Creamery is known for imaginative American cuisine, and the wine list is excellent. From the lounge, which is lined with old milk bottles, wildlife can frequently be spotted beyond the adjoining open deck.

Upstairs, guest rooms with the same bucolic view are done in cherry woodwork and modern walnut furnishings. Handmade pottery lamps and bathroom tiles—including a mosaic mural in the suite's bathroom—originated in the resident pottery shop. The tiny town of Downsville is ¼-mile down the road, where the 14-mile Red Cedar Bike Trail sails by. A friendly crew of college kids augments the family staff.

Address: *Rte. C, Box 22, Downsville, WI 54735, tel. 715/664–8354.*
Accommodations: *3 double rooms with baths, 1 suite.*
Amenities: *Air-conditioning, phone, TV, and whirlpool tub in rooms; fireplaces in common rooms, bar, lounge, restaurant.*
Rates: *$75–$105; Continental breakfast (in restaurant or in rooms). No credit cards.*
Restrictions: *Closed Jan.–Mar., restaurant closed Mon.*

The Gallery House

This neat 1861 mercantile brick building has served as a store with a family residence above it ever since its Civil War–era beginnings. The general merchandise and post-office trappings have been replaced by innkeeper and photographer Joe Hopkin's work, including pictures of Europe, Wisconsin, and points between. His wife, Jan, sells spices, teas, and gifts in the shop. Guests share their home above, where bedrooms open off a wide, hotel-like hall that's lined with paintings by local artists. The inn features antique furnishings, including family heirlooms and a brass bed. The rooms overlook a broad, white-spindled veranda, ideal for viewing barges chugging toward the nearby Mississippi River locks.

Joe and Jan treat guests to breakfast by candlelight in the dining room, which has a view of the Mississippi River. But who can watch the river when tempted with Jan's fruit soup, stuffed French toast, vegetable pâté, and other delights?

Address: *215 N. Main St., Alma, WI 54610, tel. 608/685–4975.*
Accommodations: *1 double room with bath, 2 doubles share bath.*
Amenities: *Air-conditioning, ceiling fans.*
Rates: *$49–$60; full breakfast. MC, V.*
Restrictions: *No smoking, no pets.*

Great River Bed & Breakfast

This pioneer stone farmhouse was built in 1869 by the Peterson family, who founded the community of Stockholm in 1854. The home remained in the Peterson family until 1980, when the current owners purchased it for their home. These days, they live nearby and rent the entire house to guests. In addition to having the building to themselves, guests are welcome to stroll the 45-acre farm, or just relax under the century-old trees in the yard.

The downstairs areas, including a sunporch, as well as the upstairs guest rooms and bath, are simply furnished in a Swedish farmhouse style. The original woodwork and floors are painted in shades of brick red, deep green, and dark gray-blue. White lace curtains brighten the rooms. Antique tables, chairs, and bedsteads maintain the rus-

tic feel, as does the kitchen, which includes an antique stove on which the owners prepare breakfast for guests.

The two upstairs bedrooms can be rented separately during the week, but on Friday and Saturday nights, the owners rent the entire house to only one couple or family, allowing complete privacy.

Address: *Rte. 35, Stockholm, WI 54769, tel. 715/442–5656 or 800/657–4756.*
Accommodations: *2 double rooms share bath.*
Amenities: *Woodstove in 1 room and in living room.*
Rates: *$58–$95; full breakfast. No credit cards.*
Restrictions: *No smoking, no pets. Reservations required. Closed Dec.–Feb.*

The Harrisburg Inn

Grandmotherly Carol Crisp calls her place "a view with a room"—not an understatement when used to refer to this century-old, small-town house perched high on a bluff above Lake Pepin in the Mississippi River Valley. Actually, there are four rooms lining the upper hallway, all with valley views and homey, turn-of-the-century rustic furniture, and a country look accented by colorful quilts. The two end rooms, each with old-fashioned claw-foot tubs, are the most coveted because they sport roomy balconies good for watching towboats and soaring eagles on the river and listening for the whistle of passing trains—or even for enjoying a sunrise breakfast.

Just beyond the common rooms, the large screened front porch, with its cache of wicker rockers, catches the last of the evening sun. Guests can also enjoy the view from an open deck or from the large windows of the living room while listening to the tapes from Carol's classical and jazz library.

Address: *W3334 Rte. 35, Maiden Rock, WI 54750, tel. 715/448–4500.*
Accommodations: *4 double rooms with baths.*
Amenities: *Air-conditioning, ceiling fans.*
Rates: *$58–$88; full breakfast, refreshments on arrival. D, MC, V.*
Restrictions: *Smoking on porches only, no pets.*

The Jefferson-Day House

The Miller family's pre–Civil War Italianate house is full of details that give it a gracious air. The inn's bedrooms combine historic flavor with modern luxury. The Captain's Room contains a brass bed and lace curtains; the Harbor Room sports stenciled walls and matching quilt; and the Hudson Suite holds a display of antique dolls. Guests will also find the decidedly modern addition of whirlpool baths for two. The more luxurious three-room St. Croix Suite has soft rose-and-blue accents on ivory walls and a sitting room; the bedroom features a queen-size bed and double Jacuzzi. The suite also includes a full private bath and a sunporch on which guests can enjoy a specially delivered four-course breakfast.

The inn is within walking distance of downtown Hudson and the St. Croix River. Favorite recreations include river cruises, visits to local museums, and taking in concerts and plays at the Phipps Center for the Arts.

Address: *1109 3rd St., Hudson, WI 54016, tel. 715/386–7111.*
Accommodations: *2 double rooms with baths, 2 suites.*
Amenities: *Air-conditioning, fireplace in 3 rooms, 4 double whirlpool baths, champagne.*
Rates: *$75–$159; Continental breakfast weekdays, full breakfast weekends, afternoon refreshments. MC, V.*
Restrictions: *No smoking, no pets.*

Pine Creek Lodge

When Judith Atlee built this stunning contemporary home in 1992, she included two additional bedrooms so guests could share her hilltop home. In the wood-floored living room, a large stone fireplace anchors the 25-foot vaulted pine ceiling. Picture windows offer a view of the surrounding 80 acres of woods and wild flowers, and an outdoor deck overlooks Judith's herb garden. There's a firepit for cookouts, and guests are welcome to hike, cross-country ski, or just curl up next to the fireplace with resident felines Maxine and Mitts. Breakfast, which Judith cooks to order for each guest, is served in the airy dining room or on the deck.

The South Bedroom, painted white and accented by pine ceiling beams and woodwork, is furnished with a contemporary-rustic pine bed and matching dresser. The bath includes a two-person steamroom. The North Bedroom, also white with pine trim, has a contemporary Mission-style bed and dresser accented by a stained-glass lamp; a double whirlpool tub is in the bathroom.

Address: *N447 244th St., Stockholm, WI 54769, tel. 715/448-3203.*
Accommodations: *2 double rooms with baths.*
Amenities: *Air-conditioning, 1 whirlpool bath, 1 steamroom; TV, VCR, and CD player in common room; kitchen access, masseuse on call; hiking, cross-country skiing.*
Rates: *$85; full breakfast. No credit cards.*
Restrictions: *No smoking indoors. Inquire about pets.*

The Ryan House

In 1890, Patrick Ryan, an accomplished carpenter, built this stately home for his bride, Emma, on his Bear Creek Valley farm, 4 miles from town. A farmhouse like no other for miles around, the yellow home with green shutters, capped by an elegant mansard roof, became the talk of the county.

Inside, the living room's strong suit is its original oak woodwork, pocket doors, and stained-glass windows. The dining room boasts an elegantly carved fireplace that was found in the attic: it has been restored to its rightful place of honor, warming guests breakfasting on the homemade cinnamon rolls.

A grand oak stairway leads upstairs to the guest rooms. The Hat Room is where the Ryans traditionally boarded teachers. In fact, innkeeper Lorena Weiss can recall visiting her teacher here as a little girl. The Garden Room holds Lorena's old dressing table and the four-poster bed that her husband built. There's a nice window view of the flower garden below.

Address: *U.S. 10 and Rte. V (Rte. 2, Box 28), Durand, WI 54737, tel. 715/672-8563.*
Accommodations: *1 double room with bath, 2 doubles share bath.*
Amenities: *Fireplace, TV in common room.*
Rates: *$40-$60; full breakfast, afternoon refreshments. MC, V.*
Restrictions: *No smoking indoors, no pets; closed Jan.-Mar.*

Trillium Woods

Every spring, blooming trillium carpets the maple forest surrounding this secluded home 3 miles from the college town of River Falls. The maples are the source of the syrup offered to guests having hot griddle cakes for breakfast, and in the fall their leaves turn bright shades of red and yellow. Hosts Milo and Bobby Gray encourage their guests to hike or cross-country ski through the woods, or to just relax in a hammock hung between two large trees.

The Grays have transformed this 25-year-old Cape Cod home into a calm rural retreat. The living room, with a fireplace surrounded by comfortable wingback chairs, is where guests can watch TV. A separate sitting room offers a quiet place to read. Upstairs, the Grandma Moses Room is furnished with a custom-made, queen-size cherry bed and is decorated with hand-stenciled walls and Grandma Moses prints. The Currier and Ives Room has the eponymous prints, a candlepost queen-size bed, and double whirlpool tub. The Charles Wysocki Room features a tulip motif on walls, pillows, and curtains, and is furnished with a pencil-post, queen-size canopy bed and prints of Wysocki paintings.

Address: *N7453 910th St., River Falls, WI 54022, tel. 715/425–2555.*
Accommodations: *3 double rooms with baths.*
Amenities: *Air-conditioning, fireplace, TV, hiking and ski trails.*
Rates: *$65–$95; full breakfast, snacks, evening refreshments. MC, V.*
Restrictions: *No smoking, no pets.*

Door County

Jutting into Lake Michigan like the thumb on a mitten, Door County is a 70-mile-long, 13-mile-wide peninsula that is often called the Cape Cod of the Midwest. And not without reason: Quaint coastal villages dot 250 miles of shoreline, with the waters of Green Bay on the west and Lake Michigan on the east. Lighthouses, wide sand beaches, apple and cherry orchards, quiet backroads, commercial fishing boats, and offshore islands complete the picture. Fishing, sailing, bicycling, and cross-country skiing are popular Door County sports, and most visitors at some point sample the region's famous fish boil—a 100-year-old traditional way of cooking whitefish steaks in a caldron over a wood fire (boiled red potatoes, coleslaw, and cherry pie are the de rigueur side dishes). Nearly 2 million people flock here each summer, many of them repeat summer visitors. Substantial crowds also come to view the brilliant leaf colors in autumn.

Door County was named after Portes des Morts ("Doors of Death"), a strait of water separating the peninsula from Washington Island, at the mitten-thumb's tip. The name, coined by 17th-century French explorers, derives not (as some have suggested) from the treacherous currents there, but from a bloody encounter between war parties of the Potawatomi and Winnebago tribes—an encounter from which virtually no one emerged alive. Since 1891, northern Door County has also been separated from the Wisconsin mainland by a ship canal at Sturgeon Bay, one of the busiest shipbuilding centers in the nation. The largest private motor yacht built in the United States in more than 50 years was recently completed by Sturgeon Bay's Palmer Johnson boatyard.

First-time visitors often make a circle tour via Routes 57 and 42. The Lake Michigan side of the peninsula is somewhat less settled and the landscape more rugged. It is not uncommon for the Lake Michigan side to be foggy and stormy, with choppy waters, while just a few miles across the peninsula, the bay is calm, and the skies are blue and sunny. The Green Bay side offers other advantages: warmer water for swimming, and breathtaking views of the sunset from its many limestone bluffs.

Sturgeon Bay is more or less the gateway to the peninsula; Routes 42 and 57, the main roads leading to and around Door County, converge in Sturgeon Bay. Heading up the Green Bay side of the peninsula on Rte. 42, you'll pass first through Egg Harbor, then Fish Creek, full of gingerbread Victorian houses that today house several bed-and-breakfasts and boutiques. Just north of Fish Creek lies Peninsula State Park, where you can marvel at the views from atop Eagle Bluff.

Two miles north of Fish Creek is the picturesque town of Ephraim, known as the "White Village" because its tiered hills rising from the bay are heavily covered with white wooden houses and churches. Founded in 1853 by a group of Moravians of Norwegian heritage, the town remains "dry" to this day. A short distance up Route 42 from Ephraim is Sister Bay, whose early settlers were mostly Scandinavian or German immigrants. Farther north is Ellison Bay, founded in 1870; the quiet backroads around here make for particularly good biking and hiking (nearby Newport State Park is a good camping spot). The fishing village of Gill's Rock is the next town north; the passenger ferry to Washington Island leaves from here, while the car ferry leaves from Northport, at the very tip of the peninsula.

Washington Island has nearly 100 miles of roads and is a popular cycling spot. Its population of 600 inhabits the oldest Icelandic settlement in the United States. Ferries from Washington Island take visitors on to remote Rock Island, once the private estate of millionaire inventor Chester Thordarson and now a state park permitting only backpacking and primitive camping.

Back on the mainland, retrace your route along Route 42/57 until Route 57 branches east to follow the Lake Michigan shore. Baileys Harbor, the largest village on the "lake" side of the peninsula, was named for Captain Justice Bailey, who

*found refuge there from a storm in 1844. He and his men spent
several days ashore, feasting on wild berries, and their
glowing reports soon lured settlers to the area. A few miles
south lies the quiet village of Jacksonport, where legend has it
that most of the lumber used to rebuild Chicago after the fire of
1871 was cut. Nearby Cave Point, where the hammering Lake
Michigan surf has carved elaborate grottoes into the stern
limestone, is one of the most photographed sites in all of
Wisconsin. In many respects, Cave Point symbolizes the
enduring appeal of the Door: It remains a place only lightly
touched by human hands.*

Places to Go, Sights to See

Al Johnson's Swedish Restaurant and Butik (702–712 Bay Shore Dr., Sister
Bay, tel. 414/854–2626). Tourists wait in line for hours to feast on Swedish
pancakes, meatballs, and all manner of Swedish delights. To keep them occupied
while they wait, diners are invited to go outside and watch the goats grazing on
the sod roof.

Bjorklunden Chapel (7603 Chapel La., Baileys Harbor, tel. 414/839–2216). A
replica of an ancient Norwegian church, this beautifully decorated chapel was constructed over a period of many years by the late Winifred Boynton and her husband, Donald. This labor of love is chronicled in their book, *Faith Builds a Chapel.*

Cana Island Lighthouse (Rte. Q, northeast of Baileys Harbor). Connected to
the mainland by a low stone causeway often covered with water, this 1851 lighthouse is still in use.

Cherryland Brewery (341 N. 3rd Ave., Sturgeon Bay, tel. 414/743–1945).
Located in the former train station, this lively microbrewery is open for tours
throughout the year.

The Clearing (just off Rte. 42, Ellison Bay, tel. 414/854–4088). This 128-acre oasis
is the home of a summer residential school patterned after the Danish folk tradition. Designed in 1935 by landscape architect Jens Jensen, the retreat is open to
the public on weekends for self-guided tours through the rustic buildings built to
fit the peaceful blufftop site.

Door Community Auditorium (Rte. 42, just north of Fish Creek at Gibraltar
School, tel. 414/868–2728). Nationally known musicians, dance companies, and
theater troupes perform here throughout the year. It's also the home of the
Peninsula Music Festival (tel. 414/854–4060), a three-week-long celebration of the
finest in classical music.

Door County Historical Museum (18 N. 4th Ave., Sturgeon Bay, tel. 414/743–
5809). Native American relics, pioneer items, and an early firehouse are displayed
here, daily from May through October.

Door County Maritime Museum. There are two branches of this museum, one in Sturgeon Bay (3rd Ave. and Sunset Park, tel. 414/743–8139) and the other in Gills Rock (12590 Rte. 42, tel. 414/854–2860). The Sturgeon Bay location, right next to the city's extensive modern-day shipyards, exhibits a refurbished ship's pilothouse, antique engines, turn-of-the-century sailboats, and artifacts from sunken ships; in Gills Rock you'll view nautical paintings and items illustrating the history of commercial fishing. The museum is open from Memorial Day through mid-October.

Door Peninsula Winery (5806 Rte. 42, Sturgeon Bay, tel. 414/743–7431). Wine tastings and guided tours are offered here.

Edgewood Orchard Galleries (4140 Peninsula Players Rd., Fish Creek, tel. 414/868–3579). Housed in a beautifully restored fruit barn made of stone, this is one of the premier art galleries in the Midwest. All media are represented, but special emphasis is placed on works in glass.

Fishing Charters and Guides. The waters surrounding Door County offer some of the finest and most diverse fishing in North America. For salmon, brown trout, and steelhead action, contact the Baileys Harbor Charter Fishing Association (Box 72, Baileys Harbor, tel. 800/345–5253). Walleye anglers should get in touch with the Wacky Walleye Guide Service (3798 Sand Bay Point Rd., Sturgeon Bay, tel. 414/743–5731), while smallmouth bass devotees would do well to contact Gary's Guide Service (711 Hickory St., Sturgeon Bay, tel. 414/743–1100).

Maple Grove Gallery (Rte. F between Fish Creek and Baileys Harbor, tel. 414/839–2693). It's worth a drive to visit this crafts store, featuring traditional Door County pottery and handwoven clothing, throws, pillows, and wall hangings.

Miller Art Center (107 S. 4th Ave., Sturgeon Bay, tel. 414/743–6578). Painting and graphics by Door County artists and others from the Midwest are featured in this gallery, in the Door County Public Library.

Peninsula Players (W4351 Peninsula Players Rd., Fish Creek, tel. 414/868–3287). The oldest professional summer-theater company in the nation performs hit musicals, comedies, and dramas from late-June through mid-October.

Peninsula State Park (Rte. 42, just north of Fish Creek, tel. 414/868–3258). The state's busiest park, Peninsula offers miles of bike trails, beaches, an 18-hole golf course (tel. 414/854–5791), and the American Folklore Theater (tel. 414/839–2329), which presents original musicals on an outdoor stage from late-June through late-August.

Pioneer School House (Moravia St., Ephraim). Amid period furnishings, local artists' work is on display from May to October in this 1869 schoolhouse.

The Ridges Sanctuary (Rte. Q, ½ mi north of Baileys Harbor, tel. 414/839–2802). Hiking trails wind through this beautiful 1,000-acre nature and wildlife preserve.

Sailing Cruises. Try Bella Sailing Cruises (South Shore Pier, Ephraim, tel. 414/854–2628 or Door County Sailing (10967 N. Bay Shore Dr., Sister Bay, tel. 414/854–2124).

Uncle Tom and Aunt Marge's Candy Shop (Europe Bay Rd. and Timberline Rd., Ellison Bay, tel. 414/854–4538). Uncle Tom has passed away, but Aunt Marge still welcomes visitors eager for her sublime fudge or peanut brittle.

Washington Island Tram Tours. Two operators—Washington Island Cherry Train (tel. 414/847–2811) and Viking Tour Train (tel. 414/854–2972)—run narrated tram tours of Washington Island from Memorial Day to mid-October, leaving from the ferry dock (purchase ticket with your ferry ticket at Northport or Gills Rock).

Whitefish Dunes State Park (3701 Clark Lake Rd., Sturgeon Bay, tel. 414/823–2400). This park boasts the highest sand dunes on the western shore of Lake Michigan, and what one recent poll ranked as the best swimming beach in Wisconsin.

Restaurants

Time was when dining in Door County meant fish boils, supper clubs, and ice-cream parlors—period. Good, hearty fare, to be sure, but somewhat lacking in imagination. Happily, while there are more fish boils and ice-cream parlors than ever, the level of creativity and sophistication displayed by Door County's restaurants has increased markedly in the past few years. Two of the trendsetters in this regard are **The White Gull Inn** (4225 Main St., Fish Creek, tel. 414/868–3517) and **The Inn at Cedar Crossing** (3rd and Louisiana Sts., Sturgeon Bay, tel. 414/743–4249). Critics consistently rank both among the top restaurants in Wisconsin. Fresh, regionally produced ingredients (whitefish, duckling, veal) are emphasized, and the sumptuous breakfasts are a match for the romantic candlelight dinners. The White Gull also serves what is arguably the best fish boil on the Door, presided over by master-boiler-cum-raconteur Russ Ostrand.

Currently, Door County's most exciting restaurant is **The Black Locust** (Rte. 42, at the entrance to Peninsula Park, Fish Creek, tel. 414/868–2999), where chef Christopher Kuhnz changes the menu nightly to take advantage of the harvest of the season. The decor is a bit stark, perhaps, but the food is positively voluptuous. Other innovative kitchens that stand out from the crowd include **Hotel du Nord** (Bay Shore Dr., at the north end of Sister Bay, tel. 414/854–4221), **The Common House** (8041 Rte. 57, Baileys Harbor, tel. 414/839–2708), and Trio (at the corner of Rte. 42 and Rte. E, Egg Harbor, tel. 414/868–2090).

For marvelous pies, pecan rolls, cookies, and other delights, check out the **Town Hall Bakery and Daily Special Cafe** (6225 U.S. 57, Jacksonport, tel. 414/823–2116) or **Grandma's Swedish Bakery,** which has shops in Sturgeon Bay (19 Green Bay Rd., tel. 414/743–7217) and Ellison Bay (1041 Rte. ZZ, at the Wagon Trail Resort, tel. 414/854–2385). Last but hardly least, the quintessential Door County ice cream cone is scooped at **Wilson's Restaurant and Ice Cream Parlor** (9990 Water St., Ephraim, tel. 414/854–2041).

Tourist Information

Baileys Harbor Business Association (Box 31, Baileys Harbor, WI 54202, tel. 414/839–2366); **Door County Chamber of Commerce** (U.S. 42/57, just south of

Sturgeon Bay; Box 406, Sturgeon Bay, WI 54235; tel. 414/743–4456); **Door County Fishing Hotline** (tel. 414/743–7046); **Egg Harbor Business Association** (Box 33, Egg Harbor, WI 54209, tel. 414/868–3717); **Ephraim Information Center** (Box 203, Ephraim, WI 54211, tel. 414/854–4989); **Fish Creek Civic Association** (Box 74, Fish Creek, WI 54212, tel. 414/868–2316); **Sister Bay Advancement Association** (Box 351, Sister Bay, WI 54234, tel. 414/854–2812); **Sturgeon Bay Area Advancement Group** (Box 212-C-1, Sturgeon Bay, WI 54235, tel. 414/743–3924); **Top-of-the-Thumb Association** (Box 10, Ellison Bay, WI 54210, tel. 414/854–5448; **Washington Island Chamber of Commerce** (RR1, Box 22, Washington Island, WI 54246, tel. 414/847–2225).

The Ephraim Inn

I n the picture of his son that inn owner Tim Christofferson carries in his wallet, another man is included—the Wal-Mart photographer who took the picture. Tim just wanted to make sure he remembered the guy. That's the kind of good humor Tim exudes, and inn guests feel it from the time they walk in the door. A former McDonald's marketing executive, Tim had always wanted his own business; he and his wife, Nancy, moved to Door County in 1979 when they bought Wilson's Ice Cream Parlor, overlooking the harbor in Ephraim's charming historic district. Then, in 1985, the big white house next door, where the town doctor, Dr. Sneeberger, had lived and practiced for 40 years, went up for sale. Tim and Nancy bought it and built a large addition that turned it into a sprawling horseshoe-shaped inn with a center cupola. Much to the dismay of their sons, Tim and Nancy sold Wilson's in 1987 (but it's still in operation next door) to concentrate on the inn.

The Christoffersons live in most of the old main house; all of the 17 guest bedrooms are in the new addition, where such modern essentials as soundproofing, air-conditioning, and private baths were easy to install. Each room has its own motif; often Shaker inspired, it shows up on the room's wooden key tags, the painted symbol on its door, and the hand-stenciled border on its ceiling. Shaker-style peg rails around the walls hold such decorative touches as dried flowers, grapevine wreaths, straw hats, and even chairs. The furniture is a mix of reproductions and antiques, with the couple's preference for the simple, clean lines of country furniture.

The large, harbor-view common room brings guests together around a large fireplace or in a well-stocked library nook. Full breakfasts, served in three small dining areas, may include homemade granola, fresh-baked pastries, and an Ephraim Inn omelet, a quiche-like dish of baked eggs, cheese, and spices.

The shorefront location, a decided asset, gives the inn wonderful water views and puts guests within walking distance not only of Ephraim's historic sights but also of an unspoiled beach just around a curve of the road. Not much farther up the road are Peninsula State Park and its fine 18-hole golf course.

Address: *Rte. 42 (Box 247), Ephraim, WI 54211, tel. 414/854–4515 or 800/622–2193.*
Accommodations: *17 double rooms with baths.*
Amenities: *Air-conditioning, TV in rooms; beach across street.*
Rates: *$75–$145; full breakfast. MC, V.*
Restrictions: *No smoking, no pets; 2-night minimum weekends.*

The Griffin Inn

Converted from a private house to a summer hotel in 1921, the Griffin Inn is quite a retreat, situated on 5 acres of rolling lawn shaded by maple trees. Long verandas with porch swings and a gazebo give guests plenty of places to sit and enjoy the breeze. Besides the main building, a Dutch reform–style house built in 1910, there are two cottages on the property, each with two guest units.

Innkeepers Jim and Laurie Roberts, who took over from Paul and Joyce Crittenden (now of the Church Hill Inn in Sister Bay; *see below*), added many of their own touches—on the dining-room wall hang two quilts, one made by Laurie and one by her grandmother. Handmade quilts cover the antique double beds in the guest rooms as well, and each room's decor centers on the colors of the quilts. Though the bedrooms are fairly small, they have been comfortably furnished in a collection of pieces that reflect the tastes of the various owners of the inn throughout the years.

Common rooms include the dining room, a downstairs living room with a large fieldstone fireplace where guests gather for popcorn every night, and a small library where guests can curl up on a love seat with a book.

The cottages, which are open from May through October, are a bit more rustic, with open-beam ceilings, rough cedar walls, and ceiling fans. Cottage guests can either pick up a breakfast basket each morning or make arrangements to join the main-house guests for the full family-style breakfast Laurie serves in the dining room. Laurie, who is quite a cook—she wrote two cookbooks, which are for sale at the front desk—bakes her own muffins and tea breads.

Only two blocks from downtown Ellison Bay, the inn is within walking distance of the waterfront. It sits directly on a well-traveled bike route, and is not far from Newport State Park, which has a fine Lake Michigan beach. Guests play badminton or croquet on the inn grounds, a sight that conjures up images of the inn's long past as a summer retreat.

Address: *11976 Mink River Rd., Ellison Bay, WI 54210, tel. 414/854–4306.*
Accommodations: *8 double rooms and 2 triples share 2½ baths; 4 cottages each sleep 4 people.*
Amenities: *Air-conditioning in inn, TV in cottages.*
Rates: *$75–$89; full breakfast for inn guests; Continental breakfast with full breakfast option for cottage guests. No credit cards.*
Restrictions: *No smoking, no pets; 2-night minimum weekends, 3-night minimum holidays.*

The White Gull Inn

One of the oldest lodging establishments in Door County, the White Gull Inn was founded in 1896 by a Dr. Welcker as a lodging for wealthy German immigrants who came to Fish Creek by steamer. Its current owner and manager, Andy Coulson, is a former journalist who was traveling in Australia when a friend contacted him and asked if he wanted to join a group of investors to buy the White Gull. Andy said yes—with the condition that he could run the place. The other partners happily agreed. One of Andy's first managerial decisions was to hire a new housekeeper, Jan, who proved such a prize that five years later he married her. Today Andy and Jan also own the nearby Whistling Swan (*see below*).

The Coulsons have worked hard to maintain the original feel of the white-frame inn, with its inviting front porches (upstairs and down), gleaming hardwood floors covered with braided rugs, and country-style antiques. The main entry is the focus of activity; it's here that guests watch television or gather around the large fieldstone fireplace. Besides overnight guests, crowds of people visit the inn's restaurant, famous throughout Door County for its traditional fish boils, conducted on Wednesday, Friday, Saturday, and Sunday nights in summer (Wednesday and Saturday in winter). The restaurant serves three meals a day; breakfast may include eggs Benedict, hash browns, or buttermilk pancakes.

The inn is perfectly situated: To the left is Sunset Beach Park; to the right, the charming shops of Fish Creek and then Peninsula State Park. Accommodations are spread around a number of buildings. The main house has several guest rooms, each with a comfortable wrought-iron or carved-wood bed, and each decorated with antiques, some of them once owned by Dr. Welcker himself. Behind the inn is the slightly more luxurious Cliffhouse, whose two suites have fireplaces and lush furnishings; the inn also owns three nearby cottages that make wonderful little vacation homes for families.

Address: *4225 Main St. (Box 160), Fish Creek, WI 54212, tel. 414/868–3517.*
Accommodations: *6 double rooms with baths, 3 suites; 5 cottages each sleep 2–8 people.*
Amenities: *Air-conditioning, cable TV, complimentary coffee and newspaper in rooms each morning; restaurant.*
Rates: *$86–$126; cottages $130–$215; breakfast extra. AE, D, DC, MC, V.*
Restrictions: *No pets; 2-night minimum weekends, 3-night minimum holidays.*

White Lace Inn

In 1982, a bed-and-breakfast was born when Bonnie and Dennis Statz purchased a run-down Victorian house that had been built in 1903 for a Sturgeon Bay attorney. They renovated the house outdoors and in, painting the exterior rose and cream and restoring the intricate wood paneling inside. Then in 1983, they bought the 1880s-vintage Garden House for $1 and had it moved to the grounds of their inn, right beside the flower gardens. Soon after, they bought the Washburn House, on an adjacent lot around the corner, and converted it to extra guest quarters.

"Whimsical Victorian" is the Statzes' description of the White Lace Inn's distinctive style. Massive antique Victorian furniture—not perhaps innately whimsical—has been toned down by the use of floral fabrics, fluffy pillows, and, of course, white lace. Whether it's a framed doily, lace curtains, or pillowcases, there is at least one piece of white lace in each room. Bonnie, who holds a degree in interior design, was responsible for decorating this growing inn, and she has given each room in the three buildings its own look. All bedrooms in the Garden House and Washburn House have fireplaces; all Washburn House rooms also have whirlpool baths, as do three of the Main House rooms. Bonnie personally shops at outlet stores to find thick towels for her guests. The rooms are brightened with books of poetry and photographs, and little hand-painted rocks rest on the bed pillows, gently reminding guests to remove pillow shams before retiring.

The Main House's parlor, sitting room, and dining room serve as common areas for the entire inn complex. Guests are encouraged to mingle here; cookies and other treats are served. Walk out through the white picket fence and you're on a quiet residential street, with tall shade trees and stately old houses, two blocks away from Sturgeon Bay's historic downtown district.

For Bonnie and Dennis, the inn is the realization of a dream shared since college days—owning a business. "We didn't know what kind of business we wanted, so we explored different things and came up with this," Bonnie said. "It's perfect because we like this kind of thing and we like people."

Address: *16 N. 5th Ave., Sturgeon Bay, WI 54235, tel. 414/743–1105.*
Accommodations: *14 double rooms with baths, 1 suite.*
Amenities: *Air-conditioning, whirlpool in 7 rooms, TV in 4 rooms, guest phones.*
Rates: *$48–$158; Continental breakfast. AE, D, MC, V.*
Restrictions: *No smoking, no pets; 2-night minimum weekends, 3-night minimum holidays.*

The Barbican Guest House

Don't expect to get to know your fellow guests if you stay at the Barbican Guest House—there are no common areas here for mingling—but if your aim is a romantic getaway, this is the place. All accommodations are two-room suites, decorated with thick carpets, floral-print wallpapers, and English country-house-style antiques. Each suite has a queen-size bed, a double whirlpool, its own fireplace, cable TV, a stereo, a refrigerator, and room-service breakfasts, so guests don't have to leave their rooms at all if they don't want to.

The Barbican, right in Sturgeon Bay's historic district, one block from the water, is actually two houses, both built by local lumber baron L.M. Washburn. The larger main house has a welcoming wraparound porch. Brothers Jim and Mike Pichette and Mike's wife, Cherie, bought the houses in 1986 and turned them into a bed-and-breakfast, painting them the same color: a soft mauvelike pink that perfectly communicates the romantic spirit of the inn.

Address: *132 N. 2nd Ave., Sturgeon Bay, WI 54235, tel. 414/743–4854.*
Accommodations: *11 suites.*
Amenities: *Air-conditioning, cable TV, whirlpools, stereos, in-room refrigerators.*
Rates: *$110–$150; Continental breakfast. MC, V.*
Restrictions: *No pets; 2-night minimum weekends, 3-night minimum holidays.*

The Church Hill Inn

Built in the late 1980s, the Church Hill Inn isn't a historic property, but owners Paul and Joyce Crittenden—who formerly owned the Griffin Inn in Ellison Bay and the White Apron Inn in Sister Bay—have done their best to re-create the feeling of a secluded old inn. The guest rooms are not dissimilar to what you might find in a luxury hotel, but they still are individually decorated with English antiques (many of the beds are four-posters) purchased specifically for the inn by a local dealer on her travels abroad. The two-story white-railed veranda that runs the length of the inn's front gives every room a private balcony, and each of the building's five wings has its own cozy parlor with a fireplace. At the same time, the inn offers modern amenities such as an outdoor pool, exercise room, sauna, and a whirlpool/spa (12 rooms have their own double whirlpool baths as well).

A breakfast buffet is served in a two-level dining room under a skylight; drinks and complimentary hors d'oeuvres are offered in a pub in the main parlor each evening.

Address: *425 Gateway Dr., Sister Bay, WI 54234, tel. 414/854–4885 or 800/422–4906.*
Accommodations: *32 double rooms with baths, 2 suites.*
Amenities: *Air-conditioning, cable TV, phone in rooms; whirlpool bath in 12 rooms and 2 suites; hot tub, fitness room; pool.*
Rates: *$114–$169; full breakfast. MC, V.*
Restrictions: *Smoking in designated areas only, no pets; 3-night minimum weekends.*

The Eagle Harbor Inn

Set well back from the main road, Route 42, and surrounded by birch and cedars in peaceful seclusion, this Cape Cod–style inn is the focal point of a complex of 12 vacation cottages built in the 1920s, except for Number 9, a century-old log cabin. The inn itself is the newest building on the property, having been built in the 1950s as a residence for the cottages' owners. Ned and Natalie Neddersen bought the inn in 1994.

Full breakfasts are the rule here—granola is Natalie's specialty, but Ned, who worked for 20 years as an executive chef, handles the bulk of the cooking—served in a sunny enclosed porch. Most of the cottages, convenient for families, have their own kitchens, but cottage guests can have breakfast in the inn for an extra charge. The prop-erty is within walking distance from a boat ramp and a sand swimming beach on the shores of Green Bay.

Address: *9914 Water St. (Box 558), Ephraim, WI 54211, tel. 414/854–2121.* **Accommodations:** *9 double rooms with baths; 12 cottages (9 1-bedroom, 2 2-bedroom, 1 3-bedroom).* **Amenities:** *Air-conditioning, cable TV, whirlpool in 1 room; children's playground, basketball court, grills.* **Rates:** *$61–$140; full breakfast. MC, V.* **Restrictions:** *No smoking, no pets; 2-night minimum weekends, 3-night minimum holidays.*

48 West Oak

Growing up in Sturgeon Bay, Henry Isaksen always loved this 1896 Italianate redbrick house on a quiet residential street, and when it came on the market in 1989, he knew he had to buy it. He and his wife, Jean, took the plunge, using the first floor for Henry's office (he's an architect) and turning the top floor into a small but topnotch bed-and-breakfast. There are two rooms, both with beautifully restored woodwork, hardwood floors, and turn-of-the-century antiques. The smaller one, wallpapered in plush green, has a cherry mantel over the fireplace and a stained-glass window over the double whirlpool bath. The larger room is a suite, with a good-size parlor and dining area, a separate bedroom, and a bathroom with raspberry-colored tile around the double whirlpool. The furniture and origi-nal mantels over the fireplaces blend with such up-to-date features as a microwave, refrigerator, and VCR.

Henry still works in his downstairs office, and on Tuesday nights, his barbershop quartet rehearses there. Wander downstairs to listen, and maybe they'll take a few requests.

Address: *48 W. Oak St., Sturgeon Bay, WI 54235, tel. 414/743–4830.* **Accommodations:** *1 double room with bath, 1 suite.* **Amenities:** *Air-conditioning, cable TV, whirlpool baths, phones.* **Rates:** *$90–$135. D, MC, V.* **Restrictions:** *No smoking, no pets; 2-night minimum weekends, 3-night minimum holidays.*

The French Country Inn of Ephraim

Architect Walt Fisher and his wife, Joan Fitzpatrick, were immediately drawn to this square, white-frame house in the Door County village of Ephraim. Built in 1912 for a Chicago family with 10 children, it was a classic summer beach house, with deep eaves and large casement windows to catch breezes off Green Bay, just down the road.

Like many summer houses, this one has many large open areas, which have been turned into comfy common rooms. Striving to give their inn a European ambience, Walt and Joan encourage guests to mingle. One room has a bed from an old French hotel; in another, a whole wall is covered with hats that Joan, a former teacher, once kept in her classroom to amuse students. The two-bedroom cottage, built from the house's original outside kitchen, is best for families; it's rented on a weekly basis only. The inn's country garden, with scattered flower beds and meandering paths, is Joan's pride and joy. Walt says that guests love to watch Joan mow the lawn—using, of course, an old-fashioned push mower.

Address: *3052 Spruce La. (Box 129), Ephraim, WI 54211, tel. 414/854-4001.*
Accommodations: *2 double rooms with baths, 5 doubles share 2 baths; 1 2-bedroom cottage.*
Rates: *$52–$84; cottage $475–$550 per week; Continental breakfast, evening refreshments. No credit cards.*
Restrictions: *No smoking, no pets; 2-night minimum weekends, 3-night minimum holidays.*

The Gray Goose Bed and Breakfast

Wicker furniture awaits guests on the large front porch; the Civil War–era dining table is already set for breakfast. Jack Burkhardt, a former advertising executive, and his wife, Jessie, a former nurse, are antiques dealers-cum-innkeepers who enjoy chatting with their guests, especially when the topic is the inn itself: an 1862 frame house, now painted red, with huge dormer windows affording a view of the water. They live on the inn's first floor and are always ready to offer lemonade, hot cider, popcorn, or cookies to guests looking for a snack.

In each of the bedrooms, look for Jessie's special touch—old cookie cutters hung as a ceiling border in one room, dried flower bouquets draped across the rafter in another, a border of hand mirrors around the top of one of the shared bathrooms, and, of course, a goose motif carried out in every room. Comforters and quilts accompany country-style antique furniture. It all adds up to a casual atmosphere, in keeping with the inn's quiet, wooded setting 1½ miles north of the town of Sturgeon Bay.

Address: *4258 Bay Shore Dr., Sturgeon Bay, WI 54235, tel. 414/743-9100.*
Accommodations: *4 double rooms share 2 baths.*
Amenities: *TV in guest lounge.*
Rates: *$70–$80; full breakfast. AE, MC, V.*
Restrictions: *Smoking in lounge or on porch only, no pets; 2-night minimum holidays.*

The Harbor House Inn

Else Weborg laughingly tells visitors that she never really wanted to be an innkeeper—still doesn't, as a matter of fact. But it's hard to believe this charming Danish woman, since she runs Harbor House Inn with such vigor. The house itself, its Victorian gingerbread painted in delicate shades of blue with mauve accents, was built by Else's husband's ancestors in 1904. In the mid-1980s, Else and her husband, David, a general contractor, restored the house and turned it into a bed-and-breakfast.

Guests rooms in the main house preserve a Victorian look, with turn-of-the-century furnishings. Ground-floor bedrooms have bay windows, while those upstairs have private balconies.

In 1991, Else and David added a new wing of four one-bedroom suites with floral-print fabrics and blond-wood furniture. A carriage house tucked away in the pine trees behind the main house has been turned into Troll Cottage, which preserves the stovewood construction used by the region's early Scandinavian settlers.

Address: *12666 Rte. 42, Gills Rock, WI 54210, tel. 414/854–5196.*
Accommodations: *11 double rooms with baths; 2 cottages each sleep 4.*
Amenities: *Air-conditioning, TVs, sauna, hot tub; private beach, bicycle rentals.*
Rates: *$49–$95; Continental breakfast. AE, MC, V.*
Restrictions: *2-night minimum weekends, 3-night minimum holidays.*

The Inn at Cedar Crossing

Pressed-tin ceilings, stenciled walls, secluded balconies, and a TV room just like Mom used to have are features that make the Inn at Cedar Crossing charming. The setting is convenient, if not secluded—right in Sturgeon Bay's downtown historic district, at the corner of Third Avenue and Louisiana Street, which used to be Cedar and Cottage streets (hence the inn's name). Terry Wulf bought the brick vernacular-style building in 1985, when it was just 101 years old, and restored it carefully.

Downstairs is a restaurant and pub also operated by Terry; upstairs are nine guest rooms furnished with antiques (most beds are four-posters or canopies), plus the "gathering room." Each room has its own look: golden oak in one, hand-carved

mahogany in another, painted Scandinavian furniture in another. Terry also installed oversize whirlpool tubs in half of the rooms, understanding how sore muscles can be after a day of hiking, skiing, or cycling around Door County.

Address: *336 Louisiana St., Sturgeon Bay, WI 54235, tel. 414/743–4200.*
Accommodations: *9 double rooms with baths.*
Amenities: *Air-conditioning, whirlpool in 5 rooms; restaurant.*
Rates: *$79–$135; Continental breakfast. D, MC, V.*
Restrictions: *Smoking in pub only, no pets; 2-night minimum weekends, 3-night minimum holidays.*

The Scofield House

Fran and Bill Cecil believe in letting life take them where it will. In 1987, it took them down a street in Sturgeon Bay, where they saw a gabled Victorian frame house built in 1902 by Herbert Scofield, Sturgeon Bay's mayor. They promptly bought the house, then refinished its parquet floors and massive carved mantelpieces, and gave the exterior a distinctive paint job that layers the three stories in colors of bittersweet, mustard gold, and olive green.

Special touches in the guest rooms include embossed wall coverings from England, stained-glass windows, hand-crocheted lace curtains, vintage photographs taken by the house's original owner, heirloom quilts, marble-topped dressers and washstands, and roomy antique armoires. The most impressive (and most expensive) room is the third-story suite, which has skylights, Oriental rugs, a double whirlpool, golden oak wainscoting, and a pressed-tin ceiling.

Address: *908 Michigan St. (Box 761), Sturgeon Bay, WI 54235, tel. 414/743–7727.*
Accommodations: *6 double rooms with baths.*
Amenities: *Air-conditioning, cable TV and VCR in 5 rooms, whirlpool in 4 rooms.*
Rates: *$79–$190; full breakfast. No credit cards.*
Restrictions: *No smoking, no pets; 2-night minimum, 3-night minimum holidays.*

Thorp House Inn

Unlike many historic bed-and-breakfasts, the Thorp House Inn actually began as a boardinghouse. When the original owner was killed in a shipwreck in 1903, his widow completed construction on their house and supported herself by renting rooms to tourists. In 1986, Christine and Sverre Falck-Pedersen restored it and made it a B&B again. Besides the main house, there are seven cottages (circa 1940) tucked into the cedar woods behind the inn; the Falck-Pedersens make their home in one of them. Like the main inn's guest rooms, they are furnished mostly with Victorian-era English antiques. The Falck-Pedersens expanded their complex by buying Beach House, a contemporary building just down the street, whose suites are more modern and luxurious. Christine considers remodeling an ongoing project—she's constantly looking for new additions. Her search is guided, she says, by an emphasis on authenticity and attention to detail.

Address: *4135 Bluff Rd. (Box 490), Fish Creek, WI 54212, tel. 414/868–2444.*
Accommodations: *4 double rooms with baths; 3 2-bedroom suites; 6 2-bedroom cottages.*
Amenities: *Air-conditioning, ceiling fans in guest rooms, cable TV in cottages; whirlpool in 1 room, 3 cottages, and 2 suites; fireplace in 4 cottages and 3 suites.*
Rates: *$75–$165; Continental breakfast. No credit cards.*
Restrictions: *No smoking in main house, no pets; 2-night minimum during high season, 3-night minimum holidays.*

The Whistling Swan

A sister property to the White Gull Inn (*see above*), one block away, the Whistling Swan is Jan Coulson's baby. A fastidious innkeeper, she has fussed over every detail of the smaller inn's decoration and operation, down to the bed linens that match the wall coverings, the fresh flowers on nightstands beside each bed, and the bottles of imported spring water she leaves for guests. Pastels, floral prints, and white-painted woodwork give the inn a bright, clean look. A full breakfast is served on the sunny porch, and in cold weather, Jan also serves afternoon tea in front of the fireplace in the inn's parlor.

Originally located across Green Bay in Marinette, this white frame 1887-vintage house was towed across the frozen bay one winter to its present Fish Creek location, right on Main Street. The neighborhood is full of cottages that have been converted into shops, so Jan's upscale boutique, downstairs in what used to be the house's music room, fits right in.

Address: *4192 Main St. (Box 193), Fish Creek, WI 54212, tel. 414/868–3442.*
Accommodations: *5 double rooms with baths, 2 suites.*
Amenities: *Air-conditioning, cable TV in rooms.*
Rates: *$95–$127; full breakfast. AE, D, DC, MC, V.*
Restrictions: *No smoking, no pets; 2-night minimum weekends, 3-night minimum holidays; closed weekdays Nov.–Apr. (except Christmas week).*

The White Apron

Guests at the White Apron may feel like they've checked into an old country grocery, with its storefront windows, pink awnings, and rockers on the front walk. The inn, which is listed on the National Register of Historic Places as one of the finest surviving examples of the stove-wood construction style, was a combination private home and meat market in the early 1900s. It's been a B&B now for several years, taking advantage of a pleasant location on a quiet side street off Route 42. All of Sister Bay, including its sparkling new marina, lies within easy walking distance.

The present owners, Jim and Mary Werner, took over in 1991 and stripped and varnished the floors, added a fresh coat of paint, planted extensive flower beds, and renamed the inn the White Apron. This is very much a traditional bed-and-breakfast: small, simple, and intimate. The cozy guest rooms are furnished with sturdy vintage beds, cheery linens, ceiling fans, and a few carefully chosen accessories. A full breakfast is served downstairs at the crack of nine. Mary does the cooking, balancing such staples as fresh fruit, hot-from-the-oven muffins, seasoned potatoes, and the inn's own private blend of coffee with fluffy omelets and other egg dishes.

Address: *414 Maple Dr., Sister Bay, WI 54234, tel. 414/854–5107.*
Accommodations: *5 double rooms with baths.*
Amenities: *Ceiling fans.*
Rates: *$75; full breakfast. MC, V.*
Restrictions: *No smoking, no pets; 2-night minimum, 3-night on holidays.*

Directory 1
Alphabetical

Directory 2
Geographical

Michigan

Alden
Torch Lake Bed & Breakfast *74*
Au Train
Pinewood Lodge *40*
Bay City
William Clements Inn *14*
Bay View
The Gingerbread House *73*
Beulah
Brookside Inn *60*
Big Bay
Big Bay Point Lighthouse *39*
Brooklyn
Chicago Street Inn *16*
Champion
Michigamme Lake Lodge *38*
Charlevoix
Belvedere Inn *67*
The Bridge Street Inn *72*
Clinton
Clinton Inn *16*
Coldwater
Chicago Pike Inn *23*
Detroit
Blanche House Inn *15*
Dundee
Dundee Guest House *17*
Eagle River
Eagle's Nest Bed & Breakfast *39*
Ellsworth
The House on the Hill *69*
Farmington Hills
Botsford Inn *15*
Fennville
Crane House *24*

Kingsley House *25*
Harbor Springs
Kimberly Country Estate *70*
Main Street Bed & Breakfast *73*
Holland
Parsonage 1908 *30*
Lake Leelanau
Centennial Inn *56*
Lakeside
Pebble House *31*
Laurium
Laurium Manor Inn *37*
Mackinac Island
Bay View at Mackinac *45*
Bogan Lane Inn *49*
Cloghaun Bed & Breakfast *49*
Haan's 1830 Inn *46*
The Inn on Mackinac *47*
Metivier Inn *48*
Murray Hotel *50*
1900 Market Street Inn *50*
Maple City
Leelanau Country Inn *62*
Marshall
National House Inn *26*
Northport
Birch Brook *59*
North Shore Inn *58*
Old Mill Pond Inn *63*
Petoskey
Bear River Valley *72*
The Benson House *68*
Stafford's Bay View Inn *71*
Port Huron
Victorian Inn *13*
Port Sanilac
Raymond House Inn *11*
Saginaw
Montague Inn *10*

St. Joseph
South Cliff Inn *27*
Saugatuck
Fairchild House *29*
Maplewood Hotel *30*
Wickwood Country Inn *28*
Sault Ste. Marie
Water Street Inn *40*
South Haven
Yelton Manor *32*
Suttons Bay
Lee Point Inn *61*
Tecumseh
The Stacy Mansion *12*
Traverse City
Bowers Harbor Bed & Breakfast *59*
Chateau Chantal *60*
Cherry Knoll Farm *61*
Linden Lea *57*
Neahtawanta Inn *62*
The Victoriana 1898 *63*
Union City
Victorian Villa Inn *32*
Union Pier
The Inn at Union Pier *29*
Pine Garth Inn *31*
Walloon Lake Village
Walloon Lake Inn *74*

Minnesota

Alexandria
Carrington House *131*
The Robards House *129*
Blue Earth
Fering's Guest House *142*
Cannon Falls
Quill & Quilt *106*
Crosby
Hallett House *125*
Deerwood
Walden Woods *135*

Duluth
Barnum House Bed &
Breakfast *112*
The Ellery House *114*
Fitger's Inn *118*
The Mansion Bed &
Breakfast Inn *115*
Mathew S. Burrows
1890 Inn *120*
Dundas
Martin Oaks *106*
Falcon Heights
The Rose Bed and
Breakfast *92*
Fergus Falls
Nims' Bakketop Hus
132
Glenwood
Peters' Sunset Beach
128
Grand Marais
Bearskin Lodge *113*
Naniboujou Lodge *120*
Pincushion Mountain
Bed & Breakfast *116*
The Superior Overlook
B&B *121*
Hastings
Thorwood Historic Inns
99
Lake City
Red Gables Inn *107*
The Victorian Bed &
Breakfast *100*
Lanesboro
Carrolton Country Inn
103
Historic Scanlan House
105
Mrs. B's Historic
Lanesboro Inn *97*
Little Marais
The Stone Hearth Inn
Bed & Breakfast *117*
Lutsen
Caribou Lake B&B *118*

Lindgren's Bed &
Breakfast *119*
Marine on St. Croix
Asa Parker House *83*
Minneapolis
Evelo's Bed &
Breakfast *89*
Le Blanc House *84*
Nicollet Island Inn *91*
1900 Dupont *91*
Nevis
Park Street Inn *127*
New Prague
Schumacher's New
Prague Hotel *92*
New York Mills
Whistle Stop Inn *135*
Northfield
The Archer House *101*
Dr. Joseph Moses
House *104*
Park Rapids
Heartland Trail Inn *131*
Pelican Rapids
Prairie View Estate *133*
Pequot Lakes
Stonehouse Bed and
Breakfast *134*
Preston
JailHouse Inn *96*
Princeton
Oakhurst Inn *126*
Red Wing
The Candle Light Inn
102
Pratt-Taber Inn *98*
St. James Hotel *107*
Round Lake
Prairie House on
Round Lake *142*
St. Croix Trail
The Afton House Inn
87
St. Paul
Chatsworth B&B *88*
The Garden Gate Bed

and Breakfast *89*
St. Peter
Park Row Bed and
Breakfast *140*
Sanborn
Sod House on the
Prairie *141*
Silver Bay
The Inn at Palisade
Bed & Breakfast *119*
Spicer
Spicer Castle *130*
Stillwater
The Ann Bean House *82*
Battle Hollow Bed and
Breakfast *87*
The Brunswick Inn *88*
The Heirloom Inn *90*
James A. Mulvey
Residence Inn *90*
The Rivertown Inn *85*
The William Sauntry
Mansion *86*
Vergas
Log House on Spirit
Lake and Homestead
132
Wabasha
The Anderson House
101
Bridgewaters Bed and
Breakfast *102*
Cottonwood Inn *104*
Walker
Peace Cliff *133*
Tianna Farms *134*
Welch
Hungry Point Inn *105*
Winona
Carriage House Bed &
Breakfast *103*

Wisconsin

Albany
Oak Hill Manor *197*

Sugar River Inn *198*
Alma
The Gallery House *208*
Baraboo
Pinehaven *183*
Cassville
The Geiger House *196*
Cedarburg
Stagecoach Inn *154*
Washington House Inn *155*
Cross Plains
Enchanted Valley Garden *169*
Past and Present Inn *170*
Delavan
Allyn Mansion Inn *149*
Downsville
Cedar Trails Guesthouse *207*
The Creamery *207*
Durand
The Ryan House *210*
Ellison Bay
The Griffin Inn *219*
Ephraim
The Eagle Harbor Inn *223*
The Ephraim Inn *218*
The French Country Inn of Ephraim *224*
Fish Creek
Thorp House Inn *226*
The Whistling Swan *227*
The White Gull Inn *220*
Gills Rock
The Harbor House Inn *225*
Glen Haven
The Parson's Inn *197*
Hillsboro
Mascione's Hidden Valley Villas *194*
Hudson
The Boyden House *203*

The Jefferson-Day House *209*
The Phipps Inn *206*
Janesville
Jackson Street Inn *170*
Kenosha
The Manor House *151*
La Crosse
The Country Manor *196*
Martindale House *193*
La Farge
Trillium *198*
Lake Delton
The Swallow's Nest *184*
Lake Geneva
Eleven Gables Inn on the Lake *156*
Elizabeth Inn *157*
Lawrence House *157*
Pederson Victorian Bed & Breakfast *158*
T. C. Smith Inn *158*
William's *159*
Lake Mills
Fargo Mansion Inn *166*
Madison
Arbor House *164*
Canterbury Inn *169*
Collins House *165*
Mansion Hill Inn *167*
University Heights Bed and Breakfast *171*
Maiden Rock
The Harrisburg Inn *209*
Menomonee Falls
The Hitching Post *150*
Mequon
American Country Farm *156*
Merrill
Candlewick Inn *181*
Middleton
Middleton Beach Inn *168*
Mineral Point
The Duke House *188*

The Jones House *191*
Monroe
Victorian Garden *199*
Oconomowoc
The Victorian Belle *159*
Ontario
The Inn at Wildcat Mountain *190*
Plain
Bettinger House *180*
Portage
Breese Waye *180*
Prescott
The Oak Street Inn *205*
Racine
The Mansards on-the-Lake *152*
Reedsburg
Parkview *182*
River Falls
The Knollwood House *204*
Trillium Woods *211*
Sister Bay
The Church Hill Inn *222*
The White Apron *227*
South Milwaukee
Riley House Bed and Breakfast *153*
Sparta
The Franklin Victorian *189*
Just-N-Trails *192*
Spring Green
Hill Street *181*
Stevens Point
Dreams of Yesteryear *176*
Victorian Swan on Water *184*
Stockholm
Great River Bed & Breakfast *208*
Pine Creek Lodge *210*

Notes

Notes

Notes

Notes

Notes

Fodor's Travel Guides

Available at bookstores everywhere, or call 1–800–533–6478, 24 hours a day.

U.S. Guides

Alaska

Arizona

Boston

California

Cape Cod, Martha's Vineyard, Nantucket

The Carolinas & the Georgia Coast

Chicago

Colorado

Florida

Hawaii

Las Vegas, Reno, Tahoe

Los Angeles

Maine, Vermont, New Hampshire

Maui

Miami & the Keys

New England

New Orleans

New York City

Pacific North Coast

Philadelphia & the Pennsylvania Dutch Country

The Rockies

San Diego

San Francisco

Santa Fe, Taos, Albuquerque

Seattle & Vancouver

The South

The U.S. & British Virgin Islands

USA

The Upper Great Lakes Region

Virginia & Maryland

Waikiki

Walt Disney World and the Orlando Area

Washington, D.C.

Foreign Guides

Acapulco, Ixtapa, Zihuatanejo

Australia & New Zealand

Austria

The Bahamas

Baja & Mexico's Pacific Coast Resorts

Barbados

Berlin

Bermuda

Brittany & Normandy

Budapest

Canada

Cancún, Cozumel, Yucatán Peninsula

Caribbean

China

Costa Rica, Belize, Guatemala

The Czech Republic & Slovakia

Eastern Europe

Egypt

Euro Disney

Europe

Florence, Tuscany & Umbria

France

Germany

Great Britain

Greece

Hong Kong

India

Ireland

Israel

Italy

Japan

Kenya & Tanzania

Korea

London

Madrid & Barcelona

Mexico

Montréal & Québec City

Morocco

Moscow & St. Petersburg

The Netherlands, Belgium & Luxembourg

New Zealand

Norway

Nova Scotia, Prince Edward Island & New Brunswick

Paris

Portugal

Provence & the Riviera

Rome

Russia & the Baltic Countries

Scandinavia

Scotland

Singapore

South America

Southeast Asia

Spain

Sweden

Switzerland

Thailand

Tokyo

Toronto

Turkey

Vienna & the Danube Valley

Special Series

Fodor's Affordables

Caribbean

Europe

Florida

France

Germany

Great Britain

Italy

London

Paris

**Fodor's Bed &
Breakfast and
Country Inns Guides**

America's Best B&Bs

California

Canada's Great
Country Inns

Cottages, B&Bs and
Country Inns of
England and Wales

Mid-Atlantic Region

New England

The Pacific
Northwest

The South

The Southwest

The Upper Great
Lakes Region

The Berkeley Guides

California

Central America

Eastern Europe

Europe

France

Germany & Austria

Great Britain &
Ireland

Italy

London

Mexico

Pacific Northwest &
Alaska

Paris

San Francisco

**Fodor's Exploring
Guides**

Australia

Boston &
New England

Britain

California

The Caribbean

Florence & Tuscany

Florida

France

Germany

Ireland

Italy

London

Mexico

New York City

Paris

Prague

Rome

Scotland

Singapore & Malaysia

Spain

Thailand

Turkey

Fodor's Flashmaps

Boston

New York

Washington, D.C.

Fodor's Pocket Guides

Acapulco

Bahamas

Barbados

Jamaica

London

New York City

Paris

Puerto Rico

San Francisco

Washington, D.C.

Fodor's Sports

Cycling

Golf Digest's Best
Places to Play

Hiking

The Insider's Guide
to the Best Canadian
Skiing

Running

Sailing

Skiing in the USA &
Canada

USA Today's Complete
Four Sports Stadium
Guide

**Fodor's Three-In-Ones
(guidebook, language
cassette, and phrase
book)**

France

Germany

Italy

Mexico

Spain

**Fodor's
Special-Interest
Guides**

Complete Guide to
America's National
Parks

Condé Nast Traveler
Caribbean Resort and
Cruise Ship Finder

Cruises and Ports
of Call

Euro Disney

France by Train

Halliday's New
England Food
Explorer

Healthy Escapes

Italy by Train

London Companion

Shadow Traffic's New
York Shortcuts and
Traffic Tips

Sunday in New York

Sunday in San
Francisco

Touring Europe

Touring USA:
Eastern Edition

Walt Disney World and
the Orlando Area

Walt Disney World
for Adults

**Fodor's Vacation
Planners**

Great American
Learning Vacations

Great American
Sports & Adventure
Vacations

Great American
Vacations

Great American
Vacations for Travelers
with Disabilities

National Parks and
Seashores of the East

National Parks
of the West

**The Wall Street
Journal Guides to
Business Travel**

Join us in updating the next edition of your Fodor's guide

Title of Guide:

1 **Hotel** ☐ **Restaurant** ☐ *(check one)*

Name

Number/Street

City/State/Country

Comments

2 **Hotel** ☐ **Restaurant** ☐ *(check one)*

Name

Number/Street

City/State/Country

Comments

3 **Hotel** ☐ **Restaurant** ☐ *(check one)*

Name

Number/Street

City/State/Country

Comments

Your Name *(optional)*

Address

General Comments